商务函电

段　婕　主编

西北工業大學出版社

西　安

【内容简介】 The purpose of compiling this book is to help more learners acquire basic knowledge of foreign trade practice through systematic study of international business correspondence, be familiar with various correspondence formats and common writing tips, and understand the humanistic background of different business activities as well as specific procedures, so as to enhance foreign trade exchanges.

The main aspects relating to the negotiation of transactions by means of correspondence include establishing of business relations, inquiries and replies, quotations, offers and counter offers, orders and acknowledgments, payment and packing, shipping and insurance, complaints and claims, agreements and contracts, and so on, which are all discussed in this book.

This book is suitable for students majoring in international economy and trade, and can also be used by relevant practitioners engaged in international trade for reference.

图书在版编目(CIP)数据

商务函电 ：英文 / 段婕主编. — 西安 ：西北工业大学出版社，2021.10

ISBN 978-7-5612-7442-2

Ⅰ.①商… Ⅱ.①段… Ⅲ.①国际商务-英语-电报信函-写作 Ⅳ.①F740

中国版本图书馆 CIP 数据核字(2021)第 000771 号

SHANGWU HANDIAN

商 务 函 电

责任编辑：隋秀娟 李 欣　　**策划编辑**：李阿盟

责任校对：李文乾　　**装帧设计**：李 飞

出版发行：西北工业大学出版社

通信地址：西安市友谊西路 127 号　　邮编：710072

电　　话：(029)88491757，88493844

网　　址：www.nwpup.com

印 刷 者：西安日报社印务中心

开　　本：787 mm×1 092 mm　　1/16

印　　张：17.5

字　　数：459 千字

版　　次：2021 年 10 月第 1 版　　2021 年 10 月第 1 次印刷

定　　价：58.00 元

Preface

With the further expansion of China's opening to the outside world, the development of economic globalization has made international business exchanges more and more frequent. Especially in international trade, after the buyer and the seller reach an agreement on the terms of the transaction through negotiation, the transaction is reached, and the buyer and the seller have a contractual relationship. The negotiation of international sales contract is the most important link in the whole transaction process. Although it can be carried out orally, in practice, it is mainly carried out by letter and telegram. Correspondence is not only a means of negotiating international sales contracts, but also one of the main forms of signing international sales contracts.

Business letters writing skill is a kind of practical English writing skill which integrates international business and English. In foreign economic activities, international correspondence has the function of business liaison, communication and exchanges. As a common English applied tool, it plays an important role in promoting international traders to further international markets and develop foreign trade. The course of Foreign Trade Correspondence is an important course in students' comprehensive ability training. It is an important professional course in international economy and trade, finance, management and other majors in colleges and universities. As a contact method often used in international business transactions, English is an important tool for foreign economy and trade and related business activities. This course applies to students preparing for careers in international trade, marketing, translation, business management and human resources management. The task of this course is to develop students' ability to read, translate, write, communicate and handle English business letters, to master foreign trade English, business language in trade transactions, and legal language in contracts, agreements, etc. , and to master the special styles, idiomatic formats and special vocabularies of business letters. And students should master or be familiar with the stylistic features and writing principles of all kinds of practical English in foreign trade, so as to use the knowledge and skills appropriately in future work.

This book provides examples of correspondence in various stages according to the general procedures of foreign trade and foreign affairs activities, and introduces relevant styles, expressions, special terms, abbreviations and writing skills. The main aspects relating to the negotiation of transactions by means of correspondence include establishing of business relations, inquiries and replies, quotations, offers and counter offers, orders and acknowledgments, payment and packing, shipping and insurance, complaints and claims, agreements and contracts, and so on, which are all discussed in this book. The goal is to cultivate comprehensive talents oriented to the 21st century who have solid basic language skills, broad knowledge, strong ability and lofty character, and who can skillfully use English in foreign affairs, education, economy and trade, culture, science and technology and other fields engaged in translation, teaching, management, research, and so on. Students are required to understand China's foreign economic and trade policies in their studies, to master daily business terms and foreign language idioms of foreign trade, to master general business rules, to be able to draft letters, telegrams, telexes in business exchanges, to be able to translate standardized business correspondence, and to understand and master main business means, and so on.

This book is suitable for international business English, international trade, international business and other economic management majors. It can also be used for training, further education and self-study of international trade practices. This book can also be used by companies and enterprises in the field of business information processing.

The publication of this book has been strongly supported by the Northwestern Polytechnical University Press. The editors of the press have shown their carefulness and professionalism. Here I want to express my sincere thanks! In the process of compiling this book, I have referred to a large number of researches, here I want to express my deep gratitude to the relevant authors! Due to limited knowledge and ability, there must be many flaws in the book. Please don't hesitate to correct me.

Duan Jie

July 2020

Contents

Chapter 1 An Overview of International Business Communication

Learning Objectives

a. Master the background of business letters writing;
b. Be familiar with the tips of writing effective business letters;
c. Know the features of business letters;
d. Be familiar with the categories of business letters.

Part A Introduction

In the 21st century, countries are inextricably linked to one another in trade, taking advantage of exchange rates on import and export with maximum profitability. The international market is huge, making it an essential part of any company's expansion strategy. The most well-known American companies, such as Coca-Cola, Nike and McDonald's, all have significant overseas footprints. Multiple free-trade agreements now exist between global participants that help fuel the rapid pace of globalized businesses. Organizations such as the WTO and cross-country agreements such as *North American Free Trade Agreement*(*NAFTA*) and *General Agreement on Tariffs and Trade*(*GATT*) reduce and eliminate trade barriers and tariffs, which are seen as detrimental to global corporate growth. Participating countries benefit from importing goods by acquiring a wider variety of available products, which increases local competition and in turn improves quality and decreases prices. This ideally produces a self-sustaining system in which only the best quality products sold at the lowest price survive, forcing companies to refine their production capabilities repeatedly to remain competitive.

As we know, the global economy is around our daily life. Almost everyone is engaging in international business. International business refers to the performance of trade and investment activities by firms across national borders. Firms organize, source, manufacture, market, and conduct other value-adding activities on an international scale. They seek foreign customers and engage in collaborative relationships with foreign business partners. While international business is primarily carried out by individual firms and governments, international agencies also engage in international business transactions. Firms and nations exchange many physical and intellectual assets including products, services, capital, technology, and labor.

While international business has been around for centuries, it has gained much speed and complexity over the past two decades. Today firms seek international market opportunities more than ever before, influencing the lives of billions of people around the world. Daily lives such as shopping, and leisure activities such as listening to music, watching a movie, or surfing the Internet, involve international business transactions that connect people to the global economy. International business gives people access to products and services from around the world and profoundly affects people's quality of life and economic well-being.

The growth of international business activity coincides with the broader phenomenon of globalization of markets. The globalization of markets refers to the ongoing economic integration and growing interdependency of countries worldwide. While internationalization of the firm refers to the tendency of companies to systematically increase the international dimension of their business activities, and globalization refers to a macro-trend of intense economic interconnectedness between countries. In essence, globalization leads to compression of time and space. It allows many firms to internationalize and has substantially increased the volume and variety of cross-border transactions in goods, services, and capital flows. It has also led to more rapid and widespread diffusion of products, technology, and knowledge worldwide, regardless of region.

English business correspondence refers to English letters, faxes and E-mails. It includes foreign trade (and domestic trade) of course. The purpose of this course is to help you learn how to write good business letters, faxes and E-mails by using up-to-date expressions in the simplest possible language. International business correspondence is not simply writing or information exchange. It is something that you want others to know about you, to know about your business and the way you deal with business transactions. It is by the way you create your letter that your reader can identify whether you are friendly, rude, or you just simply want to do business. Your letter shows an attitude. This is one reason why it is important to consider your way of writing. Write professionally and with courtesy. Success of business transactions is not only dependent on your ability to talk and communicate verbally, but also the way you communicate in letters. How important is leaning the proper way of writing business letters? It is one of the priorities. That's how important it is. You need to learn how to write an effective and successful business letter. This book will help you to make your written communications more effective, by guiding you through the steps and guidelines of writing effective letters. Aside from that, you will learn to see that planning is important. Gathering information and doing some research will help you. You need to connect with your customers and readers in order to build a good working relationship. If you are able to establish a good relationship, they will value you as their business partners. Skills in writing business letters are important in the success of your business. Business letters writing skills will also boost your confidence as a business person and will help boost your business as well. For globally competitive business firms, writing effective international business letters is as important as keeping their customer satisfied. Because most part of international transactions are not communicated by talking on the phone all the time, considering overseas calls are expensive, but in written communications. This book is to provide a good foundation in making international business correspondence by detailing the facts and providing practical practices involved in international business correspondence.

Part B Write Your Way to Success in International Business

The objective of communication is to obtain complete understanding between the parties involved. If you can communicate effectively, that means you have an important, and highly valued skill. Effective communication is the "lifeblood" of every company and a key to success in your business career as well as in your personal life.

Communication is so important that without it a company can not function. Since a company is a group of people associated with business, its activities require human beings to interact with each other, to exchange information, idea, plans and proposals, to coordinate and to make decisions.

Communication between people outside the company—customers, inquirers, suppliers, and the public—can have a far-reaching effect on the reputation and ultimate success of the company. Thus employees who communicate effectively can contribute in a variety of ways to the "lifeblood" of their company. Successful messages can eliminate unnecessary additional correspondence, save time and expense, build favorable impressions, enhance goodwill, and help increase company profits.

In the business community today, the importance of good communication skills is even more stressed, as it is essential that employees can use the tools of the developing information technology to communicate clearly, accurately and effectively.

Business people need to communicate with their suppliers, customers, and other stakeholders. Mastering the techniques of writing good international business letters helps to prevent misunderstandings and deliver messages effectively, so as to increase responsiveness and the chances of success.

The success of any business depends on effective communication, and letter writing constitutes an integral and indispensable part of business communications. When writing international business letters, make sure to understand the established conventions in the recipient's land, what a word or phrase means in the recipient's culture and languages, the importance of considering time zone differences, and address the letter properly.

1. Culture

Effective business letters always comply with the recipient's cultural sensitivities. For example, some cultures stress the need for very formal business letters, a stark contrast to the often casual and conversational tone of some business letters in America. For instance, applying for a license to do business or open a bank account in India requires a formal introductory letter that does not digress from the accepted style and pattern. Very often, the powers that be expect a standard letter in the recommended template, with only the names and figures changed.

In many bureaucratic cultures such as the government in India, people higher up in the echelons of power consider a letter starting with "Dear Mr. ××× " as an insult and expect a salutation of "Sir" instead.

The recommended approach for marketing pitches in America involves listing out potential uses of the product for the customer. Japanese culture, however, considers one person suggesting what another person should do inappropriate.

It is also polite to wish the recipient success at a local festival underway. Although not a mandatory requirement, it may make the recipient more responsive.

2. Languages

Use standard and consistent grammar that employs simple words with clear-cut meanings. Similarly, avoid using slang and phrases that international recipients would remain clueless in deciphering.

A major manifestation of problems related to grammar and word usage is the different meaning or connotation of some words and phrases in British English and American English. British English is in vogue in most of the Commonwealth countries.

Consider the following examples that illustrate the dangers of not understanding what a word means in the recipient's country.

While the United States requires people to drive a car on the "pavement", Britain makes it illegal to do so. The reason is that "pavement" means the "surface of the road" in American English, but means "a path with a hard surface beside the road" in British English.

A "moot" point in traditional British English is the "point to discuss". In American English, "moot" means "null and void". Thus, if an Englishman writing a business letter to an American stating, "The moot point is shipping the goods over the Atlantic.", he is stressing the need to discuss shipping logistics which is an important part of the deal. His American partner will interpret this sentence to: "The issue of shipping is of no consequence to the deal."

An Englishman once messaged his American girlfriend, "I'll give you a ring tomorrow." All he meant was that he would call her by telephone the next day. The American woman, however, thought this sentence meant that her boyfriend would offer the betrothal ceremony. The lack of understanding of the subtle difference in word meaning led to the relationship breaking off.

Even when the word's meaning is the same, the local context can make a world of difference. There is a famous story of a former minister from India on a visit to the U. S. wanting a modest bite to eat. He requested some sandwiches from a New York hotel. "How many do you want?" the room service waiter asked. The former minister, imagining small triangles of thinly sliced bread that he associated with sandwiches, replied, "Half-a-dozen." Six sandwiches arrived soon enough, each measuring a foot (about 30 centimeters) long and four inches high.

Another critical issue relates to translations. Many countries with English as a second language may interpret words differently from what the sender intends. For instance, an English movie in which a cop commands a motor cyclist to "pull over from the road" once had Italian subtitles that mean "the cop asking the driver for his sweater". Web based translation software may help in a big way, but it does have limitations. The better approach is to use simple words and sentences that leave no room for dual interpretations.

All business letters have two main functions: to ask for and give a reply to an inquiry, offer, order or complaint; to keep a record of all the important facts for ready reference. The language of old-style business letters is often long and complicated. Such letters are liable to confuse the readers. A confused and overlong letter may be put aside until someone explains its meaning, and this may mean delays. Since a letter is written for the readers, the language of modern business letters should be simple, clear and direct. The writer states the purpose of his letter briefly, and the letter is short and friendly. Such letters help the writers as well as the readers, and will probably mean an earlier reply. Nowadays, more and more people like to do business through a fax machine by sending faxes or on the web by sending E-mails. The former is the abbreviation of facsimile, which is actually an exact copy of a document, a picture or a piece of writing sent or received by an electronic system using telephone lines. The later is correspondence sent or received on the web, which is faster and more convenient than ordinary letters. At the moment, the E-commerce involves offering, ordering, inquiring, payment and complaint, etc. But all these are still based on business letters and everyday language. So, effective writing is vital to the success of business activities, which includes correct form, explicit content, compact structure, natural and conversational style.

Here are two letters. One is in an old-fashioned, pompous style of English, which is too long and complicates the messages, the other is in a simple and clear style.

Old-fashioned Style:

Dear Sir,

I beg to acknowledge receipt of your letter of the 15th inst. in connection with our not clearing our account which was outstanding at the end of June.

Please accept our profuse apologies. We were unable to settle this matter due to the sudden demise of Mr. Noel, our accountant, and as a result were unaware of those accounts which were to be cleared. We now, however, have managed to trace all our commitments and take pleasure in enclosing our remittance for £620 which we trust will settle our indebtedness.

We hope that this unforeseen incident did not in any way inconvenience you, nor lead you to believe that our not clearing our balance on the due date was an intention on our part to delay payment.

Yours,

×××

Simple and Clear Style:

Dear Sir,

I am replying to your letter of 15 July asking us to clear our June balance.

I apologize for not settling the account sooner. But due to the unfortunate death of Mr. Noel, our accountant, we were not able to settle any of our outstanding balances.

Please find enclosed our check for £620, and accept our apologies for any inconvenience.

Yours sincerely,

×××

3. Time Zone

Most people underestimate the importance of considering time zone differences when writing international business letters. Considering time zone differences becomes relevant in instances, such as greeting a person "Good Morning" when it is evening or night in the recipient's local time such as E-mails ending with the phrase "Waiting for your immediate response" when the recipient's local time is 2 am.

Proposing voice chat, video conferencing, or any other mode of real-time engagement also need to consider time zone. For instance, proposing a daily review meeting at 5 pm EST (Eastern Standard Time) in a business letter would require the Indian staff to tune in at 3:30 am in the dead of the night.

Make sure the E-mail or other mode of communication reaches the recipient preferably in the morning or well before close of business hours in the recipient's local time. Considering the recipient's time zone is a sure way to increase responsiveness.

4. Address

Another concern is the use of correct postage stamps and addresses. The basic address requirements in most parts of the world are the recipient's name, building number or name, street, city, and zip code or its equivalent. However, never assume this is always the case. For instance, United Arab Emirates Postal Service does not offer door to door delivery service and the only way to reach out to a person there by government mail service is through a Post Box number.

When in doubt, cross check the Postal Service which has a wealth of information on postal rates, standard postal article sizes, and other information for all international destinations. Not adhering to such specifications will result in delayed delivery, or worse, no delivery at all.

No one can anticipate every potential miscommunication problem, but it is still a good idea to brush up on your international business letter etiquette from time to time. If nothing else, the recipient may notice your efforts and appreciate the time and courtesy—that alone can result in a more favorable response to your letter.

Part C Three Questions about Business Letters

Communication is the process of transferring meaning. It is the sending and receiving of information through messages. The objectives of communication are to obtain complete understanding between the parties involved and get the responses required. Meanwhile, goodwill should be built up and developed between the sender and the receiver of the message. The basic tools of communication are speaking, writing, listening and reading. Writing is crucial to the modern organization because it serves as the major source of documentation. A speech may give a striking impression, but a memorandum or a letter leave a permanent record for future reference in case memory fails or a dispute arises. Besides, it is economical and can be better controlled and polished for archiving the desired objective.

Business letters are formal paper communications between, to or from businesses and usually sent through the post office or sometimes by courier. Business letters are sometimes called "snail-mail" (in contrast to E-mail which is faster). This part concentrates on business letters but also looks at other business correspondence, which includes memo, fax and E-mail.

1. What is a Business Letter?

The business letter is the principal means used by a business firm to keep in touch with its customers; often enough it is the only one channel the customers get their first impression of the firm from the tone and the quality of the letter.

Good quality paper and an attractive letterhead play their parts in this, but they are less important than the message they carry. Business does not call for the elegant language of the post, but it does require people to express themselves accurately in plain language that is clear and readily understandable.

Writing plainly does not mean that letters must be confined to a mere recital of facts, in a style that is dull and unattractive. When we write a letter, we enter into a personal relationship with our reader. Like us he has feelings and we cannot afford to disregard them. This is a necessary reminder because many people who are warm and friendly by nature became another sort of person when they sit down to write or dictate a business letter. They forget that they are "holding a conversation by post" and make use of impersonal constructions that produce a cold and aloof tone.

2. Who Writes Business Letters?

Most people who have an occupation have to write business letters. Some write many letters each day and others only write a few letters over the course of a career. Business people also read letters on a daily basis. Letters are written from a person or group, known as the sender to a person or group, known in business as the recipient. Here are some examples of senders and recipients:

business↔business

business↔consumer

customer↔company

citizen↔government official

employer↔employee

staff member↔staff member

3. Why Writes Business Letters?

There are many reasons why you may need to write business letters or other correspondence: maybe to persuade, to inform, to request, to express thanks, to remind, to recommend, to apologize, to congratulate, to reject a proposal or offer, to introduce a person or policy, to invite or welcome, to follow up, to formalize decisions.

One reason is that a great deal of business is conducted via writing. With the wide use of fax and recent development of EDI (electronics data interchange), more and more writing is involved in every part of business. Another reason is that effective business letters writers can use their writing skills to help increase their company's sales and profits by building up good relations with customers, employees, and the public. In addition, proficiency in writing gives the man or woman in business a personal advantage over less capable writers and contributes substantially to his or her self-confidence, which is a necessary quality for business success.

Example:

Dear Ms Jana,

We understand from *The Swiss Business Guide for China* that your organization is helping Swiss firms in seeking opportunities of investing in China and business cooperating with Chinese partners. To establish business relations with your organization and attract Swiss companies' investment here in ××, we write to introduce our city, the city of ××, as one of the open cities in ×× Province, China and also ourselves, Foreign Economic Relations & Trade Committee of ××, as a ×× government initiative to facilitate business relationship with foreign companies.

Our committee provides advice and assistance to ×× firms seeking to export their services, goods to foreign areas and import goods and services abroad. We also assist ×× firms in establishment of joint ventures and carry the procedures for examination and approval of joint ventures and foreign sole investment firms. Our committee can provide ×× companies with information on the world market and specific commercial opportunities as well as organize trade missions, seminars and business briefings.

Our committee facilitates and encourages investment from other countries into targeted sectors of ×× economy and maintains active promotion of ×× through its network of contacts in domestic and abroad areas.

Nowadays, we are seeking foreign investment in the field of capital construction, such as improving of tap water system and highway construction. Also, we are setting up a tannery zone in ×× County, the largest leather clothes producing and wholesaling base in North China. We invite Swiss companies with most favorable polices to set up their firms in any form on tanning, leather processing and sewage treatment.

Any information on investment projects into ×× and on business cooperation with firms in ×× is highly appreciated and will be pass on to everyone who have approached us with interest in similar project. You are also invited to our city for investigation and business tour.

Should you have any questions, please feel free to contact us. Thank you for your attention and I am looking forward to your prompt reply.

Sincerely yours,

××
Commercial Assistant

Of Foreign Economic Relations & Trade Committee of ×× City

Part D Introduction to the Course

Business correspondence or business letter is a written communication between different parties. The students are supposed to know the means through which views are expressed and ideas or information is communicated in writing in the process of business activities. The students are supposed to learn both the language and the professional knowledge (in other words, to learn the language you are going to use when you work).

1. Course Description

Business correspondence is one of the most important courses (a compulsory course) for International Business Trade major. It is designed to help students to accomplish the transition from general English learning to specialized English learning, aiming at preparation for the future business career.

2. Course Objectives

After the completion of the whole course, students are supposed to:

Comprehend and master the basic writing skills for various types of business correspondence.

Be familiar with the general conventions as well as main procedures in international trade practice.

Conduct business, make quick and correct reactions to the business information and do business concluded in real life situations.

3. Course Contents

The contents of business correspondence involve many aspects of international business trade, mainly include establishing business relations, inquiries, offers, counter offers, orders, contracts, packing, shipping, payment, insurance and claims.

4. Learning Guide

Whether you are speaking or writing, listening or reading, communication is more than a single act. Instead, it is a transnational (two-way) process that can be broken into six phases. That is, the sender has an idea; the idea becomes a message; the message is transmitted; the receiver gets the message; the receiver interprets the message; and the receiver reacts and sends feedback. Misunderstanding arise when any part of this process breaks down. Communication barriers exist between people and within organizations. Your ability to overcome these barriers determines your communication's success and effectiveness.

Effective communication benefits the organization by enhancing its image, improving cost effectiveness, raising employee morale, and increasing employee productivity. Your ability to communicate also increases your own productivity. Whether you run your own business, work for an employer, invest in a company, buy or sell products, or run for public office, your communication skills determine your success. And, regardless of the field you're in or the career you choose, your chances of being hired by an organization are better if you possess strong communication skills.

a. Achieve balance between language-learning and business-learning.

b. Achieve balance between input and output of what have been learned.

c. Achieve balance between course-book learning and simulated practice.

d. Focus on various writing patterns and writing skills of business correspondence.

e. Master the commonly-used business vocabularies and make good use of them.

Part E Features of Business Letters

Even before, the business letter was one of the most circulating papers around the world. The business world has continued with its communication and business transaction successfully using business correspondence. From announcement, to information relay, to placing of orders, acknowledgements, payment, complaints, adjustments, insurance, shipping and transportation, are all doing processing and communication and along with them are the business letters. Business letters have been widely used. Skills and sometimes, training are required for writers in order to write effective letters. Here are some of the things to remember about when dealing with business letters.

1. Letters are Permanent

Whatever is written or said in the letter will be permanently remembered or it can even be retrieved even if it has already been passed in many years. That's why a lot of letters can be used as permanent documents.

2. Letters are Powerful

Letters can be used as an authority. Sales transactions, agreements, legal documents and the like are made sure to be written in black in white. Because words said verbally can be changed and can be revocable but not what is written and signed in a black and white paper. Letters can change one request; it can confirm what has been agreed upon; it can give authorization to in-cash cheque; it can stop business communication once it is not done properly. Letters are powerful.

3. Letters are Evidence

Letters are proof that has been said or has been agreed to be done. Even in legal matters, the documentation can be used as evidence and secondary proof of what a certain person has done or has agreed on. Same is through with business, letters are evidence that this has already been forwarded and received, or this has been agreed to be done within a specified period of time, or this adjustment has been approved and promised to be given on the date mentioned. Businessmen prefer written agreements rather than merely verbal words.

A certain firm cannot deny something that has been written and signed in the business letter. That's why a written letter is usually sent after a meeting is done, that is, to confirm all that has been discussed and agreed upon during the meeting. Then, their signatures and written acceptance are requested to be given so as to make the written letter or document to be a binding agreement between them.

4. Letters Reflect Communication Level

A business letter reflects its writer's communication level. That's why it is very important to consider a guideline in making a business letter. A business letter will not only represent your company, but it will also represent you as a person and your character. It reflects how well do you manage to communicate. Time has changed and so is with business letters.

From long letters to shorter ones, from questionnaires to filling of forms, from longhand to word processing using computers, communication technology changes but to produce an effective business letter is still the same goal people need to achieve and same good relationship people need to maintain. Even with the advancement of technology and enhancement of methods, international business trades continue to exist.

Then, business letters will continue to exist as well. It will continue to circulate, to be powerful, to act as evidence. Business letters will still play a big role in the business world in the future.

Part F Researches Support International Business Letters

International business correspondence is a global tool for international business. There are various means of communication between importers and exporters such as telephone, fax, E-mail, letter, etc. Of all these, the business letter stands out as an essential business communication tool because it serves as a proof of international business dealings. It is therefore necessary for importers and exporters to learn how to write business letters. Business correspondence is utilized in many businesses.

International business correspondence plays a vital role in terms of communication in the business world. The business correspondence or business letter is a written communication between parties involved in business dealings. Business correspondence occurs between organizations, within organizations or between the customers and the organization. International correspondence is widely used in international trade. The first step taken in international correspondence is the writing of a sales letter to importers. If the importers are interested in the products, they will make inquire for catalogue, price lists, samples, after which they will make the decision to order. An order letter is written in effect to this. Correspondence generally follows a universally accepted format. Business letters are the most formal method of communication. An import/export business can be kick started at home with a telephone. There is also the need for a file system, business cards, and a machine to answer the phone calls. When the business has been established, a website address or a fax number is needed to boost communication with customers.

What is a good way to build up a successful business? The import/export business may be the right answer. Besides requiring little financial investment to start, it also offers the reputation of working with clients from all over the world. When foreign distributors who will buy the merchandise have been contacted, it is important to have a signed contract with a manufacturer that will deliver the goods. When one of the distributors asks for a firm quotation on the price of a certain quantity of goods, the next step is to go to the manufacturer and get a price quotation on the quantity of goods. The price quotation should be valid for a certain stated period. The manufacturer may agree to deliver the goods to the ship, handling the freight to that point, or arrangements might be made from the factory when necessary. The import/export business is a high profit enterprise because it involves low overhead and most of the money made in commission goes to the business owner. However, building a truly profitable business requires dedication and a good knowledge of the business.

It is necessary to have many contacts that know about the business and respect the standard or policies of the business, and can recommend it to others. Reliable agents (both home and abroad) that will help in the process of the goods delivery will also help to keep the business running smoothly. Another necessity is a good working relationship with the bank being used for the business and possibly other banks that letters of credit come into as branch transfers from foreign offices.

Orders should be treated carefully, and not with haste. It is important to investigate the manufacturers and distributors to be sure the products and sales methods are reputable. Check out the particulars of shipping and manufacturing from the foreign country. Each culture works in a specific manner. It is important to know how to work with foreign partners.

Not everyone will venture into the import/export business. It is a personal operation that can be run individually without having to answer to anyone. The benefits of negotiating in a foreign country include excitement, a touch of the exotic, and the great profit potentials. The establishment of an import/export business is secured when the proper contacts are established, and proper arrangements are concluded with reputable manufacturers, reliable shipping companies, and responsible distributors. When all costs have been counted and options have been weighed, a potential business owner needs to sell himself/herself. Next, start making inquiries and contacts. Make attempts. Analyze whether the outcome is good or not. Then make the business succeed. International business correspondence is the key to successful international business.

Part G Business Letters' Categories

There are nine kinds of business letters that will be discussed in this part.

1. Sales Letter

"Turning words into profits." That's what sales letters do. Sales letters find new customers for you and persuade them to give you a chance. A sales letter also keeps your existing customers connected to you and buying more. It brings back customers who have stopped from communicating with you and encourage them to buy from you again. Understanding how sales letters work can give you the power to create a successful business. The sales letter is also used to set-up or confirm appointments, to make announcements regarding sales promotions or store openings, to congratulate sales persons, and to introduce new products. The sales letter is in itself a sales tool.

A sales letter is used to sell, so it should be specific, complete, informative, believable, friendly, and personal. It must direct to the right audience, and appeal to the reader's needs. Paragraphs in a sales letter should be short and contain simple, everyday language. You can enclose a brochure or product sheet if you want to provide further details or add credibility of your product.

2. Inquiry Letter

Inquiry letters at some instances may also be referred to as request letters. Most inquiry or request letters are short. They can be sent by mail, telex, fax, or E-mail. It may be written as an initial contact in a business transaction. Its objective is to introduce the writer and to ask a question or to express concern that needs any specific response. A letter of inquiry seems quite simple to write, but in actual practice it is not so. Sometimes it is so confusing that the recipient is almost embarrassed. Hence, be precise, direct and straightforward, otherwise the recipient might have to write back to ask you to explain things, or it is just possible your letter won't be read at all.

3. Order Letter

Order letters deal with orders. Business deal with orders almost every day, may it be for merchandise, for services or supplies. Communications are done through letters to place an order or to acknowledge and order. In this communication between a seller and a buyer, they take it as an opportunity to establish a relationship, then eventually, loyalty that will build your company's name and will generate more revenues.

4. Complaint Letter

Errors are unavoidable occurrences in business. These usually lead to complaints. May it be a misunderstanding of the orders or delivery, or errors in the address or delays, these may lead to complaints. This is where the complaint letter comes in.

5. Adjustment Letter

The claim letter or complaint letter is the prerequisite of an adjustment letter. Granted that the complaint is justifiable, an adjustment will be made, otherwise there will be no adjustments to be made, but a letter of rejected claim.

6. Payment Letter

Issues regarding payment are what the payment letter for. There are five major methods of payment for international trade: cash-in-advance, letters of credit, documentary collections, open account, and consignment. During business transactions, there could also be some issues regarding payment like payment may either be too much, short, or delayed. Some payments are lost and are not acknowledged.

7. Transportation and Shipping Letter

Letters involved here relate to freight handling agents and companies involved in the transport. Some instances may be companies that may send a letter informing the customer about the goods to be transported or re-booking the transport. There are times where circumstances happened like damaged goods reached the customer, then a letter to inform the company is forwarded. There's several documentation involved in transport activities. There are four means of transporting goods. These are by road, rail, sea, and air.

8. Insurance Letter

Insurance has a big part in the business world. It is a means of protection for individual or companies from financial losses. To understand insurance better is to put it in a perspective where there is a risk. The primary reason of having insurance is to give payment for those who experience loss or damage. Risk is one big factor why insurance must be undertaken. Insurance will help to protect both people and business against a possible risk that will produce losses. Initially, the insurance was only for rich people who would want to protect their fellow businessmen and was only given a few rules to maintain. However, due to globalization, enlargement and development of trade especially, internationally, insurance was considered to be one important factor. The increase in the number of companies applying for insurance opens an opportunity for an insurance market. Now, the insurance business is one of the fast-rising services in business trades.

9. Banking Letter

Banks may simply be known as storage of money where bank staff looks after it. But aside from that, banks offer other services like credits, debits, inter-banking and others that may be related to money. There are also correspondence involved in banking and they are usually business-related letters. Bank supervisors used letters to build relationships with banking officials that may be able to help them in their business. Some letters serve as reminders, applications for an account and others.

Chapter 2 Business Letters Writing

Learning Objectives

a. Master the purposes and importance of business letters;

b. Become acquainted with the 8 Cs, the tone and writing rules of business letters;

c. Skillfully write effective business letters with proper preparation.

Part A Introduction

Business communication is very important. One of the most used business communication before and now is the business letter. The business letter continues to circulate locally and overseas for its purpose. A lot of areas in business are using the business letter, may it be for placing of orders, acknowledgements, adjustments, payment, insurance purposes, or even banking transactions. International business communication continues to grow, especially this time where the market is open globally. Business firms aim to be competitive. In order to do this they will not only try to conquer the market in their area, but also need to be part of the global market. One of their means to convey their messages and purposes is writing international business letters. It is then safe to say that the business letter is inevitable in the business world.

Small, medium or large business reaches success at some point. There are factors to consider in order for that success to come. One of which is the use of business letters. To start with a promotion, to announce an opening, to communicate your products available, to negotiate, to close a sale, and so on, these are just some of the areas where a business letter is involved. The proper use of business letters will give an affirmative feedback for the company. These letters serve as the representative of your company. This book will give you aid and guidelines in considering and writing a business letter. This book will particularly be concentrating on international business letters.

A business letter is a recognized way of communication between people or companies who deal with trading, may it be for goods or in service. The trade between the two entities is built and progresses as they communicate through the business letter. The business letter is considered as an official document. It is not like any other thank-you letters or postcards. This letter is issued with authority. A business letter is also an effective and influential communication tool in order to have a systematic and structured flow of information between two transacting entities. This is a letter used for essential communications. A wrong impression placed on a letter may result to a negative feedback from a reader. That's why writing a business letter needs a skill. Any person dealing with business letters is seeking for guidelines in order to convey the correct message.

A business letter is an essential document because it deals with trade concerns. It shows how professional the writer is in conveying what he wants to inform his reader and how the receiver react on the writer's concern. An international business letter is then defined as a business letter that deals with communications not only in one particular country, but also internationally. To start a business letter, you have to note that the first thing the reader would like to know is, "What is the letter all about?"

A business letter is a type of correspondence between companies or between companies and individuals, such as customers, clients, contractors or other outside parties. Business letters differ from personal letters in that they are more formal in tone and writing style. However, the tone and style can vary greatly depending on the type of the business letter.

Business letters serve a variety of purposes. They can be used to distribute or seek to obtain information. They can serve as apologies or for other troubleshooting strategies. Other purposes of business letters include use a business letter as a call to action, as an introduction, and so on.

Among the most important factors to consider while writing a business letter is the reason for writing it. The purpose of the letter is important because it helps the writer properly convey the message.

And the writer should consider to whom the letter is addressed. This step makes sure that the message the writer is trying to convey reaches the appropriate individual. For example, writing a letter of apology to the wrong individual defeats the purpose of the letter.

Meanwhile, the writer should consider the tone to use in the letter. While all business letters should maintain a certain level of formality, the tone should be different when writing a letter to someone with whom the writer has a long-established relationship in comparison to when writing to someone the writer has never met.

Business communication is a process through which the parties involved establish partnerships or relationships, negotiate terms, and complete transactions. Every company, big or small, communicates with many different firms and companies everyday. Although new information technologies are increasingly used, business letters are still the main channel and medium of business communication. Even though the way of transmission of business letters is changing, the essential act of sending a message from one person to another remains the same. Therefore, it is necessary to be aware of the importance of business letters writing. In business world, words are as important as figures. By words we make sales, create goodwill, win customers and hold old ones. Words can let us obtain credit, get bills paid, report on new ideas and products, and launch sales campaigns. So success in writing is a key to success in business.

If you want to write successful business letters, always keep in mind that you are going to have a talk with your reader. The most effective letters are messages from one real people to the other. They should be easy to read and easy to understand, and they must be friendly and courteous.

Part B Purposes and Importance of Business Letters

1. Purposes and Importance of Business Letters

There are several purposes and importance of business letters.

The primary purpose is to communicate to your reader about important facts. You must take note that to communicate in an accurate and precise manner. These facts may affect your reader's schedule or activity. For example, there is a delay in delivery. You must provide the accurate reason for the delay and when the delivery will be received. Your letter may contain the following phrases:

Please accept our apologies for the delay in the delivery of your order. There has been a miss communication between our dispatch department and the shipping agency. We are currently doing our best to fix this problem. Please expect your delivery to come in your area in a week. You should be receiving it on the 20th of this month. Again, we apologize for the inconvenience that may cause you because of this delay. We assure you that this kind of problem will not happen again in the future. Thank you for your understanding.

The second purpose of a business letter is to prompt the reader regarding an action to be done. The reader is given an instruction that needs to be replied with an action. Here is an example:

With reference to our previous meeting on last 19th of June, we have agreed to place a discount of 10% from the total amount of our orders. We are now sending you the order form which needs to be filled-out. Please send this form back to us before the 25th of June so we can arrange the shipment by the 2nd of July.

The third purpose is to make a decent impression on the reader. A business letter serves as an ambassador of the company who sent it. "A good letter is a master key that opens the locked doors." So if your letter gives a good impression on the readers, they would most likely be communicating back to you. But if your letter does not even give interest to the reader then, you lose your chance to build a relationship or a trade. Your letter must form a positive image in the reader's mind.

Here are other purpose and importance of the business letter.

a. It helps to build the business.

b. It helps to sell products or services.

c. It builds relationship and friendship.

d. It catches new customers.

e. It opens new markets.

f. It wins back lost customers.

g. It solves problems and issues between two conflicting organizations.

h. It can bring more finances or profits.

i. It can be used to collect unpaid debts.

j. It builds confidence between two transacting people or organization.

2. Important Points to Consider in Writing a Business Letter

In writing a business letter, there are also some things to be considered in order for this letter to serve its purpose. Here are some points:

A. Consider the relationship. Know your relationship with the receiver of the letter. Are you his customer? Or employer? Or supplier? Or just an acquaintance? By this you would know how to start the letter and what the contents should be. Create a goodwill with your reader. A goodwill is a friendly feeling or feeling of confidence. Many people will not respond or may not talk to you because their impressions and attitudes are formed out of reading your letter. As earlier mentioned, your letter acts as an ambassador. It represents your company.

B. Consider the timing. Is this the right time for you to send the letter? For example, your customer is declared to be bankrupt and they still have an outstanding balance. Is it the right time to send a letter demanding for the payment? Or would you rather send a letter that will comfort your customer and reminding them of the outstanding balance in a polite manner? Consider the timing for sales and promotion. This will help you get a positive feedback. Use a tone that is suited to the occasion.

C. Consider your reason for writing. Your letter must be clear enough to be understood. You should also use an active voice to ask for a particular response. Your request should be reasonable and legal. Know the purpose of your letter and use this as a guideline in writing your letter. Inform the reader what he needs to know and don't let him guess between the lines.

D. Consider your reaction if you were the receiver. If you were to receive the letter, will you be pleased? Or will you be irritated? Will you understand right away what you request or written in the letter? Is it politely done? Put yourself in the shoes of your reader and see if your letter is clear enough to be understood and politely done to be accepted. Don't use jargon that your reader is not familiar with. Consider the format.

Part C How To Create Effective Business Letters

Writing a letter indicates a mirror of who we are and how we perform business transactions. The letter we make helps us to catch customers, maintain customers, communicate with our subordinates or colleague, coordinate with our associates and so on. This is not the same letter that is lengthy or giving sugarcoated words, but it is a professional letter written to will let your reader provide a response. You don't need to write to impress your reader but you write to give your point, what you need and what is needed to be done. This letter will deal with the situation that requires response. This may even create a series of letters just to finish one transaction and this letter communication may continue to maintain good business relationship. This is a business letter.

1. Plan

One important factor in the success of any business is planning. Preparation and foreseeing all the possible areas of risks, income, and losses are all included in planning. Business letters are also part of it. A business letter without any consideration and plan will surely come to failure. Planning is also a key factor in creating a business letter.

(1) Research the facts

It is always an advantage to do a little research before making your letter. Have a chance to check on previous correspondence and find out everything you need to know about your reader. This will help you to get away from creating a poor letter. Going through a little research in the previous correspondence, you can list down some things that will help you know your reader. You may be able to know about your reader if they are committed to a business relationship, or know how to separate professional and personal relationship, or offer ideas to help improve business relationship and customer services, or are interested to reduce cost rather than waste money.

After seeing these things, try to imagine and have a visual concept of your reader. After that, have an attention to the topic you want to relay. Another important point is to make your letter simple and understandable, direct but courteous, short but complete.

(2) Consider the subject and the reader

After the research, you now have an idea of your reader. With this, you can also have an idea of what topic you are going to talk about in the letter. The facts you've gathered from your research will allow you to organize the best letter output. Making an outline is a good method to see the logical order or the idea in general. Here is an example:

Paragraph 1: (*i*) *Say thank you for the meeting held.*

(*ii*) *Be grateful for new ideas shared that can be used for business.*

Paragraph 2: (*i*) *Present the details of the meeting and present the actions to be made.*

(*ii*) *Verify for correction or any additional topics missed out.*

Paragraph 3: (*i*) *Appreciate for their support and hope for reply.*

(*ii*) *Suggest another meeting if needed.*

One good point to consider is also the interest of the reader. It is good to open your letter with a topic that will attract the interest of the reader. The letter you sent must give a good impression to the reader. In order to do this, you can imagine yourself to be the reader. How will you feel or what will be your impression upon reading your letter.

Give emphasis on the "You" attitude rather than the "I" or "We". The "You" attitude must be worked out in order to bring the best approach to your reader. One principle to remember here is writing letters to a person from a person. Write a letter to a person. Don't just merely write a letter to answer a letter. Another area to consider about your reader is, "What is your relationship with the reader?" An employer? A supplier? A customer? A subordinate? These questions will help in the way you make your letter.

One good letter maybe is difficult to write because not all people are the same. One apology letter may be accepted by a person because he understands the situation. One may reject the letter because what he cares the most is the business, and no mistake is acceptable. That's why the planning and research are very important so that you can send a letter that will really cater to the person who will be reading the letter.

2. Set Your Objective and Make Sure to Accomplish

A good letter has an objective. Your research will help you find out about your reader and the company. Your outline will give you an idea of the letter as a whole. Your objective will keep you on track and will guide you all throughout while creating the letter. Stay focused on your goal and make sure to accomplish it. Your objective should lead you to the answer, "What is the letter all about?" The reader wants a clear answer to the question. This will be enhanced by the details you will include in the letter. One general objective for all business letters is to avoid confusion, cliché, technobabble, phraseology, and inadequate conclusion that will fail to move the reader to action.

3. Components of an Effective Business Letter

Aside from planning, an effective and successful business letter should aim to consider that its content corresponds to the proper components of an effective business letter.

(1) Language

One cause of misunderstanding is the "language barrier". You have to understand that it is not enough that you have given your message; it is also important that your reader understands the message. It is significant to consider that the language you use is also the same language as your reader uses. This means that what words you use in your letter should be understandable to the reader. Do not use jargon that they are not familiar with, nor write a letter that your reader does not even have any idea what are you talking about. Your line of communication should be at the same level in such a way that you both understand what you are dealing with. It is not necessary to exaggerate with the use of words, nor decorate the letter in a way that you are moving away from the actual message. Your reader may feel overwhelmed by the use of words. Use simple and plain words. Here are some examples (See Table 2.1):

Table 2.1 Examples

Avoid these	Use these
Will you be kind enough to	Please
Come to a decision	Decide
Express a preference for	Prefer

Avoid cliché in order to have more focus on the message of your letter. Consider saying things in a more natural way instead of using frequently used expressions.

(2) Tone

Another factor to consider in your letter is the tone, "pleasant tone". The tone is the sound of the writer's voice, and this will propose something different from the literal meaning. The writer's words may imply contrast to the literal meaning of the words. A pleasant tone can be accomplished if you are natural, friendly and courteous. Your letter must be personal. Show your reader that you are not only giving statistics, but you are writing as a person. The tone of your letter should show that the writer is a human being. The letter has a human touch. If your reader feels that you are sincerely concerned not only about the business, but also personal relationships, it is most likely that you will receive a response. One point already mentioned above is the relationship of the writer to the reader. This will also have an effect on the tone of your letter. A boss or an employer who is sending a letter to his subordinate will sound different from the supplier sending a letter to his customer. Different letters are written for different purposes. Because of this reason that tonal component is important. With proper use of tone, you can make negative news as positive. But ignoring your tone, even positive news will come out to be negative. Here is an example:

The competition in this position is very tough, with many outstanding candidates.

Your credentials are very impressive, but we regret to inform you that they did not match with the current position we need. We hope that you will be able to find a position that will match with your skills and experience.

(3) Focus

The focus of your letter should be on the reader. This is having the "You" attitude. The "You" means you are putting yourself from the standpoint of the reader. With this, you see clearly what your reader's skills are, what he loves to do and hates to do. This gives a human touch on your letter. There are instances where the writer thought he is focusing on the reader and assumes that his interests and likes are the same with the reader. But the truth is not. Here are some guideline questions that you need in order to know that whether you are following the "You" attitude or not:

a. What motivation will you include for the reader to react positively with your letter?

b. What will give interest to the reader?

c. What can be the reader's perspective with regards to the topic you detailed in your letter?

At first glance, you may not know the answers to these questions. But if you will do some research and planning, take time to sit down and check in these areas, you will be able to draw clear answers. You must let your reader feel that your letter is of personal value. Here is an example of a letter with a "You" attitude:

Dear Mr. Brown,

Thank you very much for considering our agency for your insurance policy.

As your line of service is not covered in the current insurance policy program we have, we are keeping your application on-hold for future reference and further processing once our policy program is updated. We are currently working on this service to be approved. Once the approval is given after six months, we will surely exclude your application.

Should you request to pull out your application from us, we would appreciate if you will inform us immediately. We would like to inform you that your application is valuable to us. We hope that you will still consider to start a partnership with us. We appreciate your patience and your understanding on this matter.

Yours sincerely,

×××

(4) Length

"The shorter, the better." This is one of the most common rule of thumb, as long as the components of your letter are included. Different letters have different purposes. The purpose of your letter will help you in deciding how long or how short your letter will be. Here are some sentences to avoid (See Table 2.2):

Table 2.2 Sentences to avoid

Avoid these	Use these
Please see that an inquisition is conducted to ascertain the source of the fault.	Please find out the reason.
We would like to express our regret for being unable to ...	We are sorry to inform you ...
Fill-in your orders at this time considering your prompt that ...	We cannot meet your present request order immediately.

"Come right to the point." This is another point to consider. Most businessmen are busy and they will not read a very long letter. As much as possible, limit your letter to one page. Put your main topics in the first paragraph. So your reader will know what the letter is all about. Planning will help you limit your letter.

(5) Stationery

Purchasing business stationery is not something all businesses consider an important business decision that needs careful thought and deliberation. However, business stationery is very important because it not only identifies the business, but it is also an effective marketing tool. Custom stationery demonstrates professionalism and can often attract new clients. When considering business stationery, managers should consider the following benefits of creating custom designed professional stationery.

A. Business stationery projects the company's image. Establishing trust is an important part of attracting and maintaining clients. The main purpose of business stationery is to depict the company in a positive and professional manner. Professional stationery tells clients and potential clients that the business is professional and legitimate. Quality stationery will leave a long lasting impression. It is basically the face of the company.

B. Stationery helps with networking. When corresponding with clients and other businesses, business stationery is the first thing they notice. As well, when meeting potential clients for the first time at a meeting or conference, business cards are the first thing they see from the company. Quality business stationery is part of the introduction and should represent the company in a positive manner. It is important to remember that after a company representative gives a business card and leaves, the business card remains with the potential client so it is important the card depicts the company's professionalism. Custom stationery demonstrates that the business welcomes and appreciates the client's business.

C. Business stationery as a marketing tool. Because businesses are constantly sending out communications, giving out business cards, and other office related items, it is important that businesses acquire and use a variety of different types of stationery. This can include custom stationery letterheads, envelopes, business cards, pens, pencils, invoice and compliment slips, brochures, folders, roller stands, contract proposals, quotes and estimates, letters of recommendation, thanks and apology, and so on. By having a variety of different types of businesses stationery, they will be constantly marketing their businesses in a creative, professional, and non-intrusive manner. The stationery should be unique to the company with a distinct logo, memorable, in high quality, and should reflect the professionalism of the company.

D. Stationery that is uniquely customized. Companies can have stationery designed to their own specifications to meet their business needs and desires. There are professional stationery design companies that will design stationery with appropriate colors, images, and patterns. They are designed to meet the specifications and wishes of an individual business. The customer gives the stationery company a concept and design and the stationery is made according to their specific requests. The result is distinctive stationery that sets a business apart from their competition. For instance, color printed stationery with a unique business logo can catch a potential client's attention and increase the client's interest in the company.

Custom stationery is the best way to show business professionalism and show a company in a positive manner. As well, it can lead to company branding. Business stationery is an important part of increasing a company's public visibility.

In writing a business letter, it is also good to consider the materials you will be using in making your letter presentable and easy to recognize. You are selling your company by your letter address. The paper to be used should always be of the best quality. It is plain and not full of unrecognizable designs. The paper colors vary, and some may use shades of gray, brown, or blue. Some may use different colors of paper for different departments. But the best one to use is the white paper. Before, the paper size used the 8.5 inches × 11 inches, but now as the computer age has governed the business world, A4 size becomes popular. Most printers today are designed for A4 papers. But this does not eliminate the use of the 8.5 inches × 11 inches. The letterhead varies from one business to another. But the most commonly used is designed with business logo, business address, E-mail address, contact number, fax number, website address. If the company has a trademark or distinctive symbol, it is advisable to place in on the letterhead. This trademark should also be placed in every paper transaction of the company like the bills and invoices. Normally, letterheads are printed at the top of the paper. Some companies place some other information at the bottom of the paper aside from their letterhead details on top.

All business letters should be type-written. Proper spacing is important. It should be single-spaced. The font size ranges from 11 to 12 depending on the font. Your font should be formal like Times New Roman or Arial. Do not use decorative fonts. The envelope is also important. This is the first part that your reader will see. It again, leaves an impression. The address should be properly placed horizontally and vertically. Also, the address printed on the envelope should be exactly the same as the address printed in your letter. There is no restricted color of the envelope but light colors are preferable. The envelope size that is normally used is the 9 inches × 4 inches. Others may use the smaller size, 3.5 inches × 6 inches.

Part D 8 Cs of Business Letters

In the business world, business letters are widely used and are commonly circulating between transactions. It is known that business letters serve many purposes. It is used for selling, apologizing, seeking explanation, introducing a company or new product, expressing complaints, rejecting, providing an adjustment, organizing, and so on. Your letter must serve its goal and objective and aside from that, you also need to differentiate the good letter from the bad. You have to understand that a business letter is formal and it involves proper information and documentation. There is a way to measure the quality of a letter. The benchmark to use is the 8 Cs or eight characteristics of a business letter. An effective and successful letter must seek to include all these substantial qualities.

1. Clarity

Vague and unclear letters will only lead to confusion or doubts. To clear any doubt or confusion, the letter should be created with the use of precise and familiar words, as well as, the sentences and paragraphs should be constructed coordinately and supporting each other. The following paragraph in your letter should support the first and main paragraph. If you will be talking about another topic in the second or third paragraph, you fail to accomplish "clarity". Clarity is considered the cornerstone of effective communication. The writer should consider the reader's level of understanding. The letter should be logically and coherently arranged in a way that one idea will not be covering the other. Instead, each idea should stand out, but complementing each other. Good letter will bring a good result. The message of your letter must be understandable without any interpreter or translator. The language you use must be the language that everyone understands. It is important to choose the right words to use in your letter. You may have the correct idea and precise thoughts that you want your reader to know, but using inappropriate words will give another meaning to what you meant to say. Some business letters used general words instead of specific words. Most of the time, the general words only create cliché (which you need to avoid).

Here is an example of using general words:

We believe that if you will implement the use of the Inventory Automation System, it will have a considerable effect on your inventory problems.

You will notice that the writer has used three general words: considerable, effect, problems. The reader will then ask what is considerable and what could be the effect. And what are the problems you are talking about. Now, this is the best time to use specific words. Specify what considerable effect that the system will have. For example, it will make the counting of materials faster, or it will lessen the possible mistake of miscounting. Will it automatically update the inventory every time a new material will come? Mention the specific benefit and effect. And the problems should also be specified, for example, problems on human miscounting, or problem with the number of hours doing the inventory because it is still manual.

You'd better say it as:

We believe that if you will implement the use of the Inventory Automation System, you can experience the following benefits:

Fast and efficient materials counting;

Automatic update of the inventory when new materials arrived;

Computer-generated monthly report.

And eliminate the problems on:

Error of human counting;

Extra hours added for new materials to be counted and updated in the inventory;

Volume of paper works to check for monthly report.

A point that is ambiguous in a letter will cause trouble to both sides. In this way, clarity is often considered to be one of the main writing principles and language features. To achieve clearness and clarity, you must first have a clear idea of what you wish to convey in the letter, such as the purpose, the attitude, and the matter concerned. Following rules should be followed:

a. Avoid to use the words which have different or unclear meanings;

b. Pay attention to the position of modifier;

c. Pay attention to the rationality in logic.

Clarity tells the reader exactly what he or she wants and needs to know, using words and a format that make your writings totally understandable with just one reading. To achieve this, you should include illustrations, examples or visual aids to convey your

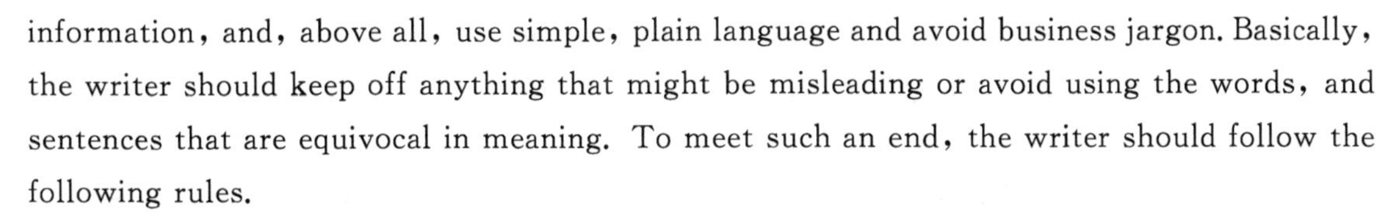

information, and, above all, use simple, plain language and avoid business jargon. Basically, the writer should keep off anything that might be misleading or avoid using the words, and sentences that are equivocal in meaning. To meet such an end, the writer should follow the following rules.

(1) Try to use concise and accessible expressions

Let us look at the following sentence:

As to the steamer sailing from Shanghai to Los Angeles, we have bimonthly direct services.

The basic meaning of this sentence is "we have direct sailings from Shanghai to Los Angels", but the word "bimonthly" has two meanings, one of which is "twice a month" and the other of which is "once every two months". You'd better not use the word like "bimonthly" of double meanings, but use the words that can express your idea clearly as follows:

a. *We have a direct sailing from Shanghai to Los Angeles every two months.*

b. *We have a direct sailing from Shanghai to Los Angeles semimonthly.*

c. *We have two direct sailings every month from Shanghai to Los Angeles.*

(2) Pay attention to the position of modifier

The basic principle for using modifiers is simply to put them as close as possible to the word or words they are modifying. Naturally, if you want to discuss a potential market, you will want to potential to appear right before market; you will not put the modifier in some distant part of the sentence.

The idea of keeping related words together—and as close together as possible—is probably the "whole idea" behind studying modifiers. Adjectives should be placed right next to the things they describe and adverbs should be placed right next to the action or the other modifiers they describe.

Let us look at the following sentences:

Your proposal for payment by time draft is acceptable to us under Order No. 115.

This sentence is poor in that "under Order No. 115" is too far away from payment by time draft.

Pay attention to the position of the modifiers:

a. *We shall be able to supply 10 cases of the item only.*

b. *We shall be able to supply 10 cases only of the item.*

The modifier "only" in the above sentences modified two different words, so the two sentences have different meanings.

(3) Pay attention to the object of the pronoun and the relations between the relative pronoun and the antecedent

Whom or what the pronoun refers to and what is the relation between the relative pronoun and the antecedent? These should be paid attention to. Generally speaking, the pronoun and relative pronoun are used to refer to the nearest noun from themselves and should be identical in person and number with the noun referred to or modified.

Let us examine the following sentence:

They informed Messrs. Smith & Brown that they would receive a reply in a few days.

In this sentence, what does the second "they" refer to, the subject "They" of the main clause or the "Messrs. Smith & Brown"? This can't be explained clearly.

It will be clear if you change the sentence into:

They informed Messrs. Smith & Brown that the latter would receive the reply in a few days.

(4) Pay attention to the rationality in logic

At first, you must pay attention to the agreement of the logical subject of the participle and the subject of the sentence.

For example:

Being a registered accountant, I'm sure you can help us.

In this sentence, the subject of the sentence is "I", but the logical subject of the participle "being" should be "you" according to inference. In order to keep the logical subject of the participle in agreement with the subject of the sentence, the above sentence should be rewritten as the following:

Being a registered accountant, you can certainly help us.

As you are a registered accountant, I'm sure you can help us.

(5) Pay attention to the sentence structure

Compare:

a. *We sent you 5 samples yesterday of the goods which you requested in your letter of May 25 by air.*

b. *We sent you, by air, 5 samples of the goods which you requested in your letter of May 25 yesterday.*

(6) Paragraph carefully and properly

Commercial letters should be clear and tidy, and easy to understand the content. So a writer should paragraph a letter carefully and properly. One paragraph for each point is a good general rule.

2. Conciseness

"Time is gold" is a saying that businessmen always consider. So, you must consider it too. Conciseness is very important for busy buyers and sellers. You can save time and effort by being concise. Using too many words will only delay decision making, so just put in the appropriate issue. But note that in using few words, you should consider not to lose the clarity or courtesy. Conciseness is a quality style. To produce a concise letter, use only the necessary information and words for efficient communication. You should not confuse conciseness with being brief. A brief letter means a short letter. But a concise letter will only use many words as needed in order to deliver the message accurately and efficiently. And note that, it includes words that will keep you on track, reaching your objective.

Another way to achieve conciseness is when you know how to begin and how to end your letter. If you will just beat around the bush and don't know where to start or end, then your letter will be a long uninteresting letter. Note that the opening of the letter is either to announce or to acknowledge. If your letter is not a reply, then you are announcing or informing your reader about your business. If it is a reply, then acknowledge your correspondent's letter. Once you know the purpose of the letter placed in the opening part, you can add details to explain it further but briefly. Don't waste too many words on unimportant matters. Your ending part is also an important part of your letter. The ending is the most likely part to be remembered. Aside from thanking or appreciating your reader, make sure that you leave your correspondent with a message that he will remember.

Conciseness is considered the most important principle in business letters writing as we now live in a world where time is money. Conciseness means to write in the fewest possible words without sacrificing completeness and courtesy. To achieve conciseness, you should avoid wordy statement and fancy language, use short sentences instead of long ones, and compose your message carefully. To achieve this, the following guidelines must be adhered to.

(1) Make a long story short and try to avoid wordiness

Make it a rule, to use no more words and pithy sentences to express your meaning clearly and concisely. Try to use a word or phrase to express your idea as much as possible instead of using long sentences or clauses. For instance, use a word to replace a phrase (See Table 2. 3):

Table 2. 3 Use a word to replace a phrase

You shouldn't use	You'd better use
at this time	now
express a preference for	prefer
enclosed herewith	here
from the point of view	as
in view of the fact that / due to the fact that	because
a draft in the amount of $ 1 000	a draft for $ 1 000

(2) Avoid the unusual or out-of-date words or jargons, and try to express your ideas in modern English

You can use these words or phrases to express your ideas in modern English (See Table 2. 4):

Table 2. 4 Express your ideas in modern English

You shouldn't use	You'd better use
consummate	complete
terminate	end
remuneration	payment
converse	talk
inst.	this month
attached hereto	enclosed is/are
acknowledge receipt of	thank you for ... I received ...
awaiting the favor of our early reply	we are looking forward to your reply
up to this writing	so far
take the liberty of	omitted

(3) Build effective sentences and paragraphs

Generally speaking, the average length for sentences should be 10 to 20 words, not over

30 ones. Usually a paragraph consists of no more than 10 lines, because short paragraphs encourage the readers to finish reading over the passage.

Let us look at the following sentence:

We would like to know whether you would allow us to extend the time of shipment for twenty days and if you would be so kind as to allow us to do so, kindly give us your reply by fax without delay.

This sentence is a bit lengthy, and is too courteous in expressions, which sounds unclear in meaning, in order to express the main idea better, this sentence may be abbreviated as follows:

Please reply by fax immediately if you will allow us to delay the shipment until April 21.

Conciseness is often considered to be the most important writing principle and language feature. It enables both parties to save time. Conciseness also means you should clearly express what you would do in a short and pithy style of writing as possible as you can. To achieve this, the following guidelines must be observed.

a. Make a long story short and try to avoid wordiness;

b. Avoid the out of date commercial jargons and try to use modern English;

c. Avoid unnecessary repeat;

d. Build effective sentences and paragraphs.

3. Consideration

Consideration gives emphasis on the "You" attitude rather than the "I" or "We". Effective communication is having an impression that you care about people and at the same time giving your best in the business you are dealing with. Interaction is important. If letters are just communicated for business reasons and no human natural interaction, then it will increase the percentage of losing a customer or supplier. Make your letter conversational. You can write in a casual way and not too strict. It is easier to understand if the letter is conversational and friendly rather than strictly business-oriented. One way of being considerate is to pay attention to letters that needs an immediate reply. If you cannot deal the problem or issue at the moment, explain why and inform them you will be writing them back again. Try to understand and respect the letter sender and don't react negatively as if you will never make any mistake. Instead, answer him with courtesy and with consideration.

Consideration means thoughtfulness. So you should always put yourself in your reader's place, which is what people now emphasize, i. e. "You" attitude, and avoid taking the writer's attitude, i. e. "We" attitude. Therefore, you should always keep in mind the receiver we are writing to, understanding his or her problems and take the positive approach.

Let's make a comparison between the following two groups of sentences.

"We" attitude:

a. *We allow a 5% discount for cash payment.*

b. *We won't be able to send you the brochure this month.*

"You" attitude:

a. *You earn a 5% discount when you pay cash.*

b. *We will send you the brochure next month.*

In addition, we should try to discuss problems in a positive way rather than in a negative way. Make a comparison between the following groups of sentences and you will find which is better. Focus on the positive approach.

Compare:

a. *We do not believe that you will have cause for dissatisfaction.* (Negative)

b. *We feel sure that you will entirely get satisfied.* (Positive)

c. *Your order will be delayed for two weeks.* (Negative)

d. *Your order will be shipped in two weeks.* (Positive)

4. Courtesy

Consideration and courtesy work together. Courtesy will nurture the goodwill and friendliness. Courtesy is as important as being clear and concise. Most effective and successful letters are done with courtesy. Some business people may tend to be cold and jargon when they create a letter. They tend to enclose themselves in the idea of "business writing". Saying "please" and "thank you" is not enough to be courteous. You have to reflect it throughout your letter. Any reader will not be interested to continue reading if he feels the letter is discourteous. Always consider how your reader will feel when he reads your letter. Avoid negatives in writing as much as possible. Negatives will make a connotation of what not to do. But in business writing, it is best to suggest positives, what to do. A letter with friendly conversation will not only be clear, but also sincere.

Courtesy plays a considerable role in business letters writing as in all business activities. It is not mere a way of showing politeness. By courtesy we mean treating people with respect and friendly human concern. In order to make a business letter courteous, try to avoid irritating, offensive, or belittling statements. To answer letters promptly is also a matter of courtesy. Following rules should be followed:

a. Change the commanding tone into requesting tone;

b. Use mitigation and avoid over emphasizing your own opinion or irritating your partner;

c. Passive voice should be adopted accordingly;

d. Try to avoid using the words with forcing tone or arousing unpleasantness;

e. Use expressions about joy and willingness, thanks and regret, etc.

Review of actual business correspondence reveals that special attention should be devoted to assuming the courtesy of business communication. Effective writers visualize the reader before starting to write. They consider the reader's desires, problems, circumstances, emotions and probable reactions to their request. Let us compare the following sentences.

a. *We are sorry that you misunderstood us.*

b. *We are sorry that we did not make ourselves clear.*

In sentence "a", the author is to put the blame on the customer for something, but in sentence "b", the author takes the initiative to bear the responsibility.

There are a lot of language styles or ways to express courtesy, some of which will be presented here for your reference as follows:

(1) Change the commanding tone into requesting tone

Change the imperative sentence into general question with the word "will" or "would" at the beginning.

For example:

a. *Will you tell us detailed information on your requirements?*

b. *Will you please tell us more detailed information on your requirements?*

c. *Would you please tell us more detailed information on your requirements?*

(2) Use the past subjunctive form

For example:

a. *Would you send us your latest catalogue and price lists on cotton piece goods?*

b. *We would ask you to make a prompt shipment.*

c. *We wish you would let us have your reply soon.*

(3) Use mitigation and avoid overemphasizing your own opinion or irritating your partner

In order to avoid overemphasizing your own opinion and irritating your partner, you should use mitigation, such as "We are afraid that ... ", "We would say ... ", "It seems to us that ... ", "We would suggest that .... ", etc.

(4) Passive voice should be adopted accordingly

In some cases, passive voice appears more courteous than active voice because it can avoid blaming the doer of the act.

For example:

a. *You made a very careless mistake during the course of shipment.*

b. *A very careless mistake was made during the course of shipment.*

c. *You did not enclose the price list in you letter.*

d. *The price list was not enclosed in your letter.*

(5) Try to avoid using the words with forcing tone or arousing unpleasantness

Some words or expressions such as "demand", "disgust", "refuse", "want you to" will arouse unpleasant feeling in audience, therefore they should be avoided or changed into some forms to express. Let us look at the following examples.

a. *demand prompt shipment from you*
request prompt shipment from you

b. *We must refuse your offer.*
We regret that we are unable to accept your offer.

(6) Use expressions about joy and willingness, thanks and regret, etc.

For example:

a. *It is with pleasure that we have reached an agreement on all the terms.*

b. *It is a pleasure for us to sign such a sales contract.*

c. *Thank you for your letter of July 9th, 2020.*

d. *We are extremely sorry that we could not answer your letter in due time.*

5. Correctness

Correctness deals with the accuracy of the figures, facts, grammar, spelling, punctuation marks and the format of the letter. The correctness of your letter can be done by using a grammar and spell check software or proofreading. Proofreading can be done by other people so as to check the other items you might have missed while proofreading your letter. Make sure that you will correct all the errors after checking and proofreading. The final version of the letter should be free from errors.

Correctness not only refers to the correct grammar rules, contents, and forms, but also accuracy in style, language and typing. To choose the right words that can most closely convey the meaning of your thoughts is one of the ways to improve the readability of your business writing. At the same time, the right tone is also significant. Usually, mistakes with tone can be avoided by using the following techniques:

a. Place more emphasis on the reader than yourself;

b. Avoid extreme cases of humility, flattery, and modesty;

c. Avoid condescension;

d. Avoid lecturing.

Correct spelling, proper grammar and punctuation will give your letter a good appearance, but they are not all the factors that correctness comprises. In business letters, you should attach great importance to this writing principle. Especially when you are giving information regarding dates, specifications, prices, quantities, discounts, commission, units and figures, etc. A minor mistake in this respect sometimes means you will make no profit or even lose out. Let us look at the following sentences to see if there is anything improper.

All offers by fax are open for 5 days.

The above sentence does not clearly explain or account for specific 5 days, and should be changed into:

All offers by fax are open for 5 days inclusive of the date of dispatch.

This contract will come into effect from Oct. 1.

The above sentence does not clearly explain whether Oct. 1 is included or not and should be changed into:

This contract will come into effect from and including October 1, 2019.

This product is absolutely the best one on the market.

This is the overstatement of the fact, and the sentence should be changed into:

This product is the best one we can supply.

We assure you that this error will never occur.

Similarly this sentence can be changed into:

We will do all we can so that we may not repeat such an error.

Correctness refers not only to correct usage of grammar, punctuation and spelling, but also to standard language, proper statement, accurate figures as well as the correct understanding of commercial jargon.

1) Avoid grammar mistakes.

a. With pronouns.

Our competitors' prices are 2%–3% lower than us (ours).

b. With verbs.

It is one of the machines that was (were) delivered last week.

c. With conjunctions.

This fridge not only is attractive (is attractive not only) in proper price, but also in good quality.

d. With subjects.

While studying the report, the telephone rang. (Wrong)
While I was studying the report, the telephone rang. (Right)

2) Avoid using overstatements.

We are well-established exporters of all kinds of goods made in Sweden. (Wrong)

We are well-established exporters of Swedish sundry goods, such as toys, buttons and stationary. (Right)

3) Accurate numbers.

5% up to 10% both inclusive

up to $40 inclusive

on or after July 10

from the 1st to 15th of March both inclusive

for five days exclusive of the day of dispatch

for 15 days exclusive of Sundays

Stg. £445.00 (Four Hundred and Forty-five Pounds Sterling only)

£15.01 (Fifteen Pounds and One penny)

5 ft. 10 in (five feet ten inches)

1/4 in pipe (pipe measuring 1/4 inch)

120 sq. ft. (120 square feet)

40 c. ft. (40 cubic feet)

28 in× 30 yds. (28 inches in width, 30 yards in length)

4) Capital letters.

Business correspondence has its special capital letter writing regulations besides the ordinary rules.

A. North, South, East, West.

When they are used for districts or areas but not for orientations:

South-West Africa

North America

West Europe

B. The name and the brand of a commodity.

"Great Wall" Electric Fan

"Three Stars" Calf Shoes

Chinese Cotton Piece Goods

C. The name of documents.

Price List

Letter of Credit

D. The name of the transportation tools.

the S. S. "Merry Captain"
the S. S. "Lucky Prince"

6. Character

This principle will make your letter special and more interesting. A writer has his own personality and it is unique. Each person has individuality. If your letter is written in your own style, considering of course the necessity of business letter, this will add interest to your letter. Rather than simply copying or stereotyping, your own style as a writer shows your character, your strong points and how confident you are in what you are saying in your letter. This principle will help you to be more positive in writing and in reaching your objective. You should not be restricted to being like someone, just bring out that distinct personality and communicate it.

7. Concreteness

In creating a business letter, you also need to consider the words you used within the letter that appeals to the reader's senses. If your letter is dull and uninteresting, the reader may just skim through it and missing the important points. This will not only give you a negative response, but also you may end up waiting for nothing. Aside from that, concreteness also includes the proper use of codes, ratios, and numbers in order for your reader to identify which of the transactions you are referring to. Definitely, there are hundreds of business transactions going on each day, it will help if you can specify the shipping code or any reference number that will point to a specific transaction.

A practical English writing is very successful and highly effective only when it contains all the necessary information to the readers (the counterpart or the public) and answers all the questions and requirements put forward by the readers. See to it that all the matters are stated or discussed, and all the questions are answered or explained. For instance, when the buyer writes a letter to accept an offer that the seller made, the buyer must state his condition of acceptance in detail or quote the evidences of the offer.

In order to verify the completeness of what you write, five "Ws" (who, what, where, when and why) and one "H" (how) should be used. For example, if what you write is a letter of order, you should make it clear that who wants to order, what he wants, when he needs the goods, where the goods to be sent and how payment will be made. If some special requirements should be presented, you could explain why you would do so.

A business letter should include all necessary information. It is essential to check the message carefully before it is sent out. As you work hard for completeness, keep the following guidelines in mind: Why do you write the letter? What are the facts supporting the reasons? Have you answered the questions asked?

Business writing should be vivid, specific and definite rather than vague, general and abstract, especially when the writer is requiring a response, solving problems, making an offer or acceptance, etc. We need to use specific facts, figures and time to stress concreteness. Try to heed the following tips:

a. Complete with the 5 Ws+1 H: Who, What, Where, When, Why, How.

b. Concreteness in action: using specific language to make the information more concrete and convincing;

c. Use concrete words.

Let us look at the following sentence:

We wish to confirm our fax dispatched yesterday.

Like "today" and "tomorrow", the word "yesterday" is a vague and general concept, which allows possibility for misinterpretation.

8. Cheerfulness

Writing a business letter is not just simply writing a letter in order to receive a response. But, you need to demonstrate a positive attitude and express joy in your letter. If your reader feels that your letter will only be a burden, then the reader will just ignore it. Let your reader feel that you are glad to have a business transaction with him. Reflect cheerfulness in your letter. Cheerfulness should already start in the opening of your letter. Remember that you need to leave a good impression to your reader. Everything that will be detailed in your letter is build from the opening.

Part E Tone of Business Letters

1. Conversational Style

A good letter should reflect the personality of the writer and needs to be pleasing to the reader. In a good letter a conversation is held. People who write with a sense of personal contact have a better chance to make what they say interesting and convincing than those who feel they are writing letters. Whatever you talk about in a letter, the language you use should be the same as if you met the person on the street, at home, or in the office. Such a language is warm and natural. It is also the language we use most and understand best.

But when faced with a writing task, many of us tend to be different. Instead of writing in friendly, conversational language, we write in stiff and stilted words. There is a misconception that big words and difficult words are preferred in business letters, but the result of such words is a cold and unnatural style—one that does not produce the goodwill effect you want your letters to have.

2. Avoid the Archaic Language of Business

Early English business writers borrowed heavily from the formal language of law and from the flowery language of the nobility. From these two sources they developed a style of letter writing that became known as the "language of business". It was a cold, stiff, and unnatural style, but it was generally accepted throughout the English-speaking world, for instance, "wherein you state as per your letter" , "take the liberty of", "acknowledge receipt of", etc. Obviously the tone is cold, out of date, and a good writer should take care to give up such stale expressions.

3. Use Positive Language and Avoid Anger

People enjoy and react favorably to positive messages. A positive tone builds the reader's confidence in the writer's ability to solve problems and strengthens personal and business relationships. Positive words are usually best for letter goals, especially when persuasion and goodwill are needed. Positive words emphasize the pleasant aspects of the goal and tend to put the reader in the right frame of mind. They also create the goodwill atmosphere readers seek in most letters.

When confronted with frustration, writers sometimes may lose temper and get angry, but rarely is anger justified in letters, because it destroys goodwill. Most of comments made in anger take many forms like sarcasm, insults and exclamation, and do not provide needed information.

The effect of angry words is to make the reader angry. With both writer and reader angry, the two are not likely to get together on whatever the letter is about. A tactful writer can refer courteously to the subject matter to avoid jeopardizing goodwill. But when pleasant, positive words have not brought desired results, negative words may be justified.

Part F Preparation before Writing

As a writer, you should make preparation for your creative works before taking up the pen. Generally speaking, the following should be borne in mind.

1. Studying Your Reader's Interest

It means that you should think of what your reader thinks.

To achieve this, you should put yourself in your reader's shoes and try to imagine how he will feel about what you write. Ask yourself constantly, "What are his needs, his wishes, his interests, his problems to be solved, and how can I meet his requirement?"

"What would be my own feelings, if I were to receive a letter of the kind I propose to write?" Try to imagine that you are receiving rather than sending the letter and emphasize the "You" attitude rather than "I" or "we" attitude.

2. Planning What You Will Write and Writing Effectively

In order to plan what you write better and to write effectively, you should draft an outline before writing. Every language has its own features. For Chinese students, English is a foreign language. They had better learn to think and write directly in English and draft an English outline before writing.

3. Writing Naturally

Writing naturally is to reveal your true feelings between lines, make sure that what you write would sound sincere and natural and try to avoid the affected words and florid style with little content. In addition, as a writer, he or she should also lean to use polite language and be considerate to the readers.

Part G Rules of Good Writing

1. Adopt the Right Tone

If a letter is to achieve its purpose, its tone must be right. Before beginning to write and think carefully about the way in which you want to influence your reader, ask yourself, "what do I want this letter to do?" and then express yourself accordingly, being persuasive, apologetic, obliging, firm and so on, depending on the effect you want to produce.

2. Write Sincerely

When you write or dictate a business letter, try to feel a genuine interest in the person you are writing to and in his problems. Say what you have to say with sincerity and make sure that it sounds sincere. Express your thoughts in your own words and in your own way. Be yourself.

3. Avoid Wordiness

Make it a rule to use no more words than are needed to make your meaning clear. Businessmen today have many letters to read and welcome the art of letter that is direct and to the point.

4. Write Clearly and to the Point

First be quite clear about what you want to say and then say naturally and with frills, in language your reader will understand just as if you were in conversation with him. For the most past, keep your sentences short and avoid the over frequent use of such conjunctions as "and", "but", "however", "consequently", the effect of which is to make sentence long.

5. Be Courteous and Considerate

Courtesy consists, not in using polite phrase (your kind inquiry, your esteemed order, your valued custom, and so on), but in showing your consideration for your correspondent. It is the quality that enables as to refuse to perform a favor and at the same time keep a friend, to refuse a customer's request for credit without killing all hope of future business.

Deal promptly with all letters needing a reply. Answer them on the day you receive them if you can. It is discourteous to keep your correspondent waiting for an answer. If you cannot deal promptly with a letter seeking information, write and explain why and say when you will write again. This creates an impression of efficiency and helps to build goodwill.

Try to understand and respect your correspondent's point of view and resist the temptation to reply as if you could not be in the wrong. If his suggestions are stupid and his criticism unfair, reply with restraint and say what you feel tastefully and without giving offense. If he sends you a rude or sharp letter, resist the temptation to reply in similar terms. Instead, answer him courteously, and lower your dignity if you allow him to set the tone of your reply.

As the buyer and the seller have both common and contradictory interests, it is very important to keep in mind the distinction between certain overlapping concepts—courtesy overdone may amount to obsequiousness. In short, any virtue overdone will bring with it some undesirable effect, and propriety is the undesirable effect, and propriety is the watchword in distinguishing the right course from the wrong.

6. Avoid Commercial Jargon

Avoid using state and roundabout phrases that add little or nothing to the sense of what you write. Such phrases were at one time common, but they have no place in modern business letters.

7. Write Effectively

In business letters writing you should use simple language, which calls for a plain style—a style that is simple, clear and easily understood. Use plain, familiar words and prefer short words to long ones if they will do just as well. Wherever possible, prefer the single word to the elaborate phrase. Express yourself in simple language so that your message is clear at first reading.

Be consistent in writing a business letter. Avoid repeating in the same sentence an important word with different meaning.

But in your efforts to avoid repetition don't make the apposite mistake of confusing your reader by using different words to express exactly the same thing. Don't say the same thing. Don't say in the same letter that goods have been sent, forwarded, and dispatched, and if you begin your letter by referring to a firm, don't change it as you go along into a "concern" or a "business", or an "organization". If you do, you will have your reader wondering whether something different is intended.

Preciseness is also required in a business letter. Use expression with precise meanings. When acknowledging a letter, refer to it by date, subject and reference number (if any). When referring to dates mention the month by name and avoid using "instant" or "inst." (for the present month), "ultimo" or "ult." (for the past month), and "proximate" or "proxy." (for the next month). Avoid using vague expressions but concrete words.

8. Avoid Monotony

In a business letter you should use either loose sentences or sentences which will make your message vivid. Short sentences are preferable to long ones because short sentences are easily understood. A succession of short sentences, however, has a disagreeable jerky effect and the best letters are those which provide a mixture of sentences of different length. Sometimes you wish to emphasize the sentence. Emphasis is also achieved by using "it is" or "it was" to introduce statements.

Unfortunately, the goods did not arrive in time. (normal order)
It was unfortunately that the goods did not arrive in time. (emphatic order)

9. Plan Your Letter

Many business letters are short and routine and can be written or dictated without special preparation. Others must first be thought about and planned. First jot down all the points you wish to cover and then arrange them in logical order to provide the plan for a letter that will read naturally and fluently. If your letter is in reply to one received, underline those parts which seek information or on which comment is necessary. This will ensure that your reply is complete.

10. Pay Attention to First and Last Impressions

If your letter is one sent in reply to another, refer in the opening paragraph to the letter you are answering, but avoid the sort of old-fashioned phrases, such as "we are in receipt of your letter ...", "we have for acknowledgement your letter ...". Although they are grammatically correct, they tend to be dull and monotonous, worm threadbare from over-use.

If a letter has been well planned and follows a logical sequence, a brief observation will usually be enough to provide the kind of ending introduced by a participle. "Thanking you in anticipation" and similar endings are no longer used in modern letter-writing. They mean nothing and serve no useful purpose.

11. Check Your Letter

Be careful to create a good first impression with your letter. Before signing, check it for the accuracy of its contents, and test its general suitability against such questions:

a. Is its appearance attractive? Is it well laid out?
b. Is it correctly spelt and properly punctuated?
c. Does it cover all essential point and is the information given correct?
d. Is what I have said clear, concise and courteous?
e. Does it sound natural and sincere?
f. Does it adopt the reader's point of view and will it be readily understood?
g. Is its general tone right and is it likely to create the impression intended?
h. Is it the kind of letter I should like to receive if I were in the reader's place?

If the answer to all the question is "yes", the letter will take the first step in creating goodwill and you may safely sign and send it.

Chapter 3 Structures and Styles of Business Letters

Learning Objectives

a. Learn about different types of business letters;

b. Master structures and styles of business letters;

c. Master principal parts and optional elements of business letters.

Part A Introduction

Because at present many business messages are sent by way of fax or E-mail instead of traditional post, and the language and styles used in the fax or E-mail messages are almost the same as those used in the letter by post, letter-writing is again regarded as quite important in international trade communicating. In today's highly developed and competitive society, communication between individuals and groups is becoming frequent and important. It serves to pass on information, to express ideas or to exchange feelings. Generally speaking, the function of a business letter is to get or to convey business information, to make or to accept an offer, to deal with various businesses. When we write a letter we enter into personal relationship with our readers. A business letter is a formal letter corresponding with other parties in regard to a particular concern or objective. There are many different types of letters, because every individual business has its own aims and interests. However, all business letters are similar in styles and formats.

1. Types

There are a number of types of business letters in the English language. Accomplished English speakers should be able to write the following types of business letters to be successful in business.

It's helpful, to begin with, gaining a clear understanding of business letters writing basics. Once you've understood the basic layout styles, standard phrases, salutations, and endings, you should continue to improve your business letters writing skills by learning to write the following types of business letters. Do you know what type of business letter you need for a task?

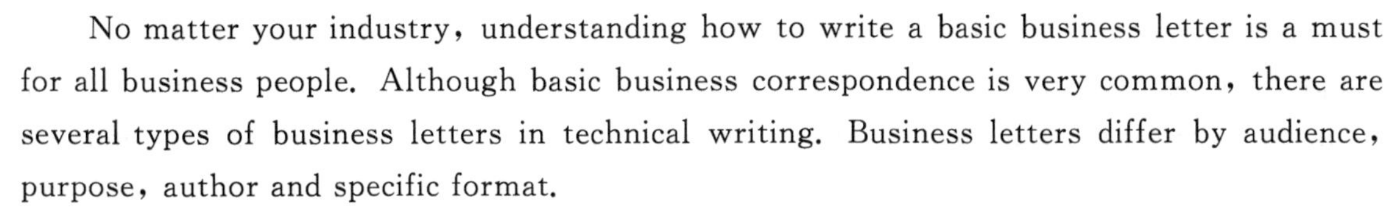

No matter your industry, understanding how to write a basic business letter is a must for all business people. Although basic business correspondence is very common, there are several types of business letters in technical writing. Business letters differ by audience, purpose, author and specific format.

(1) Cover letter

Business people use the cover letter in the job application process in order to "sell" themselves to the organization they are trying to join. Cover letters are extremely important when applying for a new position. Cover letters should include a short introduction, highlight the most important information in your resume and elicit a positive response from your prospective employer. The cover letter is the first impression you as a job seeker will make on your potential employer, and employers often use the cover letter as a litmus test to determine whether the resume is worth reading. According to the Purdue Online Writing Lab, you should write your cover letter in a narrative voice, highlighting the experiences and skills that have prepared you for the job you are seeking. The writing center at the University of North Carolina at Chapel Hill suggests writing in a tone that lies between extremely conversational and extremely formal. Use action verbs frequently when writing your cover letter, and use the help wanted ad or job description to find key words, such as "detail oriented", that should be included in your letter.

(2) Persuasive business letter

If you are writing a persuasive business letter, you are trying to convince the recipient to take actions you recommend. You may write this type of business letter to an employee, supervisor, client or colleague, or to other parties within or outside of your organization. A persuasive business letter must state the purpose (to convince) within the first few sentences. Business writing is concise because business people are stereotypically busy. It is very important for your letter to get to the point quickly and not waste time with unnecessary introductions, socializing, or details. State the course of action that you would like your reader to take within the first few lines and spend the body of the letter outlining the benefits of the action or explaining why it should be taken. Make sure to clearly include any necessary details. It is suggested that you should clearly state if you require a response.

When you write a persuasive business letter, analyze your audience. Who you are writing to will determine what information you include. For example, you would only add an introduction if the person you are writing to does not know you. In addition, a manager would find different benefits in the course of action than a client.

(3) Letters of apology

Although they are one of the most common types of business letters, letters of apology are also one of the hardest to write. You must write to "save face", allowing your business to retain integrity while offering a sincere apology for the indiscretion. Like other business letters, get straight to the point. Write the intent of the letter—to apologize—and what you are apologizing for in the first paragraph. The next paragraph should ask the related party to forgive the mistake and explain how the error was made, as well as anything that is being done to make sure it won't happen again. Finally, you should re-state your apology and offer to make up for the mistake with a discount, free merchandise or in another appropriate way. In a letter of apology, never appear to be defensive, and always provide the contact information of someone who can best address the issue.

(4) Making an inquiry

Make an inquiry when you are requesting more information about a product or service. The inquiry letter tends to include specific information such as product type, as well as asking for further details in the form of brochures, catalogs, telephone contact, etc. Making inquiries can also help you keep up with your competition.

(5) Sales letters

Sales letters are used to introduce new products to new customers and past clients. It's important to outline an important problem that needs to be solved and provide the solution in sales letters. Sales letters can be improved through the use of personalization some means in order to ensure attention.

(6) Replying to an inquiry

Replying to an inquiry is one of the most important business letters that you write. Successfully replying to an inquiry can help you complete a sale or lead to new sales. Customers who make inquiries are interested in specific information and are excellent business prospects. Learn how to thank the customers, provide as much information as possible, as well as make a call to action for a positive outcome.

(7) Account terms and conditions

When a new customer opens an account it is essential to inform him/her of account terms and conditions. If you run a small business, it is common to provide these terms and conditions in the form of a letter.

(8) Letters of acknowledgment

For legal purposes, letters of acknowledgment are often requested. These letters are also referred to as letters of receipt and tend to be rather formal and short.

(9) Placing an order

As a business person, you will often place an order. This is especially true if you have a large supply chain for your product. Make sure your order placement is clear so that you receive exactly what you order.

(10) Making a claim

Unfortunately, from time to time it is necessary to make a claim against unsatisfactory work. Clearly express your dissatisfaction and future expectations when making a claim.

(11) Adjusting a claim

Even the best business may make a mistake from time to time. In this case, you may be called upon to adjust a claim. This type of business letter is sent to unsatisfied customers making sure that you address their specific concerns, as well as retain them as future customers.

2. Formats

Professional correspondence should have a clean, polished look, which is where the proper business letter format comes in. The overall style of the correspondence depends on the relationship between you and the letter's recipient, and it can contain almost anything. Read on to learn more about business letter formats.

(1) Full block style

The full block style business letter layout is more popular than other business letter templates, and given the option, it is the one most people prefer to use. When you use this business letter format, all the information is typed flush left and margins are set at 1 to $1\frac{1}{4}$ inches all the way around. This happens to be the default setting in most word processing programs including Microsoft Word.

The left justified type is easy to read, looks crisp on the page, and leaves little room for error. If you are new to writing business letters and your company doesn't have a policy in place concerning business letter format, you may find this is a good place to start.

Full block style business letters have a formal look, however they can be used in any business situation. If you are looking for a single format that will work well in every situation, this is a good one to use.

(2) Modified block style

The modified block style business letter is the second-most popular layout. It has a clean, traditional look, with your company's return address, the date, the closing, and the signature line being started at the center point of the page.

All other elements including inside address, greeting, body, and enclosures notation are left justified, and paragraphs are followed by either double or triple spacing. Like the margins on a full block style business letter, the margins of the modified block style business letter layout are set to 1 to $1\frac{1}{4}$ inches.

Modified block style business letters are less formal than full block style letters. If you are corresponding with someone you already have a good working relationship with, the modified block style letter is a good one to use.

(3) Standard format

The standard business letter has the same look as the block style business letter, meaning that all lines are flush with the left margin. All margins should be set at $1\frac{1}{2}$ inches.

The greeting or salutation in a standard format business letter is always followed by a colon.

An optional subject line follows the salutation or greeting. This is written in all caps, and should read "SUBJECT" or "RE:" (an abbreviation for "reference"). This should be followed by a brief description of the letter's subject, an account number, or other applicable information. The subject line is often underlined.

The letter's closing is followed by a comma.

A standard format business letter has some additional, optional elements added to the closing and signature area.

If a third person, such as an assistant or secretary, typed the letter, a blank line should follow the sender's information located below the signature. The typist's initials should follow the sender's initials on a line located just below the blank line, with the sender's initials in uppercase and the typists in lowercase. For example, "KS:pj" or "MJ:ak".

On the next line, you should indicate whether a copy of the letter is being sent to anyone else with the notation "cc:" in lowercase letters. For example, "cc: John King".

On the line below that, you should indicate the presence of enclosures, if appropriate. Note that the abbreviation "Encl:" beginning with a capital "E" is used with standard business letter format. For example, "Encl: copy of invoice".

Standard format business letters are quite formal. Because they include an optional subject line, they are ideal for situations in which you need to create a formal response or communicate about an account number or case number.

(4) Open business letter

The open format business letter looks almost exactly like the block format business letter. There are two basic differences between the two layouts:

a. There is no punctuation after the greeting or salutation.

b. There is no punctuation after the closing.

The open format business letter has a clean, formal look just as the block format letter does. It is suitable for all business communications.

(5) Semi-block business letter

In this kind of business letter, all text is aligned to the left margin. As in other business letter templates, each paragraph is separated by double or triple spacing. The main difference between this type of correspondence and others is that the first line of each paragraph is indented.

The semi-block format business letter is a little less formal than the block format letter and slightly more formal than the modified block format letter. It works well in almost all situations and is a good choice if you find yourself on the fence about which format to use.

(6) Modified semi-block business letter

The modified semi-block format business letter looks almost identical to the modified block letter, with just one difference. The first line of each paragraph is indented.

The modified semi-block business letter is the least formal-looking of all business letters and is best for using when you know the recipient very well.

Regardless of which business letter format you prefer, use the following basic tips to ensure that your correspondence has a clean, professional look.

a. Save the fancy fonts for personal correspondence. Business letter format rules dictate that plain fonts like Arial, Calibri, or Times New Roman be used. Your company may have a preferred font; if so, use that one.

b. 12-point font is the standard for all business letter formats.

c. Follow the salutation or greeting with a comma or colon. In the United States, colons are sometimes preferred; in the United Kingdom, greetings are usually followed by commas. If you aren't sure which your company prefers, use a comma for all greetings other than the generic "To Whom It May Concern", which is always followed by a colon.

d. The closing, which is also known as a valediction, is always followed by a comma.

e. You can use any business letter formats with company letterhead, just skip the return address that is usually located at the top of the page.

f. Print your business letters on standard $8\frac{1}{2}$ inches × 11 inches paper. Use good quality white paper or choose a paper in a muted color like cream or gray. It is a good idea to use a matching envelope.

g. Format business letter envelopes carefully. If you are new to the process of printing envelopes, practice using a plain sheet of paper to ensure that everything is in the right place.

3. Language Style

No matter who the audience of the business letter is, be clear and concise. This is because the person receiving it is likely to only have time to scan over the letter; if they misunderstand anything, it may jeopardize further correspondence. This can be done by avoiding writing in the passive voice.

4. Main Parts

The main parts of the business letter are the date, sender's address, recipient's address, salutation, body, closing and signature.

5. Form

The form will always be by E-mail or a typed and printed document sent in the mail. An E-mail is more likely to be written in a casual tone, whereas the printed one is more likely to be formal.

6. Power of Persuasion

The business letter is often used to persuade the recipient in some way, such as an unemployed person trying to convince a manager to hire him or a lawyer trying to negotiate terms of an agreement on behalf of a client. No matter what the aim is, think of all the relevant points the reader will need to know when writing the letter.

Part B Structures of Business Letters

A business letter is one of the vital tools of communication in business organizations. To make a business letter effective we should give attention to structures/different parts of a business letter. An effective/good business letter may have the following parts:

1. Letterhead

Here the following information is highlighted:

a. The full name of the firm or individual sending the letter;

b. Address of the sender;

c. Reference number;

d. Date of drafting the letter;

e. Telephone, telex, Fax, and E-mail address of the sender.

For example:

Commerce Publications
37, Banglabazar, Dhaka-1100
Phone: 02-7170495
Cell: 0176-190865
Web:WWW. com. Pub

Ref. 110 Dx

15th, November 2017.

2. Inside Address

The address of the receiver is given here as would appear on an envelope. It helps the outward clerk to write the same address on the cover. It is also a record on the copy which serves to identify the letter for filling a purpose.

Block Form: Here all lines maintain the same margin and no punctuation is used at the end of any line.

For example:

BANI BITAN LIBRARY
40, Sadar Road
Barisal

Indented Form: Here the subsequent lines start two spaces away from the beginning of the previous line. After each line, there is a coma and a full stop is put at the end of the last line.

For example:

BANI BITAN LIBRARY,
40, Sadar Road,
Barisal.

3. Attention Line

The person who can take prompt action for the letter, his name, and department are stated here.

For example:

Mr. Mahabub, Sales Manager

4. Subject Heading

The main theme of the letter is highlighted here.

For example:

Sub: Confirmation of order for 100 GT Television.

5. Salutation

It is the complimentary greetings with which the writer opens his letter. It should be written below the inside address. The salutation is made according to the status of the receiver.

For example:

If the name is unknown: use *Dear Sir or Madam.*
If the name is known: use *Dear Mr. Hossain.*
If close friend: use *My Dear Tasir.*
If a large number of people: use *Dear Customers or Dear Subscribers or Dear Members.*

6. Body

It is that part of the letter which contains the message or the information to be communicated and therefore the most important part. It must be natural, and simple with logical sequence. It should be stated considering "You" Attitude.

7. Complimentary Close

The complimentary close is a polite way of ending a letter. There are various styles to write a complimentary close, which are given below:

Yours faithfully,
Yours truly,
Truly yours,
Yours very truly,
Yours respectfully,
Yours sincerely,
Sincerely yours,

8. Signature

It is the assent of the writer to the subject matter of the letter and is a practical necessity. It is usually handwritten and given below the complimentary close.

9. Sender's Name and Address

The person who is sending the letter, his name and address should be given for proper identification. Such identification is placed just after the signature.

For example:

Ma Jasii Hossain

Deputy Manager, Sales & Distribution

10. Enclosure

Sometimes other papers such as price list, catalog, prospectus, order, invoice, railway or lorry receipt, cash memo, check, draft, bill, etc. are enclosed with the letter. In such a case, a mention should be made of these enclosures in the letter.

For example:

Enclosures:

Peoforma Invoice
Bill of Exchange
Bill of Lading.

11. Carbon Copy

Sometimes copies of a letter have to be sent to some people other than the addressee also. In such a case, the names of those persons should be mentioned.

For example:

Copy: 1. *Mr. Hasan*
General Manager, Administration.
2. *Mr. Salam*
Deputy Manager, Sales.

12. Identification Mark

The person taking dictation of the letter and the person typing or composing the letter should be identified by their initials to the end of the letter, e. g. t, & A, etc.

13. Postscripts

Postscript (P. S.) is something written after the letter is closed, writing P. S. indicates that the writer had forgotten to include something important in the body of the letter. It is a bad practice to write a P. S. and it should preferably be avoided.

Structures/Parts of a business letter which are mention above create a good business letter. See Figure 3. 1 for the layout example of different parts of a business letter.

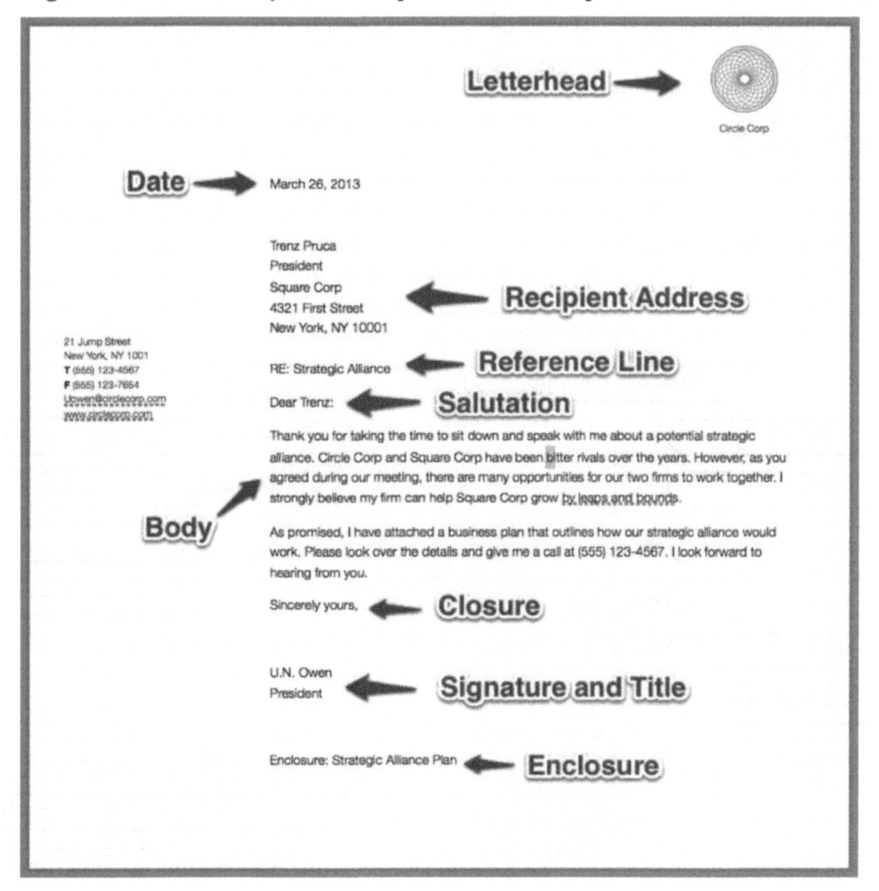
Circle Corp

March 26, 2013

Trenz Pruca
President
Square Corp
4321 First Street
New York, NY 10001

21 Jump Street
New York, NY 1001
T (555) 123-4567
F (555) 123-7654
Uowen@circlecorp.com
www.circlecorp.com

RE: Strategic Alliance

Dear Trenz:

Thank you for taking the time to sit down and speak with me about a potential strategic alliance. Circle Corp and Square Corp have been bitter rivals over the years. However, as you agreed during our meeting, there are many opportunities for our two firms to work together. I strongly believe my firm can help Square Corp grow by leaps and bounds.

As promised, I have attached a business plan that outlines how our strategic alliance would work. Please look over the details and give me a call at (555) 123-4567. I look forward to hearing from you.

Sincerely yours,

U.N. Owen
President

Enclosure: Strategic Alliance Plan

Figure 3. 1 Business letter layout example

Table 3. 1 will describe all essential structures/parts of a business letter at a glance.

Table 3. 1 Essential structures/parts of a business letter

1	Letterhead	Commerce Zone LTD. A Manufacturer of Quality Stationery Park Avenue, Baridhara, Dhaka.
2	Date	May 6,2004
3	Inside Address	Purchase Manager DEE Publication Ltd. Bangla Bazar, Dhaka.
4	Subject	Sub: Confirmation of order for 2 000 GX Ballpen
5	Salutation	Dear Sir,
6	Introduction	We are glad to receive your order for 2 000 GX Ballpen dated April 25, 2004.
7	Body	We have forwarded your Consignment and will reach on 8th July 2004. All the Business documents have been sent through Standard Chartered Bank as per your instruction and duplicate is attached herewith for your favor. We believe that you would settle our dues in time and improve our business close relations.
8	Complimentary close	Yours faithfully,
9	Signature Block	Tahsin Hossain
10	Enclosure	Duplicate of Business documents
11	Distribution	Copy: A. B. Siddique, General Manager, AdminTime Publications Ltd.

See Figure 3. 2 for the structure of business letters, which display the basic and additional components respectively.

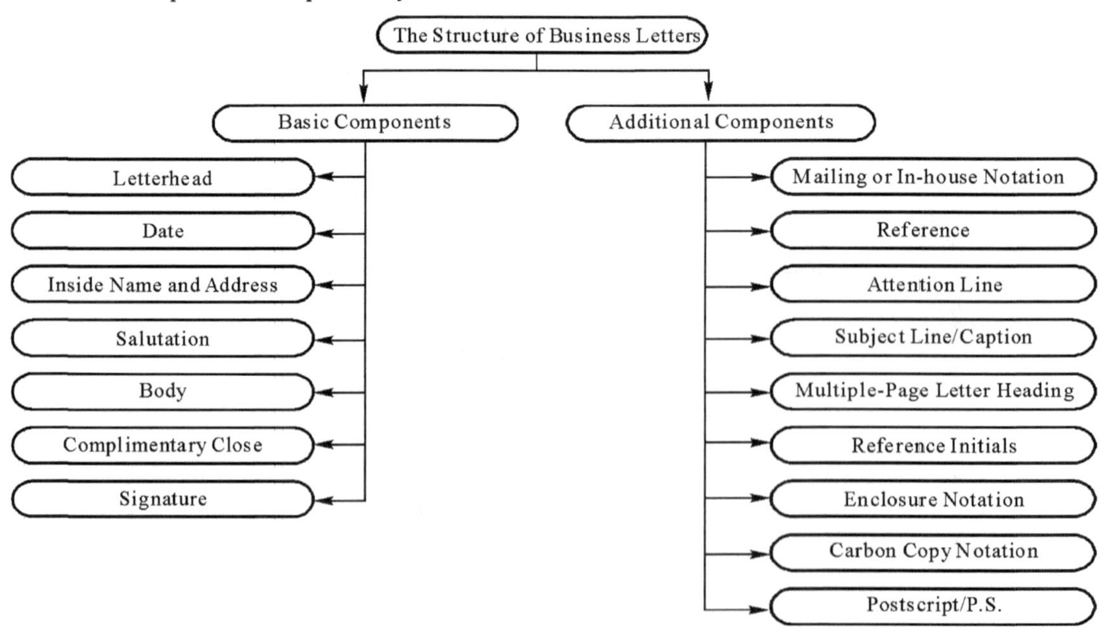

Figure 3. 2 The structure of business letters

Part C Principal Parts of Business Letters

1. Letterhead

The letterhead is the heading at the top of a letter. It usually consists of the name, address, telephone number and fax number of a company who delivers the letter. The letterhead can be typed out, but is usually printed on the companies stationary (such stationary is also called letterhead) in the up center or at the left margin of a letter. In addition, the printed letterhead may also include other items such as the company logo, website, E-mail address, etc.

Letterhead can also be called heading of the letter. It is usually placed on the top of letter. Besides the name and address, sometimes it also gives the relevant information about the sender's company, such as telephone number, fax number, internet address, etc.

It includes the essential particulars about the writer's name, postal address and zip-code, telephone and facsimile numbers.

2. Date

The format of the date line differs from country to country. The common ones are M/D/Y (typical American), D/M/Y (typical British).

e. g. 02/12/2020

This form in Britain could be taken as December 2, 2020, but in American and some other countries it would mean February 12, 2020. So the month written in letters is preferred because figures may create confusion.

The date is typed a few lines below the last line of the letterhead. Different from the place in a Chinese letter, the date in an English letter should be put above the inside name and address.

In business letters, date line is very important. You can decide from the date line whether an order is fulfilled, a contract or an agreement is in effect, or a bill is paid. Therefore, it should not be wrongly written or omitted.

Generally speaking, there are two ways in writing the date. You can write it in the logical order of day, month, year, for instance, 12th Dec. , 2020. Or you can write the date after the month and use a comma between the day and the year, e. g. Dec. 2nd, 2020. You had better use ordinal numbers for the day.

The date should be placed two or four spaces below the letterhead to the right for indented style or the left for the blocked style. The date should be written in full and not abbreviated. The preferred order of the parts that make up the date is: the day of the month, the month, the year.

3. Inside Address

The reference may include a file name, departmental code or the initials of the signer followed by that of the typist of the letter. Many letterheads provide space for references.

e. g. *Your ref*:
Our ref:

The inside address is the recipients address, which should be identical to the delivery address on the envelope. The inside address serves as the delivery address. It is typed at the left hand margin two lines below the date. The information should be given in a way like this: The address of the organization receiving the letter is typed single-spaced at the left margin. This part usually refers to the recipient's name and address. The information should be given in a way like this:

a. Receiver's name or his official title;
b. Company's name;
c. Number of the house and name of the street;
d. District, name of the town or city;
e. State or province, ZIP code;
f. Name of country.

Here is an example:

President
Shanghai Foreign Trade & Economics Training Center
89, Fuzhou RD.
Huangpu District, Shanghai, 200003
P. R. C.

Sometimes "Messrs.", which is the plural form of "Mr.", is placed as a courtesy title before the name of a company which includes a personal element. For instance:

Messrs. Evans & Sons Co. Ltd.

It consists of the correspondent's name and address. It appears exactly the same way as on the envelope. It should be placed two spaces below the date.

4. Salutation

Courtesy titles, such as "Mr.", "Ms.", etc., are commonly used to address one person. Use "Ms." if you do not know whether a lady is married or not. If there is any official position of that person, his or her official position should follow after the name.

e. g. *Mr. Smith, President*

"Messrs" is also a common courtesy title, only used for companies or firms, the name of which includes a personal element, like in "Messrs J. Henry & Co". It is not used when the name already carries a courtesy title, like "Sir James Fred & Co".

For most letter styles, place the letter greeting or salutation two lines below the last line of the inside address or the attention line (if used). If the letter is addressed to an individual, use that person's courtesy title and last name, e. g. "Dear Miss Helen". The salutation varies according to the writer-recipient relations and the formality level of the letter. "Dear Sir", "Dear Sir or Madam" or "Dear Sirs" and "Ladies and Gentlemen" can be used to address a person of whom you know neither the name nor the gender.

Sometimes some special titles may be used as the salutation. They are preceded by "Dear" and followed by the surname only, e. g. "Dear Dr. Watson", or "Dear Prof. Young". Be sure to add a colon or a comma (not a semicolon) after the salutation. Examples of typical salutations are as follows:

Dear Mr. ×× (Men)
Dear Mrs. ×× (Married women)
Dear Miss. ×× (Unmarried women and girls)
Dear Ms. ×× (Women, marital status unknown)
Dear Dr. ×× (Physicians, PHD. holders)
Dear Prof. ×× (Professors and any holder of a professional rank)
Dear Sir(s)/Madam (No specific reference, formal)
Gentlemen (No specific reference, formal)
Ladies and Gentlemen (No specific reference, formal)
To whom it may concern (You do not know yet who is the recipient)
(Dear) First name (Only close friend, informal)

The salutation is the polite greetings with which a letter begins. The customary formal greeting in a business letter is "Dear Sirs" or "Gentlemen". It should be placed two spaces below the inside address.

5. Subject Line

The subject line is placed one line below the salutation. It helps both the sender and the recipient identify the subject matter. It is used to attract readers's attention, therefore, you may underline it or make it in boldface letters. Below are some samples of the subject line:

Subject:Order No. 12345

Subject:S/C No. 345

Re:Invoice 567

Re:Your L/C No. 678

6. Body of the Letter

This is the most important part of every business letter. It is typed two lines below the salutation or subject line. No matter whether your letter is long or short, it usually consists of three paragraphs: the opening paragraph which is to give a subject introduction of the letter; the middle paragraph to discuss the details of the transaction; and the closing paragraph to end the letter in a way of summation, further request or suggestion. And when writing the letter, you should attach great importance to the principles: Clearness, Conciseness, Consideration, Courtesy, Correctness, Concreteness and Completeness. It is advisable to keep the following tips in mind:

a. Write simply, clearly, courteously, grammatically, and to the point;

b. Paragraph correctly, confining each paragraph to one topic;

c. See that your typing is accurate.

This is the most important part of a letter in which you convey the real information. Before you write it, you must consider two points as follows:

a. What is the purpose to write this letter?

b. How to present the letter in the best way?

7. Complimentary Close

This part is like bidding farewell to someone with a handshake, a wave of hand, or a kiss. Like the salutation, the complimentary close has various styles: formal, semi-formal and informal. The style shall match that of the salutation.

The complimentary close is merely a polite way to bring the letter to an end. If the salutation is "Dear Sirs", "Dear Madam or Sir", you can use "Yours faithfully", "Faithfully yours" as complimentary close.

If the salutation is "Gentlemen", "Mr. /Mrs. /Miss/Ms. White", etc. , you can use "Yours sincerely", "Sincerely yours", "Yours truly", "Truly yours", "Best wishes". Or "Best regards" can also be used in less formal letters.

It is often given from the second line below the closing sentence of the letter.

The complimentary close is mere a polite way of ending a letter. It should match the form of the salutation. The most commonly sets of salutation and complimentary close (See Table 3. 3) are:

Table 3.3 Salutation and complimentary close

Salutation	Complimentary close
Dear Sirs	Yours faithfully
Gentlemen	Yours truly
Dear Mr. ××	Yours sincerely

Some samples of the complimentary close (See Table 3.4) are:

Table 3.4 Complimentary close

Formal	Semi-formal	Informal
Yours sincerely	Sincerely yours	All the best
Yours very truly	Cordially yours	Cordially
Yours respectfully	Faithfully	Best regards

8. Signature

The signature is generally placed two lines below the complimentary close. It consists of a handwritten signature (by hand and in ink, usually illegible), the typed out name and a title. It usually consists of lines like:

a. Manual signature of the writer;

b. Typed name of the writer and his or her job title.

For example:

Yours faithfully,

The NATIONAL TRANSPORT CO.

(signature)

Zhang Wei
Manager

Part D Optional Elements of Business Letters

Optional parts of a letter are the references, the attention line, the subject line, the enclosure, the carbon copy notation, the postscript, and the identification line.

1. Attention Line

If you send your message officially to an organization, an attention line allows you to send it directly to a specific individual, officer, or department. However, if you know an individual's complete name, it is always better to use it as the first line of the inside address and avoid an attention line.

2. Subject Line

A subject line helps identify the subject of the letter. Although experts suggest placing the subject line two lines below the salutation, many businesses actually place it above the salutation. Use whatever style your organization prefers. Using a subject line will alert your reader to the content of your message and enable him or her to decide whether the letter requires immediate attention. So a subject line is often underlined or typed in capitals. For example:

RE:Claim Number ×××
Re:Tool
Subject:Order ×××

The subject line is often inserted between the salutation and the body of the letter to invite attention to the topic of the letter.

3. Enclosure

When something else is sent together with the letter, you add the enclosure to inform the reader what is enclosed. For example:

Enclosure:Sales Contract

Encls:
Packing List
Commodity Inspection certificate
Insurance Policy

If an enclosure or attachment accompanies the letter, a notation to that effect should be placed four or five lines below the signature. The word "enclosure" or shortened "enc." followed by a period or colon should be written. For example:

Enclosure:Bill of Lading
Encl. :Commercial Invoice
Enclosures:3

If something is enclosed with the letter, you may type one of the following examples at the left bottom.

Enclosure:
Enclosures:
Enclosures: 2

Encl. :
Encls. : 2
As Stated
Encs. : 2
Encls. : 2 Invoices
Encls. : 1 B/Lading
1 Photo
1 Certificate

4. Copy Notation

If copies of a business letter have been made for other individuals, a copy notation is typed one or two lines below the enclosure notation (if used). A colon following is optional. Most people prefer to use notation like CC. , cc, Cc, C. C. (all mean carbon copy). Since most copies are now photo-copied, some people use the notation CX (xerox copy), PC (photo copy), or C (copy). However, if you do not want the addressee to know that someone else is receiving a copy, do not include this notation on the original copy.

When copies of the letter are sent to others, you may type "C. C." below the signature at the left margin.

C. C. : The Bank of Osaka, Ltd., Kobe
The Osaka Chamber of Commerce & Industry

5. Postscript

The postscript (P. S.) is used to add an afterthought, aiming at the drawing of the reader's attention to a point you wish to emphasize or something you forget to mention. The note of a P. S. should be avoided as far as possible, since it may suggest that you have failed to plan your letter well. It is strongly advised to rewrite the letter instead of using the afterthought when you forget to mention something important.

As a special device, the postscript is placed two lines below at the left margin.

As a special device, the postscript has two legitimate functions.

a. Some executives occasionally add a postscript to add a personal touch to the typewritten letter.

b. Writers of sales letter often withhold one last convincing argument for emphatic inclusion in a postscript.

e. g. *P. S. ... to see you at the annual sales meeting on October 16.*

Part E　Styles of Business Letters

First, let's look at the orgnization model of a business letter

a. Introduction

explain what and why you are writing (do NOT say "I am writing because ... ");

establish a reader-reason for the communication;

summarize your message and conclusion;

b. Body

explain/present your message as clearly and specifically as possible;

follow a logical pattern;

include appropriate details and examples;

anticipate (and perhaps answer) the reader's questions;

c. Conclusion

rephrase or move towards your purpose;

specify who (you, your reader, or someone else) should take what action next;

indicates deadline(s) if applicable;

include courtesies.

In addition to business letters, this model can also be used for short memos and long reports. To note, the ability to summarize your message in the introduction will make you stand out as an effective writer.

Example:

- (Heading) China National Light Industrial Products
- Import & Export Corporation
- 82 Tian'an Men Street
- Beijing, China

Jan.30,2005(date)

- The Pakistan Trading Company (Inside Address)
- 15, Broad Street
- Karachi, Pakistan

- Gentlemen (Salutation)
- Re: Chinese Light Industrial Products (Caption)
- We thank you for your letter of Jan.10, 2005 and shall be glad to enter into business relations with your firm.
- (The Opening Sentences)
- As you know, it is our policy to trade with the people of all countries on the basis of equality and mutual benefit. We believe we shall be able, by joint efforts, to promote friendship as well as business.

- We are sending you 5 pamphlets and a price list covering part of our exports.

- Please advise what articles you are interested in at present.　(The Body of the Letter)

- Your early reply will be highly appreciated.　(The Closing Sentences)

- (The Complimentary Close) Yours faithfully, P
- CHINA NATIONAL LIGHT INDUSTRIAIRODUCTS

- IMPORT & EXPORT CORP.　(The Signature)
- (Sighed)----
- Encls:

Figure 3.3　A business letter

There are several formats for writing professional letters, such as block format, modified block format and semi-block format. There are two basic styles of letters: block form and indented form.

A. Block format. In this style, all text is left justified. Skip one line between each section.

B. Modified block format. Most content is left justified in this style, just as in the block format letter. Here are the exceptions: for your contact information and complimentary close, tab over to the center of the page, and write your information there.

C. Semi-block format. Also sometimes referred to as indented block format, this style is the same as the modified block format except that each paragraph is indented.

Any of these styles is acceptable for use in a business letter, but since the rules for the block format are so clear-cut, this may be the easiest option to select.

Many word processing programs will have templates available that will make it easier for you to format the letter appropriately. Take advantage of these templates so you can focus on the content of your letter instead of the formatting. Whichever format you choose, make sure to single-space the letter and skip a space between every paragraph and section.

Sapmle 1: Full Block Letter Format

Cleôn M. McLean
Department of English
Ontario High School
901 West Francis Street
Ontario, California, 91762

September 14th, 2015

Chaffey Joint Union High School District
211 West Fifth Street
Ontario, California, 91762

To Whom It May Concern:

A full block letter format is the most formal of the three letter formats, i. e. full block, modified block, and semi-block. With the full block format, everything except the letterhead begins at the left margin.

The date of the letter, the name and address of the receiver, the salutation, all paragraphs, the complimentary close, and the signature block all begin at the left margin. Fewer keystrokes and other adjustments are required with full block. As a result, we may see full block becoming the most common format over the next five years.

Some writers prefer full block because they see it as a crisper, cleaner look. In some cases, these writers will also choose right margin justification as a personal choice, although it is not required for the full block format.

Cordially,

Cleôn M. McLean

Sapmle 2: Semi - Block Letter Format

Cleôn M. McLean
Department of English
Ontario High School
901 West Francis Street
Ontario, California, 91762

September 14th, 2015

Veronica Partida
Chaffey Joint Union High School District
211 West Fifth Street
Ontario, California, 91762

Dear Mrs. Partida,

A semi-block letter format is the most personal and old-fashioned of the three letter formats in business today. Oftentimes the semi-block format is used for more social notes than for common business purposes.

With the semi-block format, the date, the complimentary close, and the signature block begin near the center of the page or a little to the right. In addition, all the paragraphs are indented approximately one-half inch. Only the inside address, the salutation, and the reference notes begin at the left margin. As with the modified block format, make sure that the date, the closure, and the signature block line up with each other, beginning in the center or a little to the right of center.

With all three letter formats, position the letter in the visual center of the page. A short letter should begin lower on the page to create a pleasant visual effect. Do not use right margin justification with the semi-block format because it is contradictory to the style.

Sincerely,

Cleôn M. McLean

Sapmle 3: Modified Block Letter Format

Cleôn M. McLean
Department of English
Ontario High School
901 West Francis Street
Ontario, California, 91762

September 14th, 2015

Veronica Partida
Chaffey Joint Union High School District
211 West Fifth Street
Ontario, California, 91762

Dear Mrs. Partida,

A modified block letter format is the most common of the three letter formats in business today. Most people prefer it because it has more visual balance than the full block format and is easier to work with than the semi-block format. With the modified block format, the date, the complimentary close, and the signature block begin near the center of the page or a little to the right.

All other elements, the inside address, the salutation, the paragraphs, and reference notes all begin at the left margin. When you use the modified block format, be sure the date, the closure, and the signature block line up with each other. You do not want one beginning three inches from the left margin and the other beginning four inches to the right. Avoid aligning the date and closure with the far right margin and creating a ragged left line.

If you are unsure about which format to use and you have no handy example of the receiver's style, use the modified block format. Right margin justification is a personal choice and is not required for any of the letter formats.

Respectfully,

Cleôn M. McLean

1. Indented Style

An indented letter style is a letter-writing style where the paragraphs are indented. When writing a letter using indented form, indent each paragraph. First include your name, address, phone number, and the date. This information should be located at the top of the page, either in the center, or indented on the right side of the paper. You then include the name and address of the person to whom you are sending the letter.

The paragraphs are typically indented by half an inch.

The indented letter format is not popular in modern business correspondence. Using the indented format can be an indication that the letter sender or the firm he is representing is traditional. However, someone thinks that the format does not look elegant. For a modern and sophisticated appeal, someone recommends the use of the full-block with no indention letter style.

In a composition, an indentation is a blank space between a margin and the beginning of a line of text.

The beginning of this paragraph is indented. Standard paragraph indentation is about five spaces or one-quarter to one-half of an inch, depending on which style guide you follow. In online writing, if your software doesn't allow indentation, insert a line space to indicate a new paragraph.

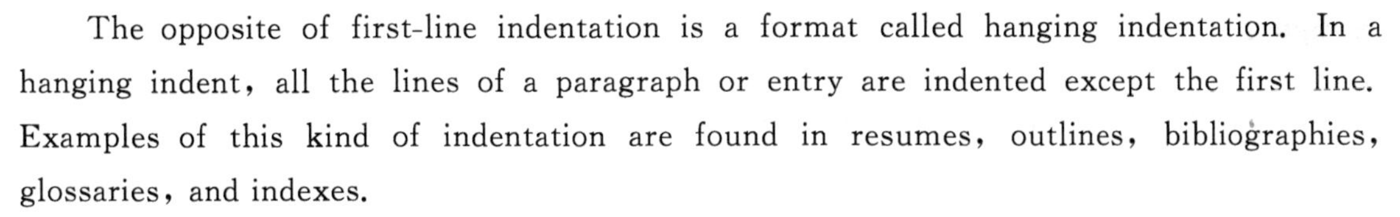

The opposite of first-line indentation is a format called hanging indentation. In a hanging indent, all the lines of a paragraph or entry are indented except the first line. Examples of this kind of indentation are found in resumes, outlines, bibliographies, glossaries, and indexes.

The main feature in this style is that each line of the inside name and address should be indented 2 – 3 spaces, and the first line of each paragraph should be indented 3 – 5 spaces.

Sample 1

THE EASTERN SEABOARD CORPORATION
350 Park Avenue, New York, 10017, USA
Telephone:2252788 Fax:2252780
E-mail:ESCO. @CA. com

January 4, 2021

Our Ref:QW9807
Your Ref:UI 87
Kanto Mercantile Corporation
2 – 1 Nihonbashi
Tokyo 89, Japan

Dear Sirs,

Price List

Here is the price list you asked about. You will be happy to know that all of the items listed on pages 5 – 7 will be marked down 30% between February and March. If you would like to take advantage of this special opportunity, please fill out the enclosed order form and return to us by the end of January.

Thank you for writing.

Yours faithfully,

THE EASTERN SEABOARD CORPORATION
James Baton
Vice President

Sample 2

Date

Dear ×××,

I hope you are doing great in the new country. I am missing you a lot here. However, I am quite aware of the fact that this opportunity is going to be great for your future. The weather is excellent on your side as well.

I have decided to resign from the current job as I have a great opportunity to apply at ××× Company. There is a vacancy for the post of administrative assistant and as you know I had been interested in this post since the beginning of my career.

I am fine and my married life is going great.

I am looking forward to seeing you in the summer vacation. Send me a message before coming so that I can make some arrangements. I have planned to have so much fun this summer.

Till next time.

LMN

2. Modified Block Form with Indented Style

In this form with indented style the sender's address is typed (or printed) in the up-middle part. The receiver's address starts from the left margin. The complimentary close as well as the signature is typed from the middle little towards the right.

Sample 1

Carol Taylor
28251 Clinton Keith
Murrieta, California 92563

14 August 2008

Joan Smith

4256 Adams Avenue
San Diego, California 92129

Dear Mrs. Smith,

Ah, there are block formats, and indented formats, modified block formats ... To simplify matters, we're demonstrating the block format on this page, one of the most common formats. For authoritative advice about all the variations, we highly recommend *The Gregg Reference Manual*, 11th ed. (New York: McGraw-Hill, 2010), a great reference tool for workplace communications. There seems to be no consensus about such fine points as whether to skip a line after your return address and before the date: some guidelines suggest that you do; others do not. Let's hope that your business letter succeeds no matter which choice you make!

Sincerely yours,

Carol Taylor

3. Full Block Style

This is the most popular business letter layout nowadays. It is the easiest to format as everything starts at the left margin. Letterhead is laid out in the center of the letter, while the rest elements of a business letter start from the left-hand side of the sheet neatly.

Open punctuation is adopted for the inside address, which means that both sender's address and recipients' address must avoid using more punctuation.

The body of the letter has double spacing between the paragraphs. Typists generally prefer the full block format, for it has a simple appearance, and is quicker to type.

The following is the indication of this style. In the full block form, every part of a letter is typed from the left margin. It is convenient to be typed with a typewriter but the layout is not so beautiful. So some businessmen us a modified block form with indented style.

When you use the block form to write a business letter, all the information is typed flush left, with one-inch margins all around. First provide your own address, then skip a line and provide the date, then skip one more line and provide the inside address of the party to whom the letter is addressed. If you are using letterhead that already provides your address, do not retype that information; just begin with the date. For formal letters, avoid abbreviations where possible.

Skip another line before the salutation. Then write the body of your letter as illustrated here, with no indentation at the beginnings of paragraphs. Skip lines between paragraphs.

After writing the body of the letter, type the closing, followed by a comma, leave three blank lines, then type your name and title (if applicable), all flush left. Sign the letter in the blank space above your typed name.

Sample 1

456 Anyplace City
Zip Code

Date

Mr. ×××
××× Corporation
Place
City
Zip Code

Dear Mr. ×××,

My friend and your former employee informed me about a job vacancy of Office Manager at ××× Corporation. I have a five-year experience of Administrative Assistant and it would be a great opportunity to work for your company.

As you can see from my resume that I had been taking the different tasks at ××× Company. I had been involved in the workflow management of the company.

Thank you for considering my application.

Truely yours,

Mr. JKL

Sample 2

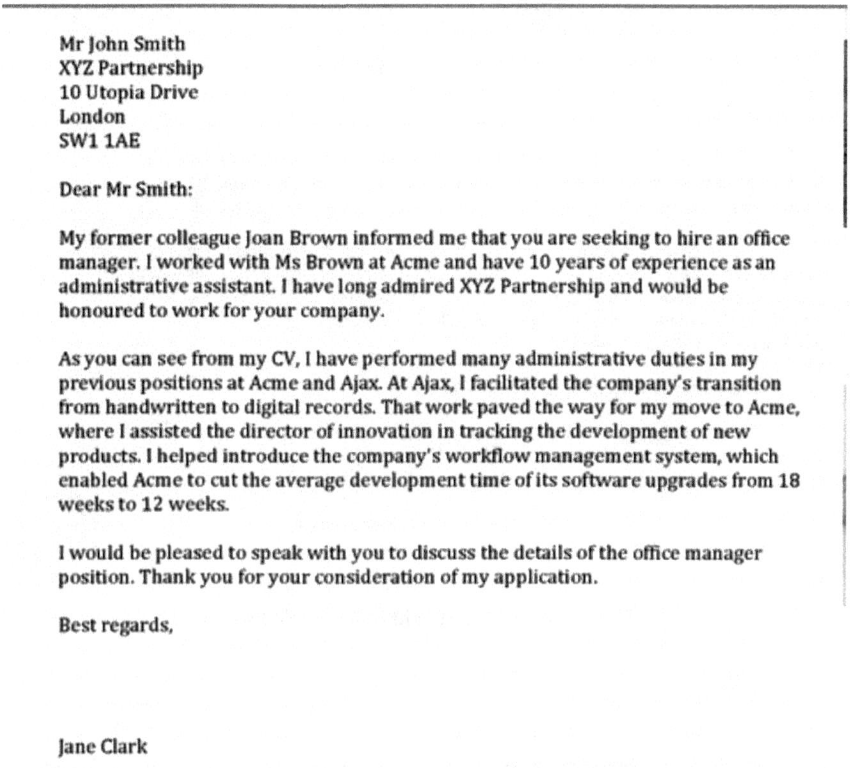

Mr John Smith
XYZ Partnership
10 Utopia Drive
London
SW1 1AE

Dear Mr Smith:

My former colleague Joan Brown informed me that you are seeking to hire an office manager. I worked with Ms Brown at Acme and have 10 years of experience as an administrative assistant. I have long admired XYZ Partnership and would be honoured to work for your company.

As you can see from my CV, I have performed many administrative duties in my previous positions at Acme and Ajax. At Ajax, I facilitated the company's transition from handwritten to digital records. That work paved the way for my move to Acme, where I assisted the director of innovation in tracking the development of new products. I helped introduce the company's workflow management system, which enabled Acme to cut the average development time of its software upgrades from 18 weeks to 12 weeks.

I would be pleased to speak with you to discuss the details of the office manager position. Thank you for your consideration of my application.

Best regards,

Jane Clark

Figure 3.4 A letter in block format

4. Semi-Block Style

A semi-block style letter is a less formal version of a block or a full-block letter with the differences being the sender's address, date, reference or attention line and complimentary closing. In addition, the signature lines are located direct center or slightly right of center, along with indented paragraphs.

Depending on the purpose and content of the letter, a semi-block format may be more desirable for less formal business correspondence, such as thank you messages or announcements of events. Letters to, and dealing with, smaller businesses with less corporate oversight and formality should use the semi-block style to create a more personalized correspondence than a standard corporate business letter.

Sample 1

1 July, 2014

Dear Katie,

I hope you are settled in comfortably in Manchester. I miss you already! But I know your new position will open up a lot of career opportunities for you. It's also great that you'll be closer to your family. And, at least for now, it's still warm!

I too have some good job news. My former boss just told me about a great position at her new company. I would still be doing administrative duties but would be managing the whole office, and it'd include a nice pay rise too. She says she's already spoken highly of me to the person I'd be working for, so I think there's a good chance it will come through.

Besides that, everything else is going pretty well..

I'm already looking forward to seeing you in December. As soon as the tickets for the winter extravaganza go on sale, I'll book us a couple of tickets. Let me know if Rob decides to come, too—if so, I'll make it three. Let's talk soon!

Until next time,
Jane

Figure 3.5 A letter in semi-block format

Sample 2

Dear Mr. Smith,

I enjoyed my visit to Company ××× today and hope to expand our business-to-business relationship in the near future. The factory tour answered many of my questions regarding production of Widget 1, but as we discussed, there are additional areas where I would appreciate greater insights into production.

My administrative assistant will be scheduling a follow-up appointment for one of our design supervisors during the week of October 8. His or her job will be to obtain additional information regarding streamlining the Widget 1 production process through improved design.

Sincerely,

Mark Jones

5. Modified Block Style

Modified block style business letters are less formal than full block style letters. If you are corresponding with someone you already have a good working relationship with, the modified block style letter is a good one to use.

Modified block layout is quite common in business letters. It is traditional and quite popular. Modified block business letters use a slightly different format from the full block business letters. In the modified block style, the return address, date, complimentary closing and the signature line are slightly to the right of the center of the paper. It is recommended to tab over to the center of the letter and not use Ctrl-E which would distort the block.

Sample 1

123 Anywhere Place
London
SW1 6DP

1 July, 2014

Ms Joan Brown
XYZ Partnership
10 Utopia Drive
London
SW1 1AE

Dear Joan:

Thank you so much for informing me of the vacancy at XYZ Partnership. I appreciate all the support you have given me throughout my career, and I would be delighted to work alongside you once again. In order to build upon my qualifications, I have applied to the evening administrative degree program at St John's College. I would greatly appreciate it if you would be willing to serve as one of my references.

In the year since you left Acme, I have taken on additional duties as Mr Jones's administrative assistant. In November, the company introduced a proprietary workflow management system, and I was charged with ensuring that each department received the upgrade on schedule. Additionally, I completed 20 hours of software training in order to input updates. As a result, I was able to pursue certification in Microsoft Office, which I received last month.

For your reference, I have also enclosed a copy of my current CV. Please let me know if you would like any additional information. Thank you once again for your help.

Regards,

Figure 3.6 A letter in modified block format

5. Standard Format

Standard format business letters are quite formal. Because they include an optional subject line, they are ideal for situations in which you need to create a formal response or communicate about an account number or case number.

At the bottom of this template, you'll see something the other business letter templates don't contain. Below the signature block are three lines of text indicating that a secretary or assistant typed the letter for the sender, that a copy was sent to another recipient, and that there are enclosures. In other business letter formats, "Enclosures:" is written out. In standard format, the word is abbreviated.

Sample 1

Your Name
Address
Phone

Today's Date

Recipient's Name
Company Name
Address

Dear ××(Recipient's Name),

SUBJECT: Type the subject here and underline it.

This standard business letter format looks very much like the block letter format. Notice that everything is left justified.

You will notice that this template contains some elements that are different from those in the other business letter formats in this chapter. First, there is a subject line. This element is optional, and can be replaced with a "RE:" line that is used to reference something specific like a previous communication or an account number. Be sure to underline this so that it stands out.

Additionally, this template has three other elements. On the line located beneath the signature block, you will notice the initials in upper case letters. A colon separates them from the assistant's initials, which are written in lower case letters. This indicates that the assistant typed the letter. If you type a standard business letter yourself, you do not need to include this element.

Beneath the initials, you will see "cc:" followed by the business partner's name. This indicates that a copy of this letter has been sent to the partner. If you write a letter like this one but don't "cc" anyone, there's no need to include this element.

Finally, you will notice the letters "encl" followed by a colon. This indicates that there are enclosures. Interestingly, the standard business letter is the only one in which you use "encl" instead of writing "enclosure" to show that a brochure, application, invoice, or other item(s) are enclosed. As you may have already guessed, you can skip the "encl" if you haven't included anything with the letter in the envelope.

Sincerely,

Your First name, Last name, and Title

YN:an
cc:Business Partner, Other entity
encl:Business letter template

6. Open Format

The open format business letter has a clean, formal look just as the block format letter does. It is suitable for all business communications.

There is one major difference between this format and the other business letter formats in this chapter. It contains no punctuation after the greeting, and no punctuation after the closing.

Summary

Depending on the purpose of your business letter, there are several formats from which you can choose. The most widely used business letter formats are full block and modified block. You can also use the memo format, which is a form of business correspondence used mostly within an organization. Remember, the format of the letter helps to establish its tone and presentation.

(1)Components of a business letter

A. The heading includes the date the letter is written. If you do not use letterhead stationery, you need to include your address above the date.

B. The address above the salutation is the letter recipient's full address. This address should match the address on the envelope.

C. The salutation is the line that begins "Dear ... ". Place a colon or comma at the end of the salutation. Use "Mr. " for men and "Ms. " for women. Try to obtain a name to which you can address your letter. If you cannot obtain a name, you should address the letter to the person's position e. g. "Admissions Officer" as a last resort, and you can use "To Whom It May Concern" as a salutation. You can also include an attention line two spaces down from the recipient's address and a subject line (if necessary).

D. The body of your letter contains your message.

The first paragraph of a typical business letter should state the main purpose and/or subject of the letter. Begin with a friendly opening; then quickly transfer to the purpose of your letter. Use several sentences to explain your purpose, but do not go into detail until the next paragraph.

The second paragraph states the specific information regarding your purpose. This may take the form of background information, statistics, or first-hand accounts. A few short paragraphs within the body of the letter should be enough to convey your message.

The closing paragraph briefly restates your purpose and why it is important. If the purpose of your letter is employment related, consider ending your letter with your contact information. However, if the purpose is informational, think about closing with gratitude for the reader's time.

E. The complimentary close should appear two lines below the last line of the body. Capitalize only the first letter of the first word and you can end the line with a comma. You can use a variety of closures: Sincerely, Sincerely yours, Yours truly, Regards, Best regards, or Best wishes.

F. Your signature should be in blue or black ink. Allow four vertical spaces for your signature.

G. The identification line contains your typed name, and, if you have one, your title, placed below your typed name. Depending on the purpose of the letter, you can position your phone number or E-mail address in place of your title.

H. Enclosure (Encl.)—attached document(s)—or Distribution (cc)—copies sent to another party—is placed two vertical spaces below the identification line.

(2)Letter formats

Sample 1 Full Block Format (See Table 3. 5)

Table 3.5 Full block format

Heading (your address and date)	20 – 54 Jackson Avenue Brooklyn, NY 11352 June 28, 2020
Address (of the person you are writing to)	Ms. Jennifer Esposito John Doe Fellowship 595 Park Avenue New York, NY 10021
Salutation	Dear Ms. Esposito,
Body	The John Doe Fellowship has always loomed on the horizon for me. Ever since I decided to major in history, I have wanted to participate in your program. From the research that I have done, I believe that your program provides its participants with an extensively detailed look at the history of the world through hands-on experience with fossils, artifacts, and other remains that compose the blueprint of our existence. I am applying for the John Doe Fellowship because I believe that it would benefit me throughout my career and allow me to further understand the ideas behind history and how it is constructed. I am a very committed and goal-oriented person with excellent interpersonal skills. My background in history involves studying many different eras and time periods. My specialty, though, is the archeological study of the ancient world and its history. During the summer of 2019 and 2020, I interned at the Metropolitan Museum of Art as a tour guide. Both times, I not only utilized my knowledge of art and history, but I also learned a lot about how that history was constructed. This experience has influenced me to intern as a tour guide at the American Museum of Natural History, where my love for the origins of history and learning from the tactile experience with artifacts increased. In the future, I would like to participate in historical research and eventually become a full-time professor of history.

Continued Table

	I believe my skills, experience, and goals make me an excellent candidate for your program. Thank you very much for considering me for the John Doe Fellowship. I am looking forward to hearing from you.
Complimentary Close	Sincerely yours,
Identification Line Title or Phone Number	Bill Lurie (419)352-5425
Signature	
Enclosures or Distribution	Enclosure

In a full block business letter, every component of the letter (heading, address, salutation, body, salutation, signature, identification, enclosures) is aligned to the left. Also, first sentences of paragraphs are not indented.

Sample 2　Modified Block Format (See Table 3.6)

Table 3.6　Modified block format

Heading (Your address and date)	123 Corona Blvd. Flushing, NY 11235 July 3, 2020
Address (of the person you are writing)	Dr. Steven Serafin, Director Reading/Writing Center Hunter College 695 Park Ave New York, NY 10065

Continued Table

Salutation	Dear Dr. Serafin:
Body	My name is Sally Eisner. I am writing this appeal to request a 4th chance to take the CUNY Proficiency Exam in June of 2020. I have taken the exam twice and missed it once. The first time, I feel that I was simply unprepared. I did not realize that I should have attended CPE workshops offered at the Reading/Writing Center. The second time, I attended the workshops and learned more about the exam; however, my Task 2 score was unsatisfactory, so I failed again. Finally, I registered for CPE tutoring at the Reading/Writing Center and studied very hard for the third time. However, on the Saturday of the exam, I had a family emergency, which caused me to miss the date. I had forgotten that I could defer the test date until after I missed it. Now, I am working hard to build on my academic skills. After a consultation with a CPE advisor at the Reading/Writing Center, I have a clear vision of what I should do in order to pass the exam. Again, I have registered for a semester of CPE tutoring at the Writing/Reading Center that I plan to attend weekly. I would really like to have a 4th chance to pass this exam because I am confident that if I work hard, I can do it. Thank you very much for considering my appeal. I hope to hear back from you soon.
Complimentary Close	Sincerely,
Signature	Sally Eisner
Identification	

In a modified block business letter, the heading, complimentary close, the signature, and identification are aligned to the right. Address, salutation, the body, and enclosures are aligned to the left. First sentences of paragraphs are indented.

Sample 3 Memo Format (See Table 3.7)

Table 3.7 Memo format

Heading	
Date:	Date:July 5, 2020
To:Name of person addressed	To: Sophia Halley, Director, Public Health Engineering (DOHMH)
From:Your name	From:Pat Godowsky, Database Manager
Subject:The purpose	Subject:Database format changes update
Text	I have made the expected changes to the database. Right now, the problems that the field inspectors experienced when they transferred their observations from their hand-held devices to the database have been resolved. A survey of the new changes shows that the field inspectors are very happy with the new system. Let me know if you need me to make any more corrections to the program.
Enclosure	Enclosure

In a memo form of business correspondence, every component of the memo is aligned to the left.

The following items should appear in the order listed below:

Date:

To: (Name of the recipient)

From: (Your name; initials of sender added in ink)

Subject: (Briefly explains the purpose of the memo)

cc: (If applicable, copies sent to another party)

Text:

Enclosure: (Optional)

(3) Usage and appearance of your letter

a. Remember to proofread your letter for these items:

- Spelling of the receiver's name
- Spelling of the receiver's place of business
- Spelling elsewhere—including your own name and business
- Typing errors
- Correct dates
- Subject-verb agreement
- Pronoun reference and form
- Punctuation

b. Checklist

- Did you type in a date to validate the letter as a record?
- Did you place a colon after the salutation?
- Did you place a comma after the complimentary close?
- Did you sign the letter below the complimentary close and above your typed name?

Part F Spacing, Margin and Envelop Addressing

1. Spacing

Most business letters are single-spaced with the exception of extremely short and one-paragraphed letters, which are usually typed with double spaces between lines. However, there should always be a double space line between paragraphs. As for the spacing between such parts as the date line and the letterhead, the signature and the complimentary close, they are described respectively in the layout of a business letter.

2. Margin

No business letters should be typed without margins, which are as necessary as the frames of a picture. The simplest method is to leave at least a one-inch margin at the left side of the letter and to keep the right margin roughly the same. The margin at the bottom of the page should be at least one and one-half times that of the side margins while the same is applicable to the top margin of plain paper without a letterhead.

3. Envelop Addressing

Envelop addressing calls for accuracy, legibility and good appearance. Like the inside address, the address on the envelope can be written in two forms: the indented form and the blocked form. Usually no punctuation is used on the envelope. No matter in which way the address on the envelope is written, it should conform to the inside address in both style and content. Generally speaking, the address of the envelope should be written in the following order:

a. Name of the addressee;

b. Number and street;

c. City, state and zip code;

d. Country.

Here are some samples of envelopes (See Figure 3.7, Figure 3.9, Figure 3.9):

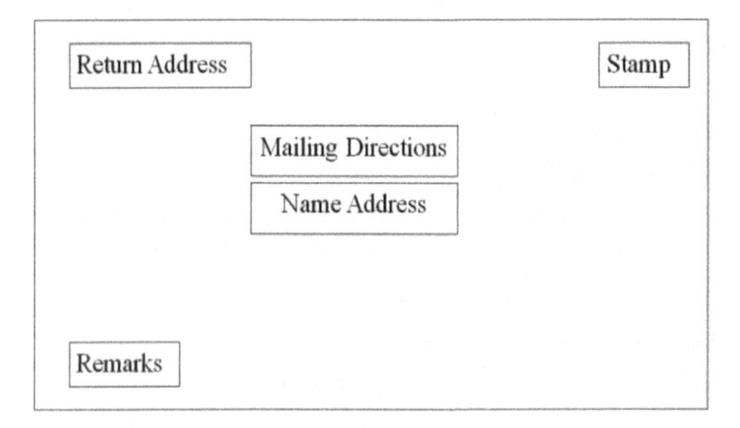

Figure 3.7　Envelope 1

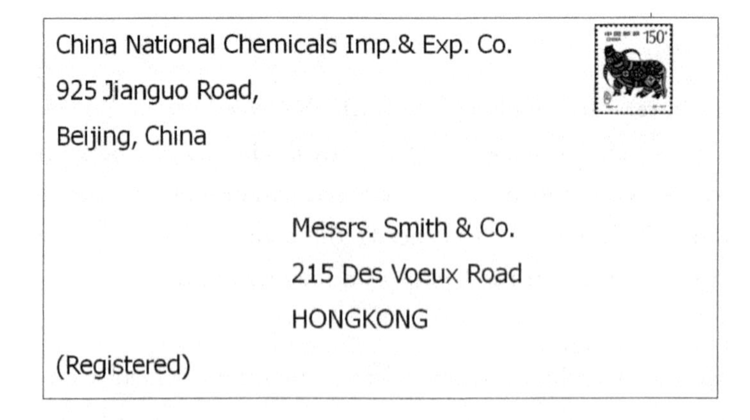

Figure 3.8　Envelope 2

Figure 3.9 Envelope 3

Business envelopes ordinarily have the return address printed on the upper left corner. The receiver's name and address should be typed about half way down the envelope.

The postmark or stamps should be placed in the up right-hand corner, while the bottom left-hand corner is for post notations such as "Confidential", "Secret", "Printed Matter", etc.

It is important to include the postcode (zip code in the U.S.A.) in order to facilitate mechanical mail-sorting.

Summary

(1) Functions of business letters

a. To ask for or to convey information;

b. To make or to accept an offer;

c. To deal with matters concerning negotiation of business.

In addition, there are letters with no other purpose than to remind the recipient of the sender's existence.

(2) Structures of business letters

letterhead, reference and date, inside name and address, salutation, subject line, body, complimentary close, signature, attention line, enclosure, carbon copy notation, postscript.

Chapter 4 Establishing Business Relations

Learning Objectives

a. Know the importance of establishing business relations;

b. Comprehend different ways to build business ralations;

c. Grasp useful expressions used in business letters.

Part A Introduction

Establishing business relations with prospective dealers is one of the important measures to maintain or expand business activities in doing foreign trade. Customers are the basis of business expansion, therefore, it is a common practice in business communications that newly established firms or firms that wish to enlarge their business scope and turnover write letters to new customers for the establishment of relations.

One can obtain such desired information as names and addresses of the firms to be dealt with through advertisements, trade directories, trade negotiations, banks, chambers of commerce both at home and abroad, commercial counselor's offices, trade presses, exhibitions and trade fairs, market surveys, inquiries received from foreign merchants, branch offices or representatives abroad, introduction of connections, business houses of the same trade and the Internet. When having obtained the desired name and address of the firm from any of the above sources, one can write a letter or a circular to the other party. Generally speaking, this kind of letter includes the following ones.

a. The source of the information, i e. how and where the writer gets the name and address of the receiver's company.

b. The intention or desire of writing the letter.

c. Self-introduction, including the business scope, branches and other necessary information.

d. The references as to the financial status and integrity of the writer's company.

e. Expectation of cooperation and an early reply.

Traders must do everything possible to consolidate their established relations with the existing customers and also develop and revitalize the trade by searching for new connections. If they are to buy some products, they may ask for samples, price lists, catalogue or other reference materials. The letters should be written politely, clearly and concisely. As regards the receiver of such kind of letter, he or she is recommended to answer in full without any delay to create goodwill, leaving a positive impression on the other party and possibly expand the trade.

To establish business relations with prospective dealers is the base of starting and developing of business. It is vitally important for both a new dealer and an old one. But by what means can a businessman secure all the necessary information about a new market and a new customer?

As we all know, no customer, no business. So we must try by all means to seek for new connections while consider consolidating the old ones from time to time. In the field of international trade, it is impossible for a firm to know other firms, especially those firms abroad. Therefore, we should, from any sources, get information on foreign firms.

Part B Ways to Build Business Relationship

Establishing business relations is the first step in dealing with and developing mutual trade. The business growth and broadening depends on the establishment of business relations. So it is a very important part to write business letters in business communication. To establish business relations is to know about your clients including financial credit, business lines and capacities, and the intention of trade contacts.

1. Channels

Well, we may establish business relations with other parties through the following channels or with the help of:

a. the advertisements in newspapers;

b. the introduction from his business connections;

c. the introduction from his subsidiaries or branches, agents abroad;

d. the market investigations;

e. attendance at the export commodities fairs;

f. visit abroad by trade delegations and groups;

g. self-introductions or enquiries received from the merchants abroad;

h. the banks;

i. the Commercial Counselor's Office;

j. the chambers of commerce both at home and abroad;

k. company's web;

l. yellow page of telephone.

2. Writing Points

a. source of information;

b. the intention;

c. line of business;

d. the reference as to the firm's finance position and integrity;

e. the expectation.

When a business company gets into an association or relationship with a new business company or an organization, it may write a letter or an E-mail to start on a good note and introduce itself properly. The E-mail written to do so is known as a new business relationship E-mail. Such an E-mail must be able to talk about the future of the relationship in general and must be polite in its tone.

Example:

To: jackmathews@yahoo.com
CC: timothyyoung@gmail.com

Subject: new business relationship E-mail

Dear Mr. Mathews,

I, Kell Anthony, the owner of Fiscal Group of Companies, am writing this mail to you to formally start this new business association between our companies. I would begin by telling you that we are very glad to be associated with your prestigious business firm and will try to take this relationship well ahead in the future.

Your company Redding London Private Limited is a respected firm which works on the same principles which we too follow. This relationship is not only beneficial for us but also for you as well and I would urge you to work towards building this into a very successful collaboration. Through mutual understanding, the right synchronization of actions and financial honesty, we must squeeze out the best possibilities for our-self.

I would like to inform you that I have signed the contract and am attaching a signed copy for your reference. Hope to have a great relationship with your firm.

Yours sincerely,

Kell Anthony

3. Contents

The following contents should be expressed in letters of establishing business relations:

A. Telling the reader how they obtain business lines and addresses.

B. Expressing the strong desire to establish business relations and co-operations.

C. Introducing the company including features, business running and types of commodities.

D. Stating what kind of products to promote or to buy.

E. If necessary, offering the information references to help understand the credit information.

F. Telling about an enclosure to help understand more about the company, such as brief introduction, catalogues, price lists and pamphlets, etc. Please remember to reply as required promptly and politely even if you are unable to meet the needs. The reason should be told in reply so as to leave space for the next dealing.

Example:

Gentlemen:

Your name and address have been given to us by the Commercial Counselor's Office of our Embassy in Pakistan.

We are now writing to you in the hope of entering into business relations with you on the basis of equality and mutual benefit and exchanging what one has for what one needs.

We are very well connected with all the major dealers here of industrial products, and feel sure we can sell large quantities of industrial goods if we can get your offers at competitive prices.

We invite you to send us details and prices, possibly also samples, of such goods as you would be interested in selling, and we shall gladly study the sales possibilities in our market. On the other hand, please favor us with a list of those goods you are interested in obtaining from us so that we might be able to quote on some and give you all the necessary information regarding supply possibilities.

We look forward to your favorable reply.

Yours faithfully,

×××

4. The Style of Letters of Establishing Business Relations

A. The company offers the wish to express the goodwill and purpose of establishing business relations.

B. The company is sincere and frank to tell the detailed information about the company so as to be accepted as a business partner.

C. Their requirements to get a reply are needed even if you disagree.

D. The language should be formal, lively and understandable by using plain, familiar expressions and varied words.

Part C　Sample Letters of Establishing Business Relations

Sample 1

A letter written by an exporter to an importer

Dear Sirs,

We come to know through the Commercial Counselor's Office of the Chinese Embassy in Morocco the name and address of your firm, in the market for textiles.

Our company specializes in exporting textile products to various foreign countries. We wish to enter into business relations with you by the commencement of some practical transactions.

To give you a general idea of the various kinds of textile products now available for export, we are enclosing here our latest brochure and a price list for your reference. We shall be pleased to give you our lowest quotation upon receipt of your detailed requirements.

We look forward to receiving from you soon.

Yours faithfully,

Joel Mandelstam

Sample 2

A letter written by an importer to a producer

Dear Sirs,

We owe your name and address to Showner Co., Ltd., through which we understand that you are interested in establishing business relations with Chinese companies for selling cosmetic products of your country.

We have been importers of cosmetic products for many years. We should appreciate the catalogue and quotations of your products, and we shall gladly study the sales possibilities in our market.

We hope you will give us an early reply.

Yours faithfully,

Alfred Liu

Sample 3

A letter written by a producer to an importer

Dear Sirs,

From the Chamber of Commerce of Beijing, we have come to know the name of your firm and take the pleasure of addressing this letter to you in the hope of establishing business relations with you.

We specialize in the exportation of various tea products, which have enjoyed great popularity in the world market. We enclose our latest catalogue for your inspection and hope that you would contact us if any item is of interest to you.

We are looking forward to your favorable and prompt reply.

Your faithfully,

Lucia Tan

Sample 4

A letter written by an import and export company to another

Dear Sirs,

You were kindly recommended to us by the Chamber of Commerce of Stockholm. We shall be pleased to enter into direct business relations with you.

Our company is one of the greatest import and export companies in China and has wide experience in all the lines we handle. We mainly export such items as electronics and electrical appliances, light industrial products and chemicals. Our imported goods include information technology products, luxurious automobiles and cosmetic products.

China is a very big market with increasing purchasing power. We would like to establish a business relation between us and to be an exclusive agent for your company in China. If you want to import some materials or products from China, we can supply all our help.

Our banker is the ×××, Stockholm branch, and it can provide you detailed information about our business and Finances.

We are looking forward to a productive trade between us.

Yours faithfully,

Charlie Qi
Manager

Sample 5

A letter written by a producer to a commercial counselor's office

Dear Sirs,

We thank you for your cooperation for our business.

We want to enlarge our trade in porcelain teacups and saucers, but unfortunately we have no good connections in Luxembourg. Therefore, we shall be obliged if you introduce us to the most capable and reliable importers in that country who are possibly interested in our products.

Your information on this respect will be highly appreciated.

Yours faithfully,

×××

Sample 6

A letter asking for information

Dear Sirs,

We have recently received a letter from Gloryshield Company in Sweden. The company introduced itself to us as one of the leading importers and wholesalers of electronic products in South Africa, and hopes to establish business relations with us and promote the sales of our products in Germany. The following is the address of the Gloryshield Company shown on the envelope of the letter sent to us:

Gloryshield Electronic Equipment Trading Co. , Ltd.
Hamlets Crossing Office Park Block 126/9 23
Melbourne Avenue Four ways Sandton 3168
South Africa

We should be obliged if you would provide us with the necessary information about the company. Any information you may obtain for us will be treated as strictly confidential.

Yours faithfully,

Perry Wang

Sample 7

Importer writes to exporter

Dear Sirs,

We have obtained your address from the Commercial Counselor of your Embassy in London and are now writing you for the establishment of business relations.

We are very well connected with all the major dealers here of light industrial products, and feel sure we can sell large quantities of Chinese goods if we get your offers at competitive prices.

As to our standing, we are permitted to mention the Bank of England, London, as a reference.

Please let us have all necessary information regarding your products for export.

Yours faithfully,

×××

Sample 8

Self-introduction by exporter

Dear Sirs,

We write to introduce ourselves as one of the largest exporters, from China, of a wide range of Machinery and Equipment.

We enclose a copy of our latest catalog covering the details of all the items available at present, and hope some of these items will be of interest to you.

It will be a great pleasure to receive your inquiries for any of the items against which we will send you our lowest quotations.

Should, by chance, your corporation not deal with the import of the goods mentioned above, we would be most grateful if this letter could be forwarded to the correct import corporation.

We are looking forward to your favorable and prompt reply.

Yours faithfully,

×××

Sample 9

Self-introduction by manufacturer

Dear Sirs,

We have learned, from the *China Daily*, that you are a leading importer of household electric appliances, and at present you are in the market for electric fans.

We, therefore, take pleasure in informing you that we are an enterprise manufacturing various electric fans and have recently produced a new model of gentle breeze electric fan entitled "Chang Feng" whose quality as well as functions has been proved by a scrupulous test, and the designs and colors have been clearly explained in our illustrated catalog enclosed.

Considering the improvements it offers, we believe you will find our "Chang Feng" a very good seller in your market.

If you have interest in dealing with us in "Chang Feng " or other types of the goods shown in our catalog, please inform us of your requirements together with your banker's name and address.

For our credit standing, please refer to the following bank: the Bank of China, ×× Branch (address) ...

Your immediate reply would be highly appreciated.

Yours faithfully,

×××

Sample 10

Self-introduction

Dear Sirs,

This is Water from SHV Company. I've been working in DVD field for more than five years. Hope that I can serve you with my professional experience from now on. Please feel free to study our offer as below.

First of all, I would like to introduce you some information about our factory. SHV Company is a professional manufacturer in producing Portable DVD Player. And SHV got the supports as below.

Staff Number: over 300
Production lines: 4 lines
Monthly capacity: 60 000 pcs
Quality control: FCC, CE, EMC, CCC, RoHS
Factory management: ISO 9001 International Quality Management System and ISO 14000 International Environment Management System
Markets: ××× from Spain, ××× from Italy, ××× from Germany, ××× from Ukraine, ××× from Bulgaria, ××× from Russia, ××× from Israel, ××× from Iran, ××× from India, ××× from Middle East, ××× from Paraguay, ××× from Panama, etc.

Now I would like to offer you the fast sale item with best price for your reference first.

Model: Item A701, 7 inches swivel screen with TV tuner, USB & Card Render
Offer: FOB Shenzhen US$50
MOQ: 1 000 pcs

Samples and more information are available for your study anytime. We appreciate your kind reply soon.

We are looking forward to our cooperation in the near future.

Faithfully yours,

×××

Exercise

Write a reply to ××× company, with the following particulars:

a. Acknowledge the receipt of their letter of June 27;

b. Agree to their proposal of establishing trade relations with you;

c. Commodity inspection will be handled by the bureau concerned in Shanghai.

Reference

Dear sirs,

With reference to your letter of June 27, we are glad to learn that you wish to enter into trade relations with us, which also meets our interest.

To give you a general idea of our products, we are sending you by air a catalogue showing various products being handled by this corporation with detailed specification and means of packing. Quotations and sample will be sent upon receipt of your specific inquiries. As we have not had the pleasure of doing business with you in the past, we would like to inform you that our goods for export are to be inspected by the Shanghai Commodity Inspection Bureau before shipment, and necessary certificates in regard to the quality and quantity of the shipment will be provided.

We are looking forward to your early reply.

Your faithfully,

×××

Chapter 5　Inquiries and Replies

Learning Objectives

a. Understand that inquiries are usually made by the buyer and are integrated with letters establishing business relations;

b. Master basic writing principles of inquiries and basic points of replies.

Part A　Introduction of Inquiries

An inquiry is usually a kind of letter or other kind of communication which is made to get the required information of the supply of certain product, service or the general information. Generally speaking, the inquirer should make all of the expression in the inquiry very specific and clear so as to enable the receiver to make the replay accordingly.

Inquiries are made when a business person intends to purchase certain goods or obtain desired services. The buyer usually sends an inquiry to invite a quotation or an offer from the seller, therefore inquiries mean potential business for both the buyer and the seller.

Based on the inquired contents, inquiries can be divided into general inquiries and specific inquiries. The writer of a general inquiry asks for general information, a catalogue, a price list, or a sample book, while that of a specific inquiry focuses on the detailed information about the specific target goods or services.

There are two kinds of inquiries. One is called general inquiry, a request for a price list, catalogue, sample or quotation of price and other terms. This kind of letter should be simple and direct in content. Another kind of inquiry is specific inquiry, an inquiry for goods of a certain specification. It is made when a buyer intents to conclude some business with the seller. When this is to be sent, many firms use a printed form for the purpose of omitting the trouble of writing a letter. Inquiry should be addressed to the company instead of an individual, only in this way, prompt attention will be received.

Inquiries can also be classified into first inquiries and inquiries for repeat orders by the relationship between the writer and the recipient. A first inquiry is employed when the letter is sent to a seller with whom the buyer has not previously done business, and inquiries for repeal orders are mostly for acquainted customers. As for the latter one, the inquiry may be very simple and most often a printed inquiry form will be enough. Our focus of this chapter will be on the writing of a first inquiry.

In a first inquiry, it is useful for the writer to tell the recipient some information about his or her own business, the kinds of goods he or she needs, and the reasons for the inquiry to win trust from the other party. Besides, the writer needs to mention how he or she obtained the seller's name and address, the market analysis of the demand for the seller's goods or services, and the materials and information that he or she wants to receive. Mostly, the writer has interest in a catalogue, a price list, the seller's discounting policy, method of payment, delivery time and samples.

The following tips are of great value in guiding the preparation of letters of inquiries.

a. State concisely and exactly the request.

b. Enumerate the questions when there are many.

c. Make a request for reply and let the seller feel the value of the information to you.

d. Show courteousness and politeness.

e. Give the seller some hope of substantial order or continued business.

The reply to inquiries should be prompt, courteous and cover all the information asked for. If you can not satisfy the inquirers' demand at the moment, you should acknowledge the letter immediately, giving the reason and assuring that you will do all you can to meet his requirement. If the inquiry is from an old client, express your appreciation of his interest in your products. If it is from a new customer, say you are glad to receive it and express the hope of lasting friendly business relation so as to create goodwill and leave a good impression on the reader.

Part B Sample Letters of Inquiries

Sample 1

Dear Sirs,

Thank you for your interest in our [services /products /services and products].

In response to your query, please find enclosed the requested details. I hope this information addresses your needs. If you require further clarifications, please do not hesitate to contact us at anytime.

We're looking forward to hearing from you soon.

Yours faithfully,

Abraham Rice
General Manager

Sample 2

Dear Sir or Madam,

Thank you for your inquiry regarding our [product or service name]. In response to your query, [list here needed information: prices, availability, etc.]. In addition to the information provided above, I have enclosed a sample [brochure, catalogue, etc.] that contains more detailed information about our products and services.

It would be my pleasure to welcome you in my office to discuss in more details your requirements and to see how I can assist you in fulfilling them. Alternatively, I can visit yours if it's more convenient.

In the meanwhile, if you have any questions or need more clarifications, please do not hesitate to contact me.

I hope to hear from you soon.

Yours faithfully,

Anna

Sample 3

Dear Sirs,

Thank you for your interest in [product or service name]. To answer your question, [list here needed information: prices, availability, etc.]. I have also attached a copy of detailed specifications and prices for your reference.

I would like to know your requirements in more detail and explain to you how our [products or services] can help you in that regard. Perhaps we can arrange a meeting [next week] at a mutually convenient time and place to discuss more.

In the meanwhile, if you have any questions or need more clarifications, please do not hesitate to contact me. In view of the demand for your products, an immediate reply is appreciated.

Looking forward to doing business with you.

Yours faithfully,

Tracy

Sample 4

Dear Mr. Li,

Thank you for contacting us regarding [product or service name]. To address your concerns, [list here needed information: prices, availability, etc.]. You can find detailed information about each product on our website [www ... com] along with specifications and images.

If you would like to know more on how we can help you, I will happily pay you a visit to discuss your requirements in detail.

In the meanwhile, if you have any questions or need more clarifications, please do not hesitate to contact me.

Thank you for considering us to be your partner.

Sincerely yours,

Gorge Rice
Manager

Enc. :Inquiry list

Sample 5

Dear Sirs,

We have been informed of your company and address through the Chamber of Commerce in Beijing. We are interested in your cotton blankets and bed-sheets for sales in the U. S. and Canadian market.

We would like you to send us details of your various ranges, including sizes, colors, prices and samples of the different qualities of material used. We trust that you will make an effort to quote us most favorable terms for large quantities.

Looking forward to establishing direct business relations with you.

Yours faithfully,

Adam Smith
Manager

Sample 6

An inquiry for sportswear

Dear Sirs,

You are recommended to us by ×× in New York that you are one of the leading sportswear dealers. Right now, we are particularly interested in importing a various ranges of sportswear.

It would be helpful if you could send us your latest catalogue and price list. If the quality of the goods comes up to our expectation and the delivery date is acceptable, we can probably let you have regular orders.

We are large dealers in textiles here and believe there is a promising market in our area for moderately priced ladies' and men's sportswear.

We are looking forward to your earliest reply.

Yours faithfully,

Paul Maidment
Manager

Sample 7

An inquiry for digital cameras

Dear Sirs,

We saw your digital cameras at the China Trade Fair in Guangzhou in October. The digital cameras you showed would be most suitable for our market. We are leading dealers of electronic products in Beijing and interested in purchasing your cameras. Would you please send us details of your cameras including the functions?

When you quote, please state terms of payment and discount you would allow on purchases of quantities not less than 1 000 sets. If your digital cameras are of good quality and the prices are in line, we will place regular large orders with you.

We should appreciate it greatly if you would give us a prompt reply.

Yours faithfully,

Zhao Tin

Sample 8

An inquiry for plastic toys

Dear Sirs,

We are very much interested in importing plastic toys from Hong Kong.

We understand that you are a leading manufacturer and sales agent of plastic products in Hong Kong. We should be obliged if you will let us have detailed information about the toy range you produce.

Please indicate any new items not yet introduced in China and send some samples if possible.

We hope that this will be a good start for a long and profitable business relation between us.

Yours faithfully,

×××

Sample 9

An inquiry for kine scopes

Dear Sirs,

As a leading importer and exporter of electronic parts, we intend to import TV kine scopes made in Japan. We would appreciate some information from you about your products.

We should be obliged if you could send us technical specifications of the product and also give us detailed information about your CIF prices, discounts, and delivery schedule.

We await your early reply.

Yours faithfully,

×××

Sample 10

An inquiry for portable typewriters

Dear Sir,

We have seen your advertisement in the *New Asia Journal* and are particularly interested in your portable typewriters, but we require a machine suitable for fairly heavy duty.

Please send me your current illustrated catalogue and a price list.

Yours faithfully,

×××

Sample 11

An inquiry for raincoats

Dear Sir,

We are a leading dealer in waterproof garments in this city. Our customers have expressed interest in your raincoats and inquired about their quality.

Provided quality and price are satisfactory, there are prospects of good sales here. But before placing a firm order we should be glad if you would send us, on fourteen day's approval, a selection of men's and women's raincoats. Any of the items unsold at the end of the period, and which we decide not to keep as stock, would be returned at our expense.

We look forward to hearing from you soon.

Yours faithfully,

×××

Sample 12

Letters between different parties

Dear Adam,

We thank you for your letter asking for our new catalogues and shall be glad to enter into business relations with your firm.

Complying with your request, we are sending you our latest catalogues and the price list covering our exports available at present and hope that you will find many items in them which interest you.

We look forward to receiving your inquiries soon.

Sincerely yours,

Frank

Reply 1

Favourite price

Dear Frank,

Thanks for your information. We are interested to buy large quantities of Angle Grinder and shall appreciate it if you would give us the best FOB Ningbo price. I have now listed below the models that are of interest:

AG105L, AG203S, AG880H

Please send us some samples for testing. We will pay the sample fees. How about MOQ?

We are waiting for your reply.

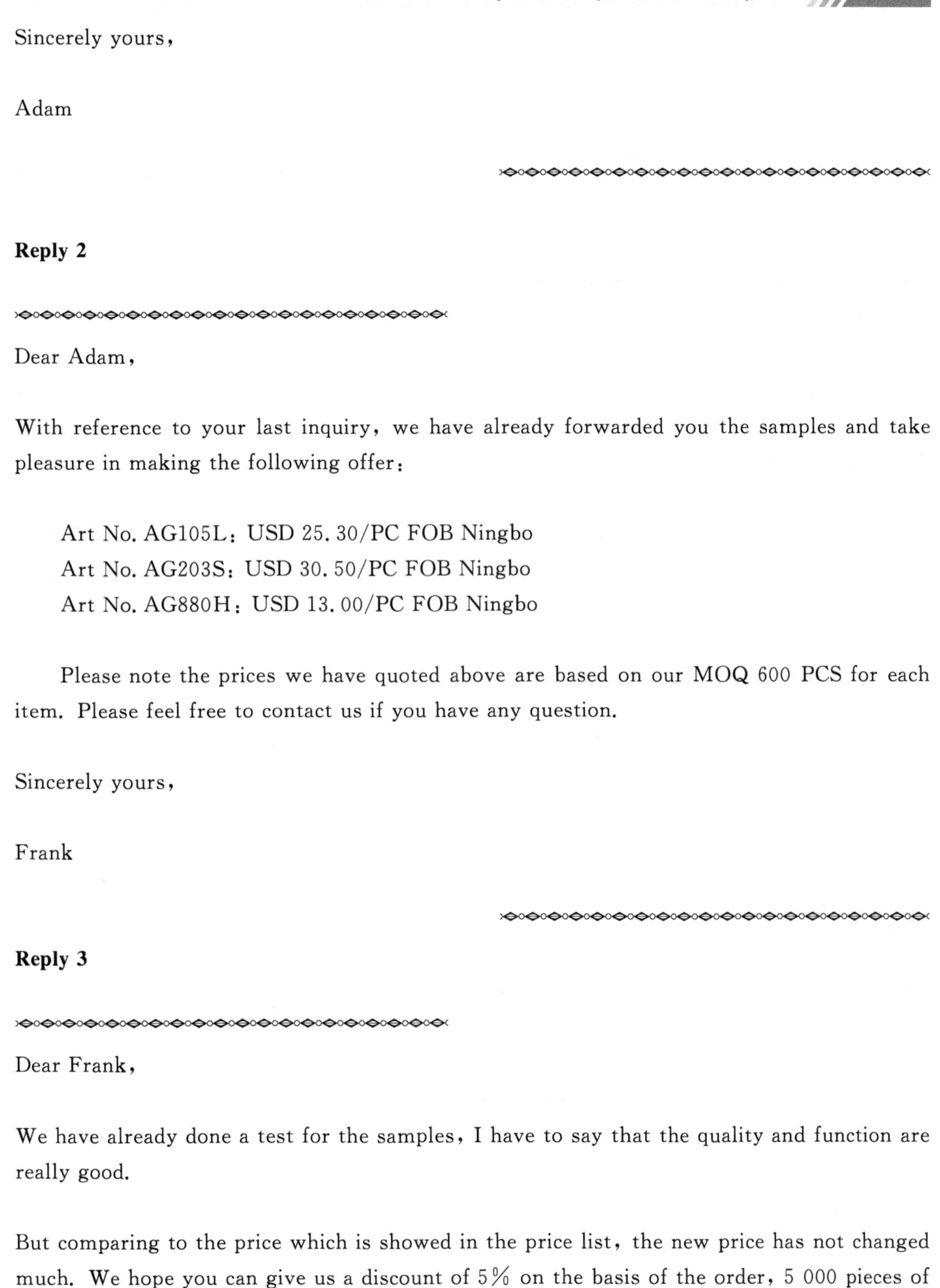

Sincerely yours,

Adam

Reply 2

Dear Adam,

With reference to your last inquiry, we have already forwarded you the samples and take pleasure in making the following offer:

Art No. AG105L: USD 25.30/PC FOB Ningbo
Art No. AG203S: USD 30.50/PC FOB Ningbo
Art No. AG880H: USD 13.00/PC FOB Ningbo

Please note the prices we have quoted above are based on our MOQ 600 PCS for each item. Please feel free to contact us if you have any question.

Sincerely yours,

Frank

Reply 3

Dear Frank,

We have already done a test for the samples, I have to say that the quality and function are really good.

But comparing to the price which is showed in the price list, the new price has not changed much. We hope you can give us a discount of 5% on the basis of the order, 5 000 pieces of Angle Grinder.

Yours sincerely,

Adam

Reply 4

Dear Adam,

The new price has already reached to the bottom of price range. You can not buy Angle Grinder of similar quality at such a price anywhere else. However, as this is the first time to do business with you, we accept your request to give you a discount of 5%.

As we have received large numbers of orders from our clients, it is quite probable that our present stock may soon run out. We would therefore suggest that you take advantage of this attractive offer.

We look forward to receiving your first order.

Sincerely yours,

Frank

Reply 5

Dear Frank,

Thank you for your letter of October 8th, 2020. We do appreciate your concession and want to accept your revised price and please send us your PI.

Yours sincerely,

Adam

Part C Introduction of Replies

1. Introduction

As mentioned above, an inquiry means potential business to be established; therefore the reply to it should be prompt and courteous and cover all the requested information. A reply to an inquiry and especially to a first inquiry should be handled with special care to create goodwill. When the goods inquired are out of stock, the seller should inform the buyer of the reason and when the goods will be available. If the goods asked have no longer been produced, or special request cannot be met, the seller needs to answer the inquiry with care and avoids making direct refusal that may offend the other party. Besides, the seller must make sure that all the questions asked in an inquiry have been answered in the reply, and if there are many questions to reply to, bullets or numbers are recommended to enumerate them.

Generally, a reply is composed of three paragraphs: the opening paragraph, the body and the closing paragraph. The opening paragraph usually begins with expressing thanks and the mention of the date the inquiry was written, often followed by a summary of what has been requested in the inquiry letter. The seller may answer the inquiry in detail in the body part and express the hope that the information offered will be useful and the expectation of a reply or an order from the buyer in the closing paragraph.

The reply to an inquiry letter example can help you to make the best response to business requests or inquiries. It is critical to the success of any business that excellent client and associate relationships are maintained, thought the best impression is made by providing the information or materials that the client or business partner has asked about. A well crafted response letter can do much to foster those good relations, and it is crucial to answer the letter authoritatively while providing the content the recipient seeks.

2. Format of the Reply to an Inquiry Letter Example

The formatting of the reply to an inquiry letter example is done in the block style. This is one of the most internationally recognized styles of business letter writing. It is both easy to read, and easy to write, and additionally has an aesthetic effect. In the block format the text is aligned to the left margin, and written in sections or "blocks". It is designed to be easily editable.

The formatting begins with the addressing; you can use your company letterhead, or type your name, address, and contact information, followed by a space, the date, another space, and the recipient's name and address like so:

Newfangled Safety Equipment Co.

62 Seven Towers,
99 Shun Koo St.
Hong Kong MX17 -001
Tel:+853 2255 4423
FAX:+852 2277 4945
E-mail:info@newfangledsafety.com

June 15, 2012

Tom Lee
Manager
Sun Lee Wholesalers Ltd
248 Yuen Fa Street M
Kowloon

A standard salutation of "Dear Mr." or "Dear Mrs." is acceptable to begin your letter. The first thing you'll want to do is to thank the customer or associate for their inquiry. This lets them know that you have received their letter and have investigated their inquiry. When you explain what action has or will be taken as a result of the enquiry, try to be brief and get right to the point. The recipient is interested in the answer to their inquiry, not much else. Take a look at the reply to an inquiry letter example.

Dear Mr. Lee,

Thank you for your enquiry about our newly developed range of fire safety and prevention products. I have enclosed our most recent catalogue, and you will find that we have quite a comprehensive inventory, including our most recently released range of construction related products.

Once you've made it clear that you received the inquiry letter, have understood its question, and explained the action taken or provided the answer required, you can let the customer or associate know what other benefits they will receive from doing business with your firm. This is a great opportunity to sell your products or services, but don't go overboard. Overselling will offend the reader, and may have the undesired effect of alienating them. Consider the approach in the reply to an inquiry letter example.

We offer our existing customers a 10% discount on all orders of products from our new range of construction related products. We would be happy to extend this offer to you if you register an account with us before June 30, 2012, and additionally as a new customer you will receive a further 5% discount on your total order.

The reply to an inquiry letter example has accomplished several things at this point. It has acknowledged receipt of the enquiry, confirmed and explained what action was or will be taken, and encouraged the customer or associate to take action. In closing you would simply establish goodwill between yourself and the enquirer, and suggest contact.

A reply to an inquiry letter should always end in a professional manner. After writing your last paragraph, sign off with a complimentary close such as "Sincerely," and your name. If writing in an official capacity, make sure you place your title underneath your printed name. The completed reply to an inquiry letter thus will look like this:

Newfangled Safety Equipment Co.
62 Seven Towers,
99 Shun Koo St.
Hong Kong MX17 - 001
Tel: +853 2255 4423
FAX: +852 2277 4945
E-mail: info@newfangledsafety.com

June 15, 2012

Tom Lee
Manager
Sun Lee Wholesalers Ltd
248 Yuen Fa Street M
Kowloon

Dear Mr. Lee,

Thank you for your inquiry about our newly developed range of fire safety and prevention products. I have enclosed our most recent catalogue, and you will find that we have quite a comprehensive inventory, including our most recently released range of construction related products.

We offer our existing customers a 10% discount on all orders of products from our new range of construction related products. We would be happy to extend this offer to you if you register an account with us before June 30, 2012, and additionally as a new customer you will receive a further 5% discount on your total order.

I hope you will find the information I have provided useful. I would be happy to have one of our account managers contact you with a view to establishing an account with us, or if you have any further questions about our products or services, you may call me directly on 2255 4423 ext 001. Thank you for considering Newfangled Safety Equipment Co. as your safety product provider. We look forward to doing business with you.

Sincerely yours,

Cindy Choi
Merchandising Manager

3. Tips and Useful Sentences

a. *Please don't hesitate to call me if I can be of any further assistance.*

b. *While I can understand your company's request for this information, it is with great regret that I cannot provide it for the following reasons ...*

c. *I refer to your enquiry regarding ...*

Part D Sample Letters of Replies

Sample 1

Dear Julia,

I hope you are doing well.

My name is Marcelo. I represent R & S Corp., from Buenos Aires, Argentina. We met each other at the Las Vegas' CES, last January. At that time we talked about your products. Actually we are WalMart's Argentina traders, relating to DVD, DivX, DVD Recorder, Portable DVD and LCD TV. I remembered that during our meeting you informed me about some prices that were suitable for us. So I'd like to know your quotation of prices—FOB China—of the following articles, for WalMart's Argentina.

DVD 5.1 full size
DVD 5.1 1/2 size with display
DivX 5.1 full size
DivX 5.1 full size with USB

This request is for WalMart's order, which will be around 20 000 pcs of each article. Please, I'll appreciate you will send me your products pictures and price. If those are different from the catalogue you gave me at the CES, just let me know which catalogue's articles you are quoting. Please answer me as soon as possible. Thanks a lot.

Hope to hear from you soon.

Yours sincerely,

Marcelo

Reply to the above

Dear Marcelo,

Thank you very much for your kind inquiry to us. Your detailed company and market information impressed us deeply. Glad to see that there is a chance for both R & S and Mizida in entering into some projects cooperation in near future.

Further to the inquiry, we would like to make you the offer as below. Photos are as attached.

DVD 5.1 full size, DVD-592, US$21, if with DivX, US$21.5
DVD 5.1 1/2 size with display, DVD-558B, US$20
DVD 5.1 full size with USB, DVD-602/561, US$23

The whole offer is upon FOB Shenzhen price.

And base on your potential quantity 20 000 pcs per item.

Wish they could meet your request.

We are ready to provide more information and samples as requested. We appreciate your comments and looking forward to working together with you soon.

Sincerely yours,

Julia
Manager

Sample 2

Dear Sirs,

Thank you very much for your kind inquiry to us. This is Alice. From now on, I will help to follow up your orders and hope my 5 years' experience and hard work can serve you better.

Regarding your inquiry, please find our reply as below.

Our products are fast sales in EU countries and America. Especially we already had steady partners in those places. And the cooperation has been lasting more than 5 years.

Regarding American market, our customers prefer healthy sleeping, so they would like to buy the mattress to protect their backbones. For example, memory mattress, independent spring mattress, surely the reel mattress you mentioned is also fast sale. Please refer to the attachments, I would like to introduce some suitable items for your market.

Currently our company is applying for the American prevailing rules CFR1633 which is standard fire protection and becoming effective in July 1st, 2020. As we know that in Los Angeles they would apply for the standard fire protection rule TB603. But now they upgrade to CFR1633. We think you might require for it, too. Please refer to the CERTIFICATION as attached.

Payment term:
30% deposit T/T in advance, 70% balance T/T before shipment.
50% deposit T/T in advance, 50% balance by irrevocable L/C at sight.

Leading time:15 days upon deposit received
MOQ:1 * 20GP, FOB Shenzhen

If you have any inquiry and need our help, please don't hesitate to contact me.

Sincerely yours,

Alice

Sample 3

Dear Sirs,

I am the purchase manager of Sound Master Company in South Africa. We are planning to import mattress. The quantity may be around 200 sets at the first time. And our boss Mike and I will visit China next month. We would like to talk to you in your factory. In order to get the visa from Chinese Embassy, can you send an invitation letter to us?

We are looking forward to hearing from you soon.

Sincerely yours,

Anson

Reply to the above

Dear Anson,

Thank you very much for your kind inquiry to us. My name is John. From now on, I will follow up your orders and offer best sales service with my professional experience.

Because we don't have your ideas about target item, I would like to offer you some fast sale items in South Africa for your easy reference first. The details are as attached. We are also inviting you to visit our website at www.××furniture.com to know more details about us.

Regarding the invitation letter, we would like to share some information with you. Normally we have to submit application form and relative necessary information to our government for approval first. As we didn't start cooperation before, the application period may be longer. In order not to affect your schedule, I would like to advise that if you have other business partners here, you'd better ask them to help you. So you may get the visa within one week.

Please take our suggestion as reference. Surely we are pleased to apply for you if you need our help. But please send us the details about the people who will come.

To catch the visit schedule and run the business soon, shall we exchange some important ideas first? We may conclude some agreements before you visit China.

We welcome your coming and visiting. And we're looking forward to our cooperation soon.

Sincerely yours,

John

Sample 4

Dear Water,

We are currently looking to expand our product line including memory foam mattresses and pillows.

I will come to China next month. In the meantime, I would like to collect as much information as possible on prices and specifications.

Please advise us at your earliest convenience.

Sincerely yours,

Michael

Reply to the above

Dear Michael,

We are glad to know that you will expand your business line on memory foam mattresses and memory foam pillows. Believe we can serve you better and better in near future.

First, please refer to the attachments for your reference. It is great that you will come to China for business. Please kindly arrange your schedule to visit our factory. We hope we can have a close talk face to face. Then we could show you our production lines and sample room. We are confident that it will make our cooperation smoothly.

When your visit schedule is available, please kindly let me know.

Sincerely yours,

Water

Sample 5

Dear Maitance,

Nice to contact with you. This is Echo from CABC (Hong Kong) International Industrial Limited. And it is my great honor to serve you in the future.

Our boss Mr. Jason, just came back from the MIDO SHOW, and I learned that you are interested in our swimming products. Here attached our updated price list for your reference. Also, please take your time to visit our website at www.cabc.com for pictures and more details.

Mr. Jason had quoted you two models in MIDO, and here we list again as below for your easy reference.

Swimming cap: CAP 800 USD 2.0 (according to your quantity of 200 pcs)
Earplug with strap: EP-200 USD 0.8 (including package)

Please contact us freely if you have any question.

We are looking forward to building business relationship with you in the near future.

Sincerely yours,

Echo

Sample 6

Dear Marcus,

How are you doing? This is Water from ××× Company, Ms. Grace's colleague. She already left the company some time ago. It's been a long time no contact with you and your company. We are glad to contact you again about external battery pack for Mobile Phone and Notebook.

I would like to update you some latest model and new offers for your reference. We hope we can enlarge our business scale. Please find the details as attached.

Looking forward to hearing from you soon.

Sincerely yours,

Water

Sample 7

Dear Andy,

This is Tina, sales representative of ××× Electronic Company. Thanks for Eden's assignment, I'm pleased to have the opportunity to contact you and take charge of our cases directly. Hope we can set long-term business relationship and expand business in the future.

Now I'm taking up your first order—2002 (DVD recorder), all the specifications and other details will be followed by me. Therefore if you have any problem, please feel free to contact me.

Further to your new order, please refer to the attachments for our quotations, we are waiting for your confirmation. Surely we will get a good delivery date for you.

Thank you for your good cooperation and your early reply will be appreciated.

Yours faithfully,

×××

Sample 8

Dear Sirs,

Thank you for your inquiry of July 23 for our BCL receiver MS-2, and we inform you that the illustrated catalogue and samples you asked for in your letter have been airmailed to you this morning.

In your letter, you asked for a special price discount of 4% off the price list. We are sorry to say that we cannot grant you such a discount, for we have to treat all customers equally. But if you raise your order to 20 000 units, we would like to offer you the requested 4% discount in accordance with our discount policy. Your payment terms by irrevocable L/C at sight are acceptable to us.

We are confident that you will be satisfied with our products both in quality and design after examining the samples, and will find that our prices are really competitive.

Your early reply will be very much appreciated.

Yours faithfully,

John Woo

Sample 9

Gentlemen:

We learn from your letter of July 2 that you are manufacturing and exporting a variety of textile machines. As there is a demand here for high-quality dyeing machines, we will appreciate your sending us a copy of your illustrated catalogue, with details of your prices and terms of payment.

Yours truly,

×××

Reply to the above

Gentlemen:

We warmly welcome your inquiry of July 15 and thank you for your interest in our dyeing machines.

We are enclosing our illustrated catalogue and price list giving the details you ask for. As for the payment terms we usually require con-firmed, irrevocable Letter of Credit payable by draft at sight.

We have already sold some of those machines to China and are now represented there by the Engineering Export Ltd, Bering. May we suggest that you contact the company directly? We think the firm may supply you with more details of our machines. We feel confident that you will find the goods are both excellent in quality and very reasonable in price.

Yours sincerely,

×××

Sample 10

Dear Sirs,

Messrs. Brown & Clark of this city inform us that you are exporters of all cotton bed-sheets and pillowcases. We are large dealers in textiles and believe there is a promising market in our area for moderately priced goods of the kind mentioned.

We would like you to send us details of your various ranges, including sizes, colors and prices, and also samples of the different qualities of material used.

When replying, please state your terms of payment and discount you would allow on purchase of quantities of not less than 100 dozen of individual items. Prices quoted should include insurance and freight to Liverpool.

I look forward to hearing from you.

Yours faithfully,

×××

Reply to the above

Dear Sirs,

We were very pleased to receive your letter of 15 March, in which you inquired about our cotton bed-sheets and pillowcases.

As requested, we are enclosing our catalogue and the price list giving the details you asked for. Also under separate cover we are sending you a full range of samples.

We are sure you will find that we use only the best quality materials for our products. And the high standard of workmanship will appeal to the most selective buyers. (advertisements)

It's understood that prices we quoted are on CIF Liverpool without engagement, subject to our final confirmation. We allow 2% discount on purchase of not less than 100 dozen of individual items. Payment is to be made by irrevocable L/C at sight.

Please feel free to contact us if you have any further questions.

We look forward to receiving your early reply.

Yours faithfully,

×××

Sample 11

Dear Sirs,

I got your business information online. We would like to cooperate with you on CARDS, and become your good partner in near future.

With more than 12 years experience in manufacturing all kinds of PVC cards, paper cards, metal cards and smart cards in China, we've grown up into a main supplier in Italy, Germany, Sweden, France, Denmark and New Zealand, etc. The daily output can reach millions of cards. Including PVC blank and printed cards, paper cards, scratch cards, magnetic cards, IC cards, game cards, gift cards, member cards, pokers, playing cards, metallic cards, phone cards, irregular-shaped cards, ATM cards, IC cards, ID cards, RFID tags, etc. We welcome your ODM projects. All sizes and thickness can be done here.

We welcome your inquiries. Please visit our official website at http://www.ucard.biz. It will be appreciated that if someone from your company could contact me freely. My E-mail is: water@ucard.biz.

Please let us become partners and start the initial cooperation soon.

Looking forward to hearing from you.

Sincerely yours,

Water

Chapter 6 Quotations, Offers and Counter Offers

Learning Objectives

a. Master specific writing requirements of quotations, offers and counter offers.

b. Distinguish and understand the writing differences between the firm offer and non-firm offer.

c. Master specific writing skills and requirements of offer responses.

Part A Introduction

1. Quotation

It is well known that there are four major steps in business negotiation: inquiry offer→counter offer→acceptance→contract.

A quotation is a promise to supply goods on the terms stated. It, however, is not legally binding as a form offer if the seller later decides not to sell.

Quotation is not an offer in the legal sense. An offer is a promise to supply goods on the terms and conditions stated, while a quotation is merely a notice of the prize of certain goods at which the seller is willing to sell. However, when sending an offer, the seller must not only quote the price of the goods he wishes to sell but also indicates all necessary terms of sales for the buyer's consideration. But, if a quotation is made together with all necessary terms and conditions of sales, it amounts to an offer.

When a seller prepares to export, he or she quotes the customer the price of the goods on receipt of the inquiry. A quotation generally includes all the necessary information requested. The prospective buyer is under no obligation to buy and the seller is not bound to sell. In brief, a quotation is not legally binding if the seller later decides not to sell. A satisfactory quotation will include the following:

a. Thanks for the inquiry if there is any;

b. The answers to all the information requested;

c. Details of prices, terms of payment, and discounts;

d. A statement or clear indication of what the price cover (e. g. freight and insurance, etc.);

e. An undertaking as to date of delivery or time of shipment;

f. The period for which the quotation is valid;

g. Additional information;

h. Hope of orders or further inquiries.

2. Offer

An offer is made when a seller promises to sell goods at a stated price and within a stated period of time. The party sending the offer is called the offerer while another party is called offeree. An offer is mostly made in response to an inquiry, while it can also be voluntarily made by the seller to regular or new customers who may have interest in his or her products without any inquiry. If so, it is required to give an undertaking that all essential terms are clearly specified. A price quotation is not an offer due to lacking of expression of a promise to sell.

Some experts divide offer into two categories: firm offer and non-firm offer. **A firm offer provides a period of validity and the acceptance made by the offeree before validity expires is effective legally, while a non-firm offer is unclear, incomplete and with reservations, and it is not binding on the offerer.** Such expressions as "reference price", "subject to our final confirmation", and "subject to goods being unsold" are often employed in the non-firm offers. A firm offer should provide complete affirmative and specific terms of business, the beginning and the ending dates and the place of the validity.

When making a firm offer, the time of shipment and the made of payment desired should be mentioned; in addition, an exact description of the goods should be given and if possible, pattern of sample. Non-firm offers are usually made by means of sending catalogues, price list, proforma invoices and quotations. They are not legally binding on the offers and cannot be "accepted", however, it can be considered as an inducement to business.

Either for a quotation or an offer, the tone should be friendly or the language should be polite. As regards the structure, a quotation or an offer is generally divided into three parts. In the first part, the seller acknowledges the inquiry and expresses thanks for the customer's interest in his or her products. The second part presents the situation of stock, the terms and conditions and the validity (for a firm offer), while the hope that the quotation or the offer will be to the recipient's satisfaction and the expectation of an acceptance are expressed in the last part.

3. Counter Offer

(1) A brief introduction

An offeree needs to make response to the offer he has received. Sometimes an offeree partly or totally disagrees with the offer but puts forward his own proposals and this is called a counter offer. If the offeree finds any terms or conditions in the offer unacceptable, he can negotiate with the seller and make a counter offer to show his disagreement to the terms of payment, packing, shipment time, quantity or the date of delivery and state his own terms and conditions. In this case, the original offer is invalid, and the counter offer actually becomes a new offer from the original offeree. The original offerer or the seller now becomes the offeree and has the full right of acceptance or refusal. He may make a reply to the buyer's counter offer. This is called a counter-counter-offer. This process can go on for several rounds till business is concluded or called off.

In writing a counter offer, one has to state the terms most explicitly and use words carefully to avoid ambiguity or misunderstanding. When a buyer rejects an offer, he should write to thank the seller and explain the reason for rejection. A letter of counter offer is usually composed of three parts. The first paragraph is designed to acknowledge the receipt of the offer and express the buyer's thanks. The explanation of the reasons to make the counter offer and the raised new terms and conditions are presented in the second part which can be divided into separate paragraphs. The buyer may use the last part to express his hope for a prompt reply or put forward his suggestions to do business together.

When it comes to real estate, both buyers and sellers tend to involve themselves in a day-long negotiation. The aim of the negotiation would be getting the best deal for both sellers and buyers with mutual satisfaction. In some cases, wherein the buyer is not satisfied with the deal and terms on purchasing the property, they submit a purchase offer letter indicating their expectations. The seller may not accept the revised terms and deals sent by the buyers. To make this ongoing negotiation smoother and successful, a seller can create a counter offer letter that addresses fair deals in short.

In a nutshell, using a counter offer letter ensures that the seller won't miss potential buyers. Creating a perfect real estate counter offer letter should not be a big task for you.

(2) Several kinds of counter offers

a. Counter offer on price;

b. Asks for reduction of minimum quantity;

c. Counter offer on payment terms;

d. Asks for earlier delivery;

e. Asks for changing the package;

f. Counter offer on the discount of the goods;

g. Asks for more commission.

(3) The key structure of counter offers

a. Opening paragraph: Express your thanks with a courteous sentence.

b. Transitional paragraph: Counter offer

• Express your difficulties to accept the offer and give your reasons.

• Express your conditions (suggestions) to counter offer.

c. Closing paragraph: Express your hope for acceptance of counter offer.

(4) How to write a real estate counter offer letter?

Step 1: study the buyer's original offer

It is obvious that the buyer always quotes the price very low from the original tag in the initial purchase offer. So it is always essential for a seller to give a glance at the buyer's offer and determine the things which he likes and dislikes. Apart from the price, the buyer may also specify replacement of the home's roof, walls, floor or any other expensive replacements with the short closing tenure. In this event, you can't expect the closing date to be so long from the negotiating schedule. It might be too soon or too long. Therefore, it is important to study the buyer's offer before creating a counter offer letter in order to make it more pertinent to the buyer's expectations.

Step 2: address your concerns

Make sure that the counter offer letter you write addresses your concerns. The things like changing the total price consideration, replacement options and closing date are the most common in the counter offer letter. If the buyer's purchase offer is not up to the market, you can highlight it in the letter indicating the market price. If you are not willing to do expensive replacement works on the property, ensure you have stated it in the letter. You can recommend your buyer a range of acceptable closing dates if you have an issue with the closing date stated by the buyer. However, you need to draft a counter letter which communicates your concerns in order to make a successful deal.

Step 3: connect with the buyer personally

It is important that you use phrases that inspire your buyer to accept the deal. If you are familiar with the buyer's expectations, you can move the selling process as per their wishes. The deals on pricing, repairing services, etc., must be acceptable by your buyer. So before writing the letter, make sure you know their expectations and create it according to that.

Step 4: let them know how serious you are

It is always good to let your buyers know about your commitment towards making the deal. Writing a counter offer letter earlier, quoting the reasonable price, informing them about the present market price and neighbourhood standards are the important things to add to the counter offer letter. This makes you more reliable and trustworthy and gets you a good deal.

Step 5: keep it short

The necessity of writing a counter offer letter is to convince your buyer to make the deal on your terms and offers. Here the buyer won't feel tedious to read the letter which has multi pages. Hence, make the letter short, that it should be of a one-page letter addressing the whole story.

Step 6: stick to the format

A professional counter offer letter must follow a certain format. Here you need to know how to organize the letter. A perfect counter offer letter must be of a business letter format which addresses the letter to the buyer. Start with the proper header which mentions the contact information. There are three elements in the letter likely introduction, the body of the letter and conclusion. Each section states your interests in making the deal. Conclude the letter by leaving a section for the signature of the seller.

Before writing a counter offer letter make sure you have clear reasons for denying the purchase offer sent by your buyer previously. You will get the best deals and additional advantages if you state logical reasons in the letter. Be honest with the reasons and phrases you address in the counter offer letter. In order to maintain strong communication with your buyer, you must know how to present an interesting counter offer letter. Since most of the buyers don't want their purchase offer to be counter offered by the seller, they don't show interest in reading the full page. Here, crafting a simple counter offer letter which makes them feel comfortable to read the full page is essential.

It is up to the buyer whether to accept the counter offer or not. However, if they are not agreed with the revised terms, they will make the second counter offer. Therefore it will continue until both parties come to a mutual satisfaction stage. To eliminate the letter to be countered, you as a seller of the property must showcase necessary information in the first counter offer itself.

Part B Sample Letters of Quotations

Sample 1

Dear Sirs,

Thank you for your order of 25 October for 24 000 bed sheets. We welcome you as one of our customers.

We are pleased to confirm our acceptance as shown in the enclosed Sales Contract in duplicate. Please sign and return one copy to us for our file.

Please open your L/C by the end of October. We will arrange for immediate shipment provided your L/C reaches us in time.

We hope that this initial order will be just the beginning of many, and that we may have many years of pleasant business relations together.

Yours faithfully,

×××

Sample 2

Dear Sir,

We were very pleased to receive your letter of 5th April answering our advertisement for typewriters and, as requested, enclose a copy of our latest illustrated catalogue and current price list.

We think the "Portable 95" is a machine that would suit your purpose very well. It weighs 6.5 kg and is a bit heavier than the usual portable, but it is good for heavy duty and at the same time conveniently portable when carried in its case.

We have one of these machines in stock and we shall be pleased to arrange for you to try it. Although costs have been rising since March, we have not yet raised our pries, but may have to do so when present stocks run out. We therefore advise you to place your order with us at once.

Yours faithfully,

×××

Sample 3

Dear Sir,

Thank you for your letter of 10th March. We are gratified to receive your request for men and women's raincoats on approval.

As we have not previously done business together, perhaps you will kindly agree to supply either the usual trade references, or the name of a bank to which we may refer. As soon as these inquiries are satisfactorily settled, we shall be happy to send you the items you mention in your letter.

We sincerely hope this will be the beginning of a long and pleasant business association. We shall do our best to make it so.

Yours faithfully,

×××

Sample 4

Dear Sirs,

We thank you very much for your letter of October 17, asking for our washing machines Model HTW 11 and Model HTW 14.

We, as being requested, enclose our latest price list of this month and details of our conditions of sales and terms of payment. We have examined your proposal to place an order for a minimum number of our washing machines in return for a special allowance, but we feel it would be better to offer you a special allowance on the following sliding scale basis.

On purchases exceeding an annual total of:
US$ 10 000 but not exceeding US$ 20 000......... 1%
US$ 20 000 but not exceeding US$ 30 000......... 2%
US$ 30 000 but not exceeding US$ 40 000......... 3%
US$ 40 000 and above.......................... 4%
No special allowance could be given on annual total purchase below US$ 10 000.

We feel that the above arrangement would be more satisfactory to both of us and can assure you that these goods are very popular in the European markets, of which we have had much experience.

We look forward to your acceptance of our proposal and to your orders.

Yours faithfully,

W. H. Ausman

Sample 5

Dear Sirs,

We thank you for your inquiry of September 23, and are pleased to send you our quotation for the goods you required as follows:

Commodity: "Polar Land" brand down jacket NFT13
Size: Large (L), medium (M), small (S)
Color: Brown, marine blue, yellow, green
Quantity: 800 pieces
Price: US $ 50.00 per piece CFR Philadelphia
Shipment: November

You are cordially invited to take advantage of this attractive quotation. We are anticipating a larger order from Canada, and that will cause a sharp rise in price.

We look forward to receiving your order.

Yours faithfully,

×××

Sample 6

Dear sirs,

We well received your inquiry in canned mushroom pieces & stems dated on ××. As per your requirement, we quote the price as below:

Name of item: canned mushroom
Pieces & stems specification: 24 tinned/ctn n.w: 425 g g.w: 227
Packaging: normal export brown carton box with buyers brand
Quantity: 1 700 ctn /container
Price: US $ 7.80 cfr dammam
Payment terms: l/c at sight
Delivery date: no later than 30/12/2019

Term of validity:27/10/2019

If any query, please feel free to let me know.

Best regards.

Tracy
Manager of MINC

Sample 7

BRIGHT STATIONERY CO.
125 SUNFLOWER PLAZA SINGAPORE
FAX:065 - 7890023

SHANGHAI LINSHENG TRADING CO. LTD.
548 YANPING ROAD
Shanghai, China
FAX:0086 - 021 - 57234621

DATE:07 - MAR. - 01

Dear Sales Manager,

Thank you for your fax and your catalogue.

We have concluded several successful transactions of similar products with other traders in your region. Recently we have received several inquiries from our customers and find that the Art. No. 7003 is closest to their requirements except that they require packing in wooden cases instead of in cartons. Therefore we wonder whether you can comply with the requirement or not. Meanwhile, please note that your after-sale service must be well in the position to meet our customers' demand for free replacement of spare parts. For your reference, we would like to state some of our general terms and conditions as follows:

1) Our usual term of payment is by D/P at 30 days'sight.
2) If the transaction is concluded on the CIF or CFR Singapore basis, the buyer must have the right to appoint the forwarding company.

3) The goods, before being loaded at the port of shipment, must be inspected by an inspection institution agreeable to the buyer in the presence of the buyer's representative.

We hope the above terms and conditions are acceptable to you and may become the basis of our future business. By return E-mail, please inform us of your banker and quote us your best prices for Art. No. SBT－121, 7003 & SDM－02, based on FOBC5 SHANGHAI and CIFC5 Singapore. You have every reason to believe that given your prices are competitive, large orders are sure to follow.

We are awaiting your early reply.

Yours sincerely,

BRIGHT STATIONERY CO.
Manager
POLLY ENDSON

Part C Sample Letters of Offers

Sample 1

Dear Sirs,

Re: SWC Sugar

We have received your letter of July 17, 2019 asking us to offer 10 000 metric tons of the subject sugar for shipment to London and appreciate very much your interest in our product.

To comply with your request, we are quoting you as follows:

Commodity: Superior White Crystal Sugar
Packing: To be packed in new gunny bags of 100 kgs. each
Quantity: Ten Thousand metric tons
Price: U. S. Dollars 105 per metric ton CIF London
Payment: 100% by irrevocable and confirmed letter of credit to be opened on our favor and to be drawn at sight

Shipment: one month after receipt of letter of credit

Your attention is drawn to fact that we have not much ready Stock on hand. Therefore, it is imperative that, in order to enable us to effect early shipment, your letter of credit should be opened in time if our price meets with your approval.

We are awaiting your immediate reply.

Yours faithfully,

×××

Sample 2

A firm offer for corn and wheat

Dear Sir or Madam,

We thank you for your letter dated December 7, asking us to make an offer for corn and wheat CIF Hong Kong.

We E-mailed you this morning offering you 2 000 metric tons of corn at US$137 per metric ton, CIF Hong Kong, for shipment during May and June 2019. This offer is subject to the receipt of your reply before April 15, 2020.

Please note that we have quoted our most favourable price and are unable to entertain any counter offer. With regard to wheat, we have to tell you that all the lots we have now are under offer and we cannot supply from stock. However, if you make us a suitable offer, we may seek help from our supplying channels and there is still a possibility of supplying them to you.

There has been a heavy demand for corn and wheat in the last 3 months and this has resulted in increased prices. However, you may take advantage of the strengthening market if you send an early reply.

Yours faithfully,

Dirk Bogarde

Sample 3

A firm offer for hard-nut crackers

Dear Sirs,

We thank you for your fax of October 17 asking us to make firm offers for hard-nut crackers. We are pleased to know you are interested in our products.

We are offering you 500 sets of hard-nut crackers at U. S. $ 8 per set CFR Livorno or any other Italian main port for shipment during November/December, 2019. This offer is firm, subject to receipt of reply by us before the end of October.

Please see to it that we have quoted our most favorable price and are unable to entertain any counter offer.

Our stock level on hand has been quite low owing to heavy commitment, and we hope you can place an early order.

Yours faithfully,

Amy Lowell

Sample 4

An offer for Dreamland-musician toys

Dear Sirs,

Thank you for your letter of July 13, in which you asked for an offer from us for 10 000 sets of Dreamland-musician M-532 toys.

We are now making you the following offer: 10 000 sets of Dreamland-musician M-532 toys, at U. S. $ 9.00 per set on FOB Shanghai basis for shipment in September 2019 with payment to be made by an irrevocable sight L/C.

We feel you may be interested in some of our other toys and therefore enclose our latest illustrated catalogue and a supply of sales literature for your reference.

We are looking forward to your order.

Yours faithfully,

Tom Liu

Sample 5

An offer for CD/VCD/MP3 players

Dear Sirs,

We have received your letter of March 17 and are pleased to make you the following offer subject to your reply reaching us by March 31, 2020.

Commodity: CD/VCD/MP3 player
Model: KW3739
Color: Blue
Quantity: 10 000 sets
Price: At U. S. $ 87. 00 each set FOB Tianjin
Shipment: In May
Payment: By L/C at sight to be opened through a bank acceptable to us.

We are expecting large orders from importers in other countries and that will cause a sharp rise in price. Therefore, we hope you may take advantage of this attractive offer.

We look forward to your prompt reply.

Sincerely yours,

Arthur Xie

Sample 6

A non-firm offer for woolen mixed blankets

Dear Sirs,

We have received your letter of November 11, asking us to offer you woolen mixed blankets. We are pleased to be told that there is a great demand for our products in Stockholm. In compliance with your request, we are making you the following offer subject to our final confirmation.

Commodity: woolen mixed blankets, different colors and pattern assortment
Size: Large (L), medium (M) and small (S)
Packing: Blankets are wrapped in plastic bags and packed in standard cardboard cartons
Price: CFR Stockholm per dozen in US Dollars; L:245, M:235, S:225
Payment: By irrevocable L/C payable by draft at sight

The Chinese woolen mixed blankets are of good quality and have fine workmanship and design. They are moderately priced, as known to all. You will certainly agree to that when you have examined our samples and quotation.

If you need any further information about our products, please let us know. We hope the above will be acceptable to you.

We are looking forward to your order soon.

Yours faithfully,

Thomas Campion

Sample 7

A non-firm offer for cotton jackets

Dear Sirs,

We thank you for your letter dated October 27, and are willing to enter into business

relations with you on the basis of equality and mutual benefit. At your request, we take pleasure in making you a special offer, subject to our final confirmation, as follows:

Commodity: "Showner" brand cotton jackets NO. 33
Quantity: 500 dozen
Size: L/XL/XXL/XXXL
Color: White, red, yellow, blue
Price: U. S. $ 2 000 per dozen CIF Sydney
Shipment: One month after receipt of L/C
Payment: By a 100% confirmed, irrevocable L/C in our favor payable by draft at sight to reach the sellers one month before shipment and remain valid for negotiation in China till the 15th day after shipment

We hope that the above will be acceptable to you and assure you of our best service at any time.

We are looking forward to your prompt reply.

Yours faithfully.

John Chung

Part D Sample Letters of Counter Offers

Sample 1

A counter offer for price

Dear Sirs,

Thank you so much for your offer, but after we carefully studying, we found your price is too high. We know your goods are in high quality, compared with the items which produce in Europe.

But, your price are higher than your competitor 5%-10%. So, we do hope you kindly reduce the price approximately 5%, say U. S. $ 7. 40/ctn. I think this concession should be acceptable by you.

Yours sincerely,

Tracy
Manager of MINC

Sample 2

Dear Sir,

Subject: Counter offer

We have been very pleased with your product, as you know. However, we find that we can obtain a price of $4.00 per hundred with a local firm. This is fifty cents per hundred lower than your price.

If you can see your way clear to meeting these figures we would be pleased to place with you an order that will carry us for the rest of this year. That order is likely to be one of the largest that we have ever placed with you.

Sincerely yours,

×××

Sample 3

Dear Sir,

Subject: We regret that we cannot accept your counter offer.

In reference to your E-mail of August 1, we cannot make a better offer than the one we suggested to you, and we feel that offer itself is most generous under the circumstances.

In checking our books, we find that you have purchased from us twice as much the first three months of this year as you did in the first three months of last year. This indicates to us that you have been successful in retailing our merchandise.

We hope that upon reconsideration you will be able to accept our offer. We have been very pleased to have you on our list of accounts.

Yours sincerely,

×××

Sample 4

Dear Sirs,

We have received your offer of October 21 for 500 sets of washing machines Model HTW 11 and Model HTW 14 at US$35 000 with 3% discount.

In reply, we regret to inform you that the prices you quoted are found too high. We trust the quality of your produces and would welcome the opportunity to do business with you. May we suggest that you give us more discount, say 5% on your quoted price of US$35 000? We believe that would help to introduce your goods to our market. Should you be prepared to grant us that rate of discount, we would be pleased to come to terms and place with you an order.

We are anticipating your early reply.

Yours faithfully,

W. Philips
Business Manager

Sample 5

A counter offer for down jackets

Dear Sir,

We thank you for your offer of November 7, and the samples of "Polar Land" brand down jacket NFT13.

We know clearly that the quality of your jackets is very good, but we find your price is rather too high for our local market. Information indicates that the price of your products is around 20% higher than that of the Indonesia origin.

Such being the case, we have to ask you to consider if you can make a reduction in your price, say 15%. As our order would be no less than 800 pieces, you may think it worthwhile to make a concession. As the market is declining, we hope you will consider our proposal most favorable and fax us your acceptance, thus we may push the sales of your products.

Yours faithfully,

William Carols

Sample 6

A reply to counter offer for down jackets

Dear Sirs,

We thank you very much for your letter of December 3, in which you asked us to reduce our price of "Polar Land" brand down jacket NFT13 by around 15%.

While appreciating your good wish to push the sales of our products, we regret to say that we cannot bring our price down to that low level at this stage. For your information, our "Polar Land" brand down jackets NFT13 have been well established in Netherlands, and there is a steady demand for them.

We trust it will not be difficult for our products to get a footing in your local market if you could see your way to do some marketing work. Please rest assured that we would always do our best to help you and promote the sales of our goods in your area.

Yours faithfully,

John Lesseter

Sample 7

A counter offer for DVD players

Dear Sirs,

We thank you for your fax offer of June 7 for 3 000 sets of Gloryfield brand DVD players. We appreciate the good quality of your goods, but unfortunately we are not in a position to accept the offer on your terms. Your prices are on rather high side.

To step up the trade, we suggest you make some concessions, say 4%, on your quoted prices, and we feel confident that it would help to push the sales of your goods in our market. If you can do so, we will place our order with you immediately. We hope you will not lose this chance so that you will benefit from this expanding market.

We will appreciate it very much if you could consider our counter offer most favorably and fax us your acceptance at your earliest convenience.

Yours faithfully,

Andrew Stanton

Sample 8

A counter offer for CD/VCD/MP3 players

Dear Sirs,

We learn from your letter of June 12 that you offer us 10 000 sets of CD/VCD/MP3 player KW3739 at US$ 87.00 per set.

We regret to say that we find your price is rather high, and it will be difficult to convince our clients at your price. We believe you are familiar with the market, and you cannot ignore the fierce competition from suppliers in Southeast Asian countries.

We suggest that you make some allowance, say 8% on your offered price. Since our order is large, it is worthwhile to make a concession. We hope you will consider our counter offer most favorably.

Look forward to your early reply.

Yours faithfully,

Andrew Stanton

Sample 9

A counter offer for hiking boots

Dear Sirs,

We note from your letter of April 23 that you are interested in our hiking boots but find that our offer of March 17 is a bit high.

We regret to say that we cannot comply with your request. To accept the prices you suggested would leave us little or no margin of profit on our sales. We have received many inquiries from importers in other countries and information shows that our price is fixed at a reasonable level.

We thank you again for your prompt response to our inquiry and offer, and would like to take this opportunity to conclude some transactions with you.

We are awaiting your early and favorable reply.

Yours faithfully,

×××

Sample 10

A counter offer for hiking boots

Dears Miss Anna,

Thank you for you letter of November 24, in which you asked us to reduce our prices by 10% on our water-proof hiking boots X-5. But regretfully enough, we are unable to entertain your counter offer, since your request of cutting the price by 10% will leave us no margin of profit on our sales.

However, on considering our long-term relations, we should like to make a concession and grant your request to lower the prices of our products. After careful study and consideration, we suggest a reduction of 6%, instead of the 10% you requested, should your order exceed 12 000 pairs.

We are anticipating your prompt reply.

Yours sincerely,

Robert De Niro

Sample 11

A counter offer for compasses

Dear Sirs,

We have received your letter of August 7, informing us that you can supply us 15 000 AZ-3467 all-weather compasses at US$ 349.00 per set FOB Tokyo.

To be frank with you, we like the design and craftsmanship of your compasses, but your price is rather too high to be acceptable. As you know, the price of compasses has been declining in the last six months. We have to point out that manufacturers in other countries, including South Korea, are actually lowering their prices according to a market survey made by us recently.

Due to this situation, it is impossible for us to accept your price. If you can make a reduction in you price, say 10%, we might come to terms.

We hope you will consider our counter offer most favorably and look forward to your early reply.

Yours faithfully,

×××

Sample 12

A counter offer on the price

Dear Sirs,

We thank you for your offer by telex of September 3 for 5 000 pieces of the goods at U.S.D. 9.50 per piece CIF Hamburg.

We immediately contacted our customers and they showed great interest in the quality and designs of your products. However they said your price is too much on the high side, i. e, 10% higher than the average. They told us if you can reduce your price to U.S.D. 8.55 per piece, they will increase 1 000 pieces to the quantity. So there is a good chance of concluding a bigger transaction with them if you can meet their requirement. We hope you will take advantage of this opportunity so that you will benefit from the expanding market.

We await your favorable reply with great interest.

Yours faithfully,

×××

Sample 13

Buyer asks for reduction of minimum quantity

Dear Sirs,

Re: Your offer No. 123

We thank you for your fax of April 4 offering us six designs of Ornamental Cloth. However we regret to inform you that the minimum of 10 000 yards per design is too big for this market.

In case you can reduce the minimum to 7 000 yards per design, there is a possibility of placing orders with you, because a consider able quantity of this material is required on this market for manufacturing curtains, bed sheets, etc.

Your early reply will be highly appreciated.

Yours faithfully,

×××

Sample 14

A counter offer on payment terms

Dear Sirs,

We thank you for your quotation of February 3 for 1 000 sets of Panasonic 2188 Color TV. We find your price as well as delivery date satisfactory, however we would give our suggestion of an alteration of your payment terms.

Our past purchase of other household electrical appliances from you has been paid as a rule by confirmed, irrevocable letter of credit at sight. On this basis, it has indeed cost us a great deal. From the moment to open credit till the time our buyers pay us, the tie-up of our funds lasts about four months. Under the present circumstances, this question is particularly taxing owing to the tight money condition and unprecedented high bank interest.

In view of our long business relations and our amicable cooperation prospects, we suggest that you accept either "Cash against Documents on arrival of goods" or "Drawing on us at 60 day's sight".

Your first priority to the consideration of the above request and an early favorable reply will be highly appreciated.

Yours faithfully,

×××

Sample 15

Buyer asks for earlier delivery

Dear Sirs,

Re: ×××

We refer to your offer of March 13 for 2 000 pieces of the subject articles.

As our customers urgently need the goods, they request us to telex you to shift your delivery time from "the end of July" to "on or before June 15", or they will get the goods from other resources.

In order to promote your business, please accept this condition. We await your pleasant reply.

Yours faithfully,

×××

Chapter 7 Orders and Acknowledgments

Learning Objectives

a. Master writing requirements of orders and acknowledgments.

b. Be familiar with the writing format of the order confirmation letter.

Part A Introduction

1. Order

An order is the buyer's request to supply a specified quantity of goods to the terms stated. It is an offer to buy.

The order from a buyer is an offer to buy. Going through inquiry, quotation and several rounds of offer and counter offer, the seller and the buyer come to an agreement and the buyer may place an order with the seller. An order can be sent by a letter, a printed order form, a fax or an E-mail message. Usually well-known customers will probably use a form while a new customer or one placing a single order often writes a letter.

No matter what forms the buyer may choose, the order must be accurate, clear, specific and complete. The buyer must make the seller know clearly the exact goods he wants. The language of an order letter should be definite, exact and simple, Experiences show it is important that the buyer should pay special attention to spelling and any decimal point. The writer is strongly recommended to double check all price calculations to avoid making mistakes before sending the letter.

An order may include the descriptions of the following specific items:

a. Name of commodity;

b. Quality requirements and specifications;

c. Quantity;

d. Price;

e. Packing and marking;

f. Terms of delivery;

g. Terms of payment;

h. Documents.

A letter of order is mostly composed of three parts. The buyer prepares the first part to refer to the previous contact, and describes the details of the order in the second part, followed by the last part that states the terms and form of payment, the anticipated date of delivery and the mode of transportation.

The essential qualities of an order are accuracy and clarity. An order or an order letter should:

a. Include full details of description, quantity, price, quote article number, if any;

b. State mode of packing, port of destination, time of shipment;

c. Confirm the terms of payment as agreed upon in preliminary negotiations.

Sometimes, buyers will seek to protect themselves by making their order subject to certain penalties should the contracted terms not be fulfilled.

The buyer's obligations:

a. To accept the goods supplied, provided they comply with the terms of the order;

b. To pay for them according to the terms agreed upon;

c. To check the goods as soon as possible (failure to give prompt notice of faults to the seller will be taken as acceptance of the goods).

The seller's obligations:

a. To deliver goods exactly of the kind ordered, and the agreed time;

b. To guarantee that the goods to be supplied are free from faults of which the buyer could not be aware at the time of purchase.

If faulty goods are delivered, the buyer can demand either a reduction in price, or replacement of the goods, or cancellation of the order. He may also be able to claim damages.

2. Acknowledgment

Upon receipt of an order, the seller should acknowledge it in good time. If the goods ordered are available, the seller had better lose no time to state his acknowledgement and repeat the terms in the letter of order. The seller, in the acknowledgement, may praise the buyer for his or her wise order, express thanks to longtime customer or deliver a hearty welcome to a new customer. Quite often a letter of acknowledgement includes the following contents:

a. Acknowledgement of the order with expressions of thanks;

b. Restatement of the shipping instructions and the terms of payment;

c. Favorable comments on the goods ordered;

d. Recommendation of other products likely to be of interest;

e. Hope for further orders.

When the seller cannot accept an order because the goods required are out of stock or the price and the specifications have been changed, he or she should write a rejecting letter with utmost care immediately so as to alleviate or eliminate the negative impact on future business with the customer.

First order, that is orders from new customers, should most certainly be acknowledged by letter. The letter should:

a. Express pleasure at receiving the order;

b. Add a favorable comment on the goods ordered;

c. Include an assurance of prompt and careful attention;

d. Draw attention to the other products likely to be of interest;

e. Hope for further orders.

Part B Sample Letters of Orders

Sample 1

Placing an order

Dear Mr. Gilson,

Re: Order for 2 000 Pairs of Sheep Leather Gloves

Please dispatch to us 2 000 pairs of sheep leather gloves as per the terms stated in your offer May 5.

Would you please take special care of the quality of the package of this order? The leather should be of the same quality as that used in the sample. We hope that you can pack each pair in an airtight polythene bag, a dozen pairs of gloves in a box and then 20 boxes to a strong seaworthy wooden case. We will order more if the first order with you prove to be satisfactory.

We are enclosing our Purchase Confirmation No. 2009-308 in duplicate for your signature. Please sign and return one copy for our file. Upon receipt of your confirmation, an L/C will be issued.

Sincerely yours,

Sample 2

An order for marmalade

Dear Mr. Carter,

Please ship us orange marmalade as per the following terms:

Quantity: 15 000 jars
Description: Orange marmalade, Quality A2
Price: U. S. $ 2. 10 per jar CIF Zhuhai
Shipment: By December 10,2009
Mode of Transport: Ocean freight
Payment: 5% special discount

We are awaiting your acknowledgment.

Faithfully yours,

×××

Sample 3

Dear Sir,

We are pleased to receive your order No. BD/135 Canned Beef. We accept the order and are enclosing our Sales Confirmation No. 354 in duplicate of which please sign and return one copy to us for our file. We trust you will open the relative L/C at an early date.

As to the Items A and B, we shall arrange delivery as soon as we get your L/C, and for items C and D we shall ship accordingly.

Hoping the goods will turn out to be your entire satisfaction and we may have further orders from you.

Yours faithfully,

×××

Sample 4

Dear Sirs,

We are really sorry for the inconvenience you had with the defective model of the computer. We received a letter stating that you would like a different model.

We will definitely replace the computer for you. If you can please send the computer with the original bill and we will transport the model you requested. We assure you that this would be a model you like and you will not face any problem. Last model was from the lot which was missed out from the stages of testing. It happens very rarely but we apologize for our mistake and assure you that we will be providing you with the new model as soon as possible.

Please accept the discount coupon which you can avail on the next purchase and we appreciate your patience and thank you for your business. We hope you will allow us to serve you in the future.

Your sincerely,

×××

Sample 5

An order of canned beef

PURCHASE ORDER

No. BD/135

Messrs: China National Cereals, Oils & Foodstuffs

Import & Export Corp, Shaanxi Branch 130 LianHu Rood, Shaanxi, China

We confirm our agreement on purchase of the following goods:

Description: A-I Grade Canned Beef of the following four specifications:

A. 225 GM net weight

B. 350 GM net weight

C. 425 GM net weight

D. 450 GM net weight

Quantity:(Case)

A. 500

B. 400

C. 400

D. 600

Packing:By standard export case of 120 cans each

Unit Price: CIF net New York per case in U. S. dollars

A. 36. 20

B. 40. 50

C. 50. 60

D. 38. 40

Payment:100% by irrevocable letter of credit opened immediately through First National City Bank, N. Y. and drawn at sight.

Delivery:For Item A and B:Prompt shipment

For Item C and D:One month after receipt of L/C

Shipping Marks:On each and every case, the following shipping mark should be stenciled

Remark:In addition to the ordinary shipping documents, please also submit Certificate of Origin for each shipment. BD Co. , Ltd.

Sample 6

An order for peanuts

Dear Sirs,

We have received your letter of March 7 and now place an order with you at your revised price:Fifty metric tons of Peanuts at US $700 per metric ton CFR Dalian for shipment in May.

Enclosed is our Purchase Confirmation NO. 137 in duplicate. Please sign and return one copy for our records at your earliest convenience.

We are arranging for the establishment of the covering letter of credit and shall let you know by fax as soon as it is opened.

We stress the importance of making punctual shipment within the validity of the L/C, and any delay in shipment would be harmful to our future business.

Yours faithfully,

Liu Guanru

Sample 7

An order for hiking shoes

Dear Sirs,

Thank you for your offer of October 11 for hiking shoes and the samples you sent us.

Having examined your samples carefully, we found the quality of materials used, the prices and the workmanship are up to our requirements. We are pleased to send you an order for the following items on the understanding that they will be supplied at the prices mentioned.

500 pairs of men's hiking shoes:
Size and quantity: 40 (100 pairs), 41 (100 pairs), 42 (200 pairs), 43 (100 pairs), each pair at U. S. $ 140 CIF Shanghai

400 pairs of women's hiking shoes:
Size and quantity: 39 (50 pairs), 38 (100 pairs), 37 (150 pairs), 36 (100 pairs), each pair at U. S. $ 125 CIF Shanghai

Our order is subject to your acceptance of our usual terms of payment, i. e. cash against documents.

We expect to find a good market for the above and hope to place further and larger orders with you.

Yours faithfully,

×××

Sample 8

An order for machine tools

Dear Sirs,

We have received your letter of January 3 and thank you for the catalogue and price list enclosed. We are satisfied with the quality and specifications of your products after we studied the pamphlets.

We are sending you one copy of our sales confirmation NO. 4345 placing an order with you for your machine tools with the value totaling US $ 85 000. As these goods are urgently needed, please make shipment of the goods before the end of February.

We will instruct our bank to open our confirmed irrevocable L/C in your favor the moment we receive your confirmation on the order.

There is a great demand for machine tools in our market, and the subsequent orders will be in large quantities.

We are looking forward to your early reply and confirmation.

Yours faithfully,

Robert De Niro

Sample 9

An order for lamps

Dear Sirs,

Subject: TM - T12 Lamps

Further to our discussions through fax and E-mail, we should like to confirm details of ordering the subject goods:

Quantity	Description	Amount
6 000 sets	TM－T12 Lamps	U. S. $150 000. 00

The above price are quoted on CFR Dalian basis.

Packing: Each set in a box, 12 sets to a cardboard carton and 60 sets to a wooden case.
Shipment: To be made in three equal monthly installments, beginning from June, 2019.
Payment: By confirmed, irrevocable L/C payable by draft at 60 days sight to be opened 30 days before the time of shipment.

We would like you to send us your acknowledgement of this order as soon as possible.

When we receive your acknowledgement, we will arrange to apply for L/C.

We look forward to your reply.

Yours faithfully,

×××

Sample 10

An order for transistor radios

Dear Sirs,

We confirm our agreement on purchase of the following goods:

Description of Article: "Satect" brand transistor radio
Model: GML-268 Hi-sensitivity 9-band receiver
Quantity: 4 800 sets
Price: US$ 55. 00 per set CIF Rabat
Packing: Each set is packed in a polybag then in a box, 12 sets to a cardboard carton and 96 sets to a wooden case.
Delivery: As we need the goods urgently, please deliver them within 40 days after receipt of the order.
Payment: By irrevocable documentary letter of credit opened through Bank of ×× and drawn at sight.

Shipping marks: Mark the cases with our initials TNS in a circle, under which comes the destination RABAT with order number SY 2356 below again.

We trust that you will give special care to the packing of the goods lest they should be damaged in transit.

Yours faithfully,

×××

Sample 11

Offering rayon in place of watered silk

Dear Sirs,

Thank you for your fax of yesterday (April 3) with your order No. 456 for 5 000 meters of 100 cm wide watered silk.

We are sorry we can no longer supply this silk. Fashions constantly change and in recent years the demand for watered silk has fallen to such an extent that we have ceased to produce it.

In its place we can offer you our new "Gossamer" brand of rayon. This is a finely woven, hard wearing, non-creatable material with a most attractive luster. The large number of repeat orders we regularly receive from leading distributors and dress manufacturers is clear evidence of the popularity of this brand. At the low price of only Stg. 1. 80 a meter this rayon is much cheaper than silk and its appearance is just attractive.

We are sending you by parcel post a sample cutting for your reference hoping you may be interested in our new article. We are awaiting your order with keen interest.

Yours faithfully,

×××

Sample 12

Rejecting ordered price

Dear Sirs,

We refer to your Order No. 345 and regret to say that we are not able to accept your bid price for Frozen Rabbit Meat.

As you may be aware that the prices for foodstuffs have gone up sharply owing to the rough weather. So it is impossible to purchase supplies at economic prices. Moreover, we have improved our packing method, as you may have seen from our samples, which cost us a lot. The price, therefore, is 8% higher than your bid.

For the market is firm with an upward tendency, we advise you to accept our price without delay. In view of our long business connection we will definitely keep supplies available for you if you amend the price in your order within 5 days.

Yours faithfully,

×××

Sample 13

Rejection for the reason of no supply

Dear Sir,

Re: Your Order No. 456

Referring to the 50 metric tons of Silicon Steel Sheet under your Order No. 456, we regret to tell you that we have no stock of the goods you required for the time being and do not expect further deliveries for at least another two months. Before then you may have been able to obtain the goods elsewhere, but if not we will revert to this matter as soon as our new supplies come up.

We are enclosing 2 copies of our catalog coveting all the articles available at present. If you need any of the items please inform us. We assure you that your requirement will receive our prompt attention at all times.

Yours faithfully,

×××

Sample 14

Rejecting buyer's delivery terms

Dear Sirs,

Thank you for your Order No. 93120 for 3 000 sets of "Haier" Brand Color T. V. , but since you make delivery before Christmas a firm condition, we deeply regret that we cannot supply you at present.

The manufacturers are finding it impossible to meet current demand for their stock is exhausted but consecutive new orders are pouring in. Though the workers are speeding up the production, the buyers still have to wait. Another client of us placed, through us, an order for 500 sets a month ago, and is informed that his order could not be dealt with until the beginning of February next year.

We are sorry that we can't meet your requirement this time. But if you are interested in other brands, please let us know.

Yours faithfully,

×××

Sample 15

Declining the order because of delayed loading

Dear Sirs,

We thank you very much for your order No. 135 of October 30. We regret having to refuse this, but the delivery date stipulated by you does not give us sufficient time to ship your order.

The minimum period necessary where goods have to be prepared for shipment is five to six weeks. We are anxious to serve you but are sure you will see the need for giving us a little more time to suit your requirement.

Yours faithfully,

×××

Sample 16

Refusing to orders due to limited production equipment

Dear Sirs,

We thank you very much for your order November 3. After careful consideration on your request, however, we have come to the conclusion that it would be better for us to decline your order in this case.

In order to reach the limit you required in your specifications we would have to install a large amount of special equipment at our plant, and this would not be possible before next January next year without interrupting our normal production.

We are really very sorry not to be in a position to accept your order, but hope that you will understand our situation. Please let us have any other inquiries, as we shall be only too pleased to meet your requirements if it is within our power.

Yours faithfully,

×××

Sample 17

Declining the order due to the higher price

Dear Sirs,

We thank you for your order No. 228 asking for the shipment during September. However we regret our inability to book the order at the prices we quoted four months ago.

As you know well, wages and materials have risen considerably in these days in addition to the increase of taxes and we are reluctantly compelled to adjust our prices in order to cover these increases. The lowest prices we can quote now are as follow:

Model PA-218 $ 258　　Model PB-318 $ 298　　Model PC-428 $ 328

We do not want to influence you, but we think it is fair to mention that we shall have to increase those prices substantially again when our old stock of the goods is exhausted.

Please inform us by return whether you may book your order at these prices. We should be able to guarantee shipment during September as requested.

Yours faithfully,

×××

Sample 18

Trial order

Dear Sirs,

We thank you for your letter of March 23. We have studied your catalog and price list and have chosen five models for which we enclose our order.

We would like to stress that this is a trial order and if we are satisfied with your shipment, you can expect our regular repeat orders. To avoid any difficulties with the customs authorities here, please make sure that our shipping instructions are carefully observed.

For our credit standing we refer you to the ×× Bank, Ltd. , ×× and International Trading Co. , Ltd., ××.

Yours faithfully,

×××

Sample 19

An order for washing machines

Dear Sirs,

In reply to your counter offer of September 23, we are sending you this confirming letter and are pleased to place an order with you as follows:

Commodity: "Super Cleaner" brand washing machine
Model: AZ - 6732
Quantity: 10 000 sets
Price: U. S. $ 386. 00 per set
Delivery: By the end of October
Packing: In firm, plastic-lined, waterproof cases
Payment; Draft at sight under irrevocable L/C

Since we are in urgent need of the above goods, please confirm this order by return. We expect to find a good market for washing machines and hope to place further and large orders with you in the near future if this initial order turns out to be satisfactory.

Yours faithfully,

Stanley Kubrick

Part C Sample Letters of Acknowledgments

There are several writing tips for acknowledgments.

1. Draw an Outline

Business people write the acknowledgment letter for various reasons. Hence, it is better to draft an outline so that you are right on the target. The outline will also provide you points to be discussed. For example, you need to write for acknowledging receipt of a price list. Keep the documents ready and circle the elements you want a clearer view on. It could be the freight charges, price, delivery, payment terms, etc. Make two columns with headings as "Accepted" and "To be Discussed", and fill them accordingly. Decide on the logical order of the information and organize it accordingly.

2. Start with a Rough Letter

No one can write a perfect letter at one go. There will be some addition and deletion before it is ready for mailing. Hence, draft a rough letter first using the outline you have drawn in the first step. Don't bother about the spelling and grammatical mistakes. Simply put down your thoughts as they come to you. You can keep the editing for the later stage. Once the letter is complete, read it twice. Mark the mistakes and change the sentence wherever it does not sound professional or is difficult to understand. Try to make the letter concise with only needed contents. The key rule is to start the letter with a positive tone regardless of whether you are accepting or rejecting the offer. In both the scenarios, the letter tone has to be polite.

3. Timely Respond

You need to accept, or decline anything you are asked for within 48 hours of receiving the acknowledgment source. This way, the sender will not have to keeping guessing about your response. If there is a genuine reason for the delay in writing, you must apologize it and produce a convincing reason for not acting in time.

Sample 1

An acknowledgement letter of an order for transistor radios

Dear Sirs,

Thank you for your Order NO. 2356 for GML-268 Hi-sensitivity 9-band receivers and assure you that all the items you required are in stock.

We confirm with you the following order for transistor radios at the prices stated in your letter of October 14:

Description of article: "Satect" brand transistor radio
Model: GML-268 Hi-sensitivity 9 - band receiver
Quantity: 4 800 sets
Price: US $ 55.00 per set CIF Rabat
Packing: Each set is packed in a polybag then in a box, 12 sets to a cardboard carton and 96 sets to a wooden case.

Truly yours,

×××

Sample 2

An acknowledgement letter of an order for washing machines

Dear Sirs,

Thank you very much for your order for our SC-Y12 full-automatic washing machines, and it draws our immediate attention.

The prices and terms of payment you suggested are acceptable, and you may rely on us to give your order prompt attention. We will arrange shipment accordingly and shall send you the shipping advice and the invoice at the time of shipment by the end of July.

We are working on your order and will keep you informed in time of the progress. I am sure you will be pleased to collect good comments about our products from your consumers, and build up a market for the product in your region.

Yours faithfully,

Carlos M. Luis

Sample 3

A confirming letter for an order for hiking boots

Dear Sirs,

We have pleasure in receiving your order and would like to thank you for your cooperation and assistance rendered to us. We are confident that you will be satisfied with our service and the quality of our goods.

We confirm that the X-7 all-weather hiking boots you ordered are in stock and can be supplied at the prices stated in your letter of July 8. Enclosed is our Sales Confirmation NO. 438 in duplicate, a copy of which is to be countersigned and returned for our records.

It is understood that a letter of credit in our favor covering the above mentioned goods will be established immediately. We wish to point out that the stipulations in the relevant credit should strictly conform to the terms stated in our Sales Confirmation in order to avoid subsequent amendments.

Your prompt reply and the related L/C at the earliest date will be appreciated.

Yours faithfully,

John Clive

Sample 4

Dear Sirs,

Please supply the following goods:

Electric Typewriter PA-311 10 sets @ $ 300 $ 3 000;
Portable Typewriter HA-261 10 sets @ $ 70 $ 700.

Delivery: By the end of March, 1980
Term: Draft at sight under irrevocable L/C

Invoice: Commercial Invoices in triplicate

The order No. 233 must be stated on all invoices and correspondence. Final shipping instructions will follow.

Please confirm this order by return.

Yours faithfully,

×××

Sample 5

Dear Sirs,

Thank you for quotation of May 23, and we note that the total cost of the 200 units is $10, 000 C. I. F. Keelung. We agree to this price, and would ask you to accept this letter as our official order for the goods in question.
Please ship at the first available opportunity. Payment is being made by Banker's Draft today. However, in view of the fact that we have now been doing business with you for a year we would appreciate quarterly settlement of our accounts.

Yours faithfully,

×××

Sample 6

Dear Sirs,

We refer to our letter of March 10 when we stressed the importance of dispatching our order No. 816 so that it may reach here by April 30.

As we have not received any information from you that goods have been sent, we have no alternative but to cancel this order. We regret this action, but you will appreciate that we have no other way, as our customers insist on delivery by that date.

Yours faithfully,

×××

Sample 7

Dear Sirs,

Thank you for your letter of August 23, with which you sent us details of your produce PH-61. We have now seen the samples and are prepared to give them a trial order, provided you can guarantee shipment on or before September 30.

The enclosed order is given strictly on this condition, and we reserve the right of cancellation and refusal of delivery after this date. Upon receipt of our acceptance, we will open a letter of credit immediately.

Yours faithfully,

×××

Sample 8

Dear Sirs,

We have received your letter of September 10 and enclose our order No. 285 for 6 sets of your classical furniture.

We note that you have asked for a minimum order of 6 cabinets because of special size we require. At the moment, however, we have no use for more than 6 sets. We hope that you will oblige us and accept the order at the price of $300.

We look forward to your prompt acceptance.

Yours faithfully,

×××

Sample 9

Dear Sirs,

We are pleased to place the following order with you if you can guarantee shipment at Hong Kong to Keelung by March 30.

a. 5 units of European furniture No. FA - 23;
b. 3 pieces of Persian Carpet No. TC - 18.

Kindly confirm acceptance of our order by return and send advice of shipment with three copies of your invoice with B/L to our office in Taipei. We will send the bank draft upon receipt of them.

Yours faithfully,

×××

Sample 10

Dear Sirs,

Thank you very much for your order of August 10 for five hundred units of electronic lighters. All these items are in stock, and we can guarantee shipment to San Francisco well before September 30. As requested we will inform you of the date of dispatch immediately upon completing shipment.

Yours faithfully,

×××

Sample 11

Dear Sirs,

We are very glad to receive your order for 50 units of classic furniture to be supplied to your own specifications. As we mentioned in our previous letter, shipment for the furniture made to the supplied specifications is not usually possible in less than five months, but we would like to help you and to give your order special priority.

You may rest assured that your furniture will be ready for shipment by September 30. We will inform you when your order is ready for dispatch and shall be pleased to assist you to the best of our ability at all times.

Yours faithfully,

×××

Chapter 8 Payment by Letters of Credit

Learning Objectives

a. Master writing requirements of the letter of credit;

b. Know how the letter of credit works;

c. Know different types of letters of credit.

Part A Introduction

Paying for goods supplied in home trade is a fairly simple matter because payment can be made either in advance or within a reasonably short period after delivery. But this problem is much more complicated in foreign trade. Must the seller wait perhaps several months for his money or shall the buyer pay several months before he not even sees his goods? Clearly, the seller runs certain risks of non-payment if he surrounds goods before payment has been made. As it is not often possible for the seller personally to collect payment before delivery, the appointment of agents for this purpose in the importers' countries becomes necessary. This function is usually entrusted to the banker, who has branches or correspondent bank in most towns or cities overseas.

Payment is the most important and complicated part in business and settlement of foreign trade may be made in many ways, such as payment in advance, open account terms, consignment sales, etc. But the most often adopted methods of payment in international trade are as follows: collection, remittance and letter of credit.

Did you know that when exporting there are ways to secure payment from your foreign buyer so that if they do not pay you—you still get paid? A letter of credit is one method of payment that your export business can leverage to insure against foreign buyer nonpayment. If you export goods or services, you may have your foreign buyer pay in advance of delivery. A letter of credit gives your business a high level of certainty that you will be paid for the goods or services that you export, offering one of the more secure methods of international payment.

Letter of credit (abbreviated to L/C) is the most commonly used means of payment in international trade, as it can ensure that an exporter gets his money when he dispatches his goods—not when they are received by the customer, thus giving the exporter the largest possible protection.

The procedure for a letter of credit begins with completion of the contract. When a contract of transaction is signed, the buyer is usually under obligation to establish a letter of credit with his bank within the time stipulated in the sales contract (confirmation). However, there may be circumstances where the buyer fails to establish L/C, or it does not reach the seller in time; then a letter, a fax or whatever media is considered safe and quick has to be used to urge buyer to expedite the L/C or to give notification of its whereabouts. When urging establishment of L/C, the first message conveyed should be polite, indicating that the goods ordered are ready but the relevant L/C has not yet arrived. If the first message has no response from the buyer, a second one will be sent, though still restrained in tone, to let the recipient feel your disappointment and concerns.

When the seller finds that there are some discrepancies or some unforeseen special clauses to which he or she does not agree in the L/C, the seller should send an advice to the buyer, asking him or her to make an amendment to the L/C. Sometimes an unexpected event may take place to goods supply, shipment, etc. , which will require timely amendment to the original L/C.

Not only can the seller ask for amendment to an L/C, the buyer can likewise ask for amendment if he or she finds something in the L/C needs to be altered. The usual procedure is that the buyer should first obtain consent from the seller and then instruct the opening bank to amend the L/C. The request for L/C amendment is usually made by fax or even E-mail.

Besides the date of shipment, which is usually stipulated in the L/C, every L/C has its expiry date. In order to leave sufficient time to the seller to make out the shipping documents and the bank to make their negotiation, the date of shipment and the expiry date of the L/C should be made at least two weeks apart.

Sometimes the seller may fail to get the goods ready for shipment in time or the buyer may request that the shipment be postponed for one reason or another; then the seller will have to ask for extension of the expiry date as well as the date of shipment of the L/C.

If the beneficiary is satisfied with the credit or the amendment to the credit, he arranges for the goods to be shipped. Meanwhile, he prepares the documents in accordance with the credit. Of all the documents, the more essential is the bill of exchange, which the exporter draws on the issuing bank. The bill of exchange is made payable at sight or within certain days after sight, according to the credit. Besides, other documents the exporter will have to prepare under a letter of credit include commercial invoice, the packing list and any other documents the importer specifies in the L/C.

After the goods have been shipped and the bill of lading has been obtained, the beneficiary delivers all the documents to the negotiating bank with the credit. The bank checks the documents against the credit. If it is satisfied that they are in order, the bank pays the beneficiary right away, in case the accompanying draft is payable at sight, or within a certain period of time after sight, in case the credit is accompanied by a time draft.

When the applicant's bank has ascertained that all the instructions in the credit are complied with, it pays its correspondent, debits the L/C amount to the applicant's account in the manner agreed on, and releases the documents. With these, the importer is able to take delivery of the goods covered by the L/C.

1. What is the Purpose of a Letter of Credit?

The primary purpose of a letter of credit is to guarantee payment. Although the conditions of a letter of credit may vary based on your situation and the bank's regulations, letters of credit essentially let you capitalize on the bank's credit instead of relying on your own.

2. How to Acquire a Letter of Credit?

To obtain a letter of credit, the buyer simply applies for one through the company's bank. It is always preferable to request a letter of credit from a bank with which you have an established relationship, as opposed to applying at a new bank.

3. What is a Letter of Credit?

A letter of credit, or "credit letter" is a letter from a bank or financial institute guaranteeing that a buyer's payment to a seller will be received on time and for the correct amount. In the event that the buyer is unable to make a payment on the purchase, the bank will be required to cover the full or remaining amount of the purchase. It may be offered as a facility.

Letters of credit are often used within the international trade industry. Due to the nature of international dealings, including factors such as distance, differing laws in each country, and difficulty in knowing each party personally, the use of letters of credit has become a very important aspect of international trade.

A letter of credit is a legal document that transfers responsibility for collecting payment for shipped goods and services from your business to your foreign buyer's bank. The letter of credit stipulates that if your foreign buyer is unable to pay for the goods that you exported to them, your foreign buyer's bank will pay your business instead. In other words, if your buyer has a letter of credit covering a shipment, your buyer's bank has promised that you will receive payment for that shipment, even if the foreign buyer does not pay. Banks collect a fee for issuing a letter of credit.

4. How a Letter of Credit Works?

Because a letter of credit is typically a negotiable instrument, the issuing bank pays the beneficiary or any bank nominated by the beneficiary. If a letter of credit is transferable, the beneficiary may assign another entity, such as a corporate parent or a third party, the right to draw.

Banks typically require a pledge of securities or cash as collateral for issuing a letter of credit. Banks also collect a fee for service, typically a percentage of the size of the letter of credit. The *International Chamber of Commerce Uniform Customs and Practice for Documentary Credits* oversees letters of credit used in international transactions.

Step 1: You and your foreign buyer agree through a contract that you will export goods or services to a buyer for a set price. You ask your buyer to obtain a letter of credit, which will guarantee that you receive payment for your exports.

Step 2: Your foreign buyer applies for a letter of credit through a bank, which assesses the buyer's credit risk. If the bank approves of the buyer, the bank issues a letter of credit to the buyer.

Step 3: In the United States, your bank evaluates the foreign buyer's letter of credit and forwards it to your business.

Step 4: You export the purchased goods or services to the buyer and document that you sent the goods or services to the buyer as originally agreed upon in the contract. You then submit the documents to your bank as proof that you provided the goods or services to your buyer.

Step 5: Your bank sends the shipping documents to your buyer's bank and waits for your buyer's bank to pay.

Step 6: Your buyer's bank receives the documents, removes money from the buyer's account at that bank, and sends the money to your bank.

Step 7: Your bank receives the money from your buyer's bank and deposits the funds into your account.

When a merchant needs financing to buy products, suppliers often rely on the business' reputation when deciding whether to extend credit. This is relatively easy to do when the supplier has worked with the same buyers for years, or they have a strong standing in the industry.

When the business is half the world away, however, lending can be a riskier proposition. One way to resolve this issue is the use of a banker's acceptance (BA).

A banker's acceptance is a short-term issuance by a bank that guarantees payment at a later time. It is often used in importing and exporting, with the importer's bank guaranteeing payment to the exporter. It differs from a post-dated check in that it is seen as an investment and can be traded on a secondary market.

Applying for a banker's acceptance is similar to applying for a short-term, fixed-rate loan; the borrower goes through a credit check and sometimes extra underwriting processes. Similar to buying a Treasury bill, an investor on the secondary market might buy the acceptance at a discounted price, but still get the full value at the time of maturity.

(1) How it works

Banker's acceptances are time drafts that a business can order from the bank if it wants additional security against counterparty risk. The financial institution promises to pay the exporting firm a specific amount on a specific date, at which time it recoups its money by debiting the importer's account.

A banker's acceptance works much like a post-dated check, which is simply an order for a bank to pay a specified party at a later date. If today is Jan. 1, and a check is written with the date "Feb. 1", then the payee cannot cash or deposit the check for an entire month. This can be thought of as a maturity date for a claim on another's assets.

(2) Critical distinctions

Perhaps the most critical distinction between a banker's acceptance and a post-dated check is a real secondary market for banker's acceptances; post-dated checks don't have such a market. For this reason, banker's acceptances are considered to be investments, whereas checks are not. The holder may choose to sell the BA for a discounted price on a secondary market, giving investors a relatively safe, short-term investment.

BAs are frequently used in international trade because of advantages for both sides. Exporters often feel safer relying on payment from a reputable bank than a business with which it has little, if any, history. Once the bank verifies, or "accept" a time draft, it becomes a primary obligation of that institution.

The importer may turn to a banker's acceptance when it has trouble obtaining other forms of financing, or when a BA is the least expensive option. The advantage of borrowing is that the importer receives the goods and has the opportunity to resell them before making payment to the bank.

(3) Obtaining a banker's acceptance

Banker's acceptances can be created as letters of credit, documentary drafts, and other financial transactions. If you are trying to obtain an acceptance, approach a bank with which you have a good working relationship. You need to be able to prove or offer collateral against, your ability to repay the bank at a future date. Many, but not all banks offer acceptances. A banker's acceptance operates much like a short-term, fixed-rate loan. You go through a credit check and possibly additional underwriting processes. You are also charged a percentage of the total acceptance to purchase it.

If you are looking to purchase a banker's acceptance for a short-term investment, there is a relatively liquid secondary market for partially aged banker's acceptances. They are normally sold at prices near or below the London Interbank Offer Rate, or LIBOR.

Like most money market instruments, a banker's acceptance is a fairly safe and liquid investment, especially if the paying bank is in good financial health with a strong credit rating.

(4) Discounting the acceptance

To understand banker's acceptances as an investment, it's important to understand how businesses use them in global trade. Here's one fairly typical example. An American company, Clear Signal Electronics, decides to purchase 100 televisions from Dresner Trading, a German exporter. After completing a trade agreement, Clear Signal approaches its bank for a letter of credit. This letter of credit makes the bank the intermediary responsible for completing the transaction.

Once Dresner ships the goods, it sends the appropriate documents—typically through its own financial institution—to the paying bank in the United States. The exporter now has a couple of choices. It could keep the acceptance until maturity, or it could sell it to a third party, perhaps to the very bank responsible for making the payment. In this case, Dresner receives an amount less than the face value of the draft, but it doesn't have to wait on the funds.

When a bank buys back the acceptance at a lower price, it is said to be "discounting" the acceptance. If Clear Signal's bank does this, it essentially has the same choices that Dresner had. It could hold the draft until it matures, which is akin to extending the importer a loan. More commonly, though, it replenishes its funds by rediscounting the acceptance—in other words, selling it for a discounted price on the secondary market. It could market the BAs itself, especially if it's a larger bank, or enlist a securities brokerage to perform the task.

(5) Acceptance as an investment

Since acceptance is a short-term, negotiable agreement, it acts much like other money market instruments. Like a Treasury bill, the investor buys the bank draft at a discounted price and gets the full face value upon maturity. The difference between the discount and face value determines the yield. In most cases, the maturity date is within 30 to 180 days.

Banker's acceptances do not trade on an exchange, but rather through large banks and securities dealers. As such, most dealers don't supply bid and ask prices, but rather negotiate the price with the prospective investor, often a fund manager.

The pricing of these drafts largely depends on the reputation and size of the paying bank. Those with a strong credit rating can usually sell their acceptances for a lower yield, as they're believed to have little chance of defaulting on their obligation. Institutions that sell a large volume of BAs also enjoy an advantage in this regard.

While banks often sell their acceptances through dealers in New York and other major financial centers, they may use their branch network to supplement sales. The bank's staff will often contact local investors, who are generally interested in smaller transactions, not those of $1 million or more that many fund managers pursue. Local investors often accept a smaller yield and, because the bank circumvents dealers, its selling expenses can be much less.

(6) Risks and rewards

A banker's acceptance is a money market instrument, and like most money markets, it is relatively safe and liquid, particularly when the paying bank enjoys a strong credit rating. The bank carries primary responsibility for the payment. Because of the tremendous risk to its reputation, if it can't fund an acceptance, most banks that provide acceptances are well-known, highly rated institutions.

However, even if the bank lacks the necessary cash to make the payment, the investor receives added protection from other parties involved in the transaction. The importer is secondarily liable for the acceptance, and the exporter has a contingent obligation. In fact, any investors that have bought or sold the instrument on the open market carry any obligation for the draft.

An acceptance provides the opportunity for a modest profit, with yields generally somewhere above those of T-bills. Liquidity generally isn't an issue because most bankers' acceptance maturities are between one and six months. And since they don't have to be held until maturity, holders have the flexibility to resell them if they so choose.

Banker's acceptances are issued at a discount to their face value and always trade below face value, much like a T-bills. The holder of a $ 100 000 acceptance might not want to wait until maturity to receive those funds, so the holder can sell the acceptance to another party for, say, $ 990 000. While some market risk could be involved for those operating in the secondary market, the high liquidity and short maturity of these instruments make that unlikely.

(7)The bottom line

A banker's acceptance can be a sound investment for those seeking to balance higher-risk investments in their portfolio, or for those focusing on asset preservation. On the risk/reward spectrum, a BA is toward the very bottom, just ahead of the Treasury bill.

Because banker's acceptance pricing is negotiated between buyer and seller, investors who do their research stand the best chance of getting a competitive rate. This is especially true given the volatile nature of BA pricing. In the course of a single day, yields can go up or down significantly. As such, it's important to look up yields on a reputable website before making a purchase. In light of the bank's primary obligation for an acceptance, any quotes should reflect its reputation and credit rating.

5. What are the Alternatives to a Letter of Credit?

A letter of credit is a useful tool for export businesses, ensuring foreign buyer payment. However, it is also burdensome and expensive for foreign buyers, making a letter of credit less than ideal when marketing the sale of certain goods and services and when competing against other businesses.

As an alternative, an exporter can either require payment up front,or offer some form of open account terms. Offering open account terms allows your business to be more flexible regarding payment for goods and services and could allow your business to "seal the deal" when competing overseas. As such, exporters are increasingly offering payment terms that are less constraining by providing more flexible credit terms on an open account basis. This includes providing credit to foreign buyers you deem to be creditworthy, allowing them to pay your business for goods and services at a later date and time than the initial point of sale.

The Export-Import Bank of the United States (Ex-Im Bank) offers a variety of products and services that complement or can substitute for a letter of credit. Export Credit Insurance insures against nonpayment for U. S. made products and services sold overseas, while the Working Capital Guarantee program can provide your business access to the pre-export capital required to capture sales.

6. Different Types of Letters of Credit

A letter of credit is a payment method that smoothes the way for international trade or other transactions. With a letter of credit, buyers and sellers can reduce their risk and ensure timely payment and delivery of goods or services. Learning about different types of letters of credit can help you choose which one to use and understand what you're working with.

(1) Commercial letter of credit

This is a standard letter of credit that's commonly used in international trade, and may also be referred to as a documentary credit or an import/export letter of credit. A bank acts as a neutral third party to release funds when all the conditions of the agreement have been met.

(2) Standby letter of credit

This type of letter of credit is different. It provides payment if something fails to happen. Instead of facilitating a transaction, a standby letter of credit provides compensation when something goes wrong. Standby letters of credit are very similar to commercial letters of credit, but they are only payable when the payee (or "beneficiary") proves that they didn't get what was promised. Standby letters of credit are like insurance that you'll get paid, and they can be used to ensure that services will be performed satisfactorily.

(3) Confirmed (and unconfirmed) letter of credit

When a letter of credit is confirmed, another bank (presumably one that the beneficiary trusts) guarantees that payment will be made. Exporters might not trust a bank that issues a letter of credit on behalf of a buyer (because the exporter is not familiar with that bank, for example, and is not sure if payment will ever arrive), so they might require that a bank in their home country confirm the letter. If the issuing bank fails to pay—and the exporter can meet all of the requirements of the letter of credit—the confirming bank will have to pay the exporter (and try to collect from the issuing bank later).

(4) Back to back letter of credit

A back to back letter of credit allows intermediaries to connect buyers and sellers. Two letters of credit are used so that each party gets paid individually: An intermediary gets paid by the buyer, and a supplier gets paid by the intermediary. The final buyer and the intermediary use a "master" letter of credit, and the intermediary and supplier use a letter of credit based on the master letter.

(5) Revolving letter of credit

A revolving letter of credit can be used for multiple payments. If a buyer and seller expect to do business continually, they may prefer not to obtain a new letter of credit for every transaction (or for every step in a series of transactions). This type of letter of credit allows businesses to use a single letter of credit for numerous transactions until the letter expires (typically up to one year).

(6) Sight letter of credit

Payment under a sight letter of credit occurs as soon as the beneficiary submits acceptable documents to the appropriate bank. The bank has a few days to review the documents and ensure that they meet the requirements in the letter of credit. If the documents are compliant, payment is made immediately.

(7) Deferred payment letter of credit

With this type of letter of credit, payment does not happen immediately after the documents are accepted. Some agreed-to period of time passes before the seller is paid. A deferred payment letter of credit is naturally a better deal for buyers than for sellers. These are also known as term or usance letters of credit.

(8) Red clause letter of credit

With a red clause, the beneficiary has access to cash up front. The buyer allows for an unsecured loan to be issued as part of the letter of credit, which is essentially an advance on the rest of the payment. The seller or beneficiary can then use the money to buy, manufacture, or ship goods to the buyer.

(9) Irrevocable letter of credit

An irrevocable letter of credit cannot be changed without authorization from all parties involved. Almost all letters of credit now are irrevocable, because revocable letters of credit simply do not provide the security that most beneficiaries want.

Part B Sample Letters of L/C

1. Asking for Opening L/C

Sample 1

Dear Sir or Madam,

We shall be very glad if you will arrange to open an irrevocable letter of credit for US $ 16 200 in favor of the Qingdao Trading Company, the credit to be valid until September 3. Enclosed is an application form for documentary credit.

The credit which evidences shipment of 5 000 cases of cutlery may be used against presentation of the following documents: 2 Bills of Lading in triplicate, one copy of Commercial Invoice, Packing List, Certificate of Insurance and Certificate of Origin.

The company may draw on your New York office at 90 days for each shipment.

Yours faithfully,

Susan Block
Manager

Sample 2

Dear Mr. Gao,

Please open an Irrevocable Letter of Credit for US $ 40 000 in favor of the Medic Medical Equipment Ltd. , the credit to be valid until October 30.

The documents, which may be used against negotiation, are as follows: Bills of Lading, Commercial Invoice and Packing List in triplicate.

The conditions of shipment of 400 sets of medical equipment are as per S/C No. 987: Transshipment is prohibited and partial shipments are permitted.

We enclose the application form for the L/C and would be pleased if you can open the L/C as soon as possible.

Yours sincerely,

Wang Wei
Manager

Sample 3

Dear Sirs,

Re: Advising the Establishment of L/C

It's a great pleasure to have reached an agreement on Excavator Type ××× with you two weeks ago. As we have required, you have to effect the shipment of the goods as soon as possible. Therefore we have already established our L/C No. ××× dated May 28 for Sales Confirmation No. ××× through the Bank of China, Beijing Branch, valid until July 12. Please make the shipment in time.

As to the quality and the performance of your products, we think it is necessary for you to keep them in exact accordance with the samples. Any inconsistency with the required quality and performance of the products will be detrimental to our future business.

Sincerely yours,

×××

2. Urging Establishment of L/C

Sample 1

Dear Sirs,

With reference to the 5 000 dozen shirts under our Sales Confirmation No. 504, we would like you to know that the date of delivery is approaching, but up to the present we have not received the covering Letter of Credit. Please do your utmost to expedite its establishment so that we may process the order as agreed.

In order to avoid subsequent amendment, please see to it that the L/C stipulations should be in strict conformity with the terms of the contract.

We look forward to receiving your favorable response earlier.

Yours faithfully,

Liu Yun
Manager

Sample 2

Dear Mr. Bernstein,

As of today, we have not received your L/C covering 3 000 TAMs you are buying from us. Please check your Purchase Contract AS-166 and you will see that you have promised to open the covering credit before the end of August. Are you having some problem that we can help you with?

Your order has been made up for quite some time and on the other hand, the demand for our products has been extremely great recently. Mr. Bernstein, we hope you can understand that we cannot afford to keep the goods for you too long.

For your benefit, please expedite the L/C, which must reach us before September 18.

If this is not feasible, please call or write me today. Thank you.

Sincerely yours,

Zhou Qiang

Sample 3

Dear Sirs,

Re: Urging the Establishment of L/C

We wrote a letter to you on August to confirm having received your Order for ×× sets of Drilling Machines Type ××× and we, accordingly, enclosed the original of our Sales Confirmation No. ×××, which stipulates the shipment should be made by the end of October and the L/C should reach us one month before the shipment date. Now the shipment date is approaching, but your L/C has not been received by us. We think your immediate attention should be called on to this matter.

Therefore, we have to write to you again for urging your establishment of the above-mentioned L/C in order to enable us to execute your order smoothly.

We thank you for your cooperation.

Truly yours,

×××

3. Amendment to L/C

Sample 1

Dear Mr. Oscar,

We thank you for L/C No. 378 for 20 M/T of crabs against S/C No. EX55. But much to our regret, **there are two discrepancies between the L/C and the S/C. Hereby we list them below for your attention:**

a. It is stipulated in our S/C No. EX55 that shipment should be made on or before 31st of October, but the L/C states: "latest shipment date: 20th of October, 2019".
b. Our S/C states, partial shipment and transshipment allowed, whereas the L/C says that transshipment is prohibited.

We would like you to make the above-mentioned amendments immediately.

We won't be able to ship the goods in time if the amendments come too late.

We are waiting for your quick reply.

Sincerely yours,

Cheng Gang
Manager

Sample 2

Dear Oscar,

We have received your letter of credit No. 395. under S/C No. EX56. **On examination, we find two points, which do not conform to the stipulations of** S/C No. EX56.

Please amend the L/C as follows:
a. The total value of your order should be US$ 250 000 instead of US$ 150 000.
b. Add the wording: "five percent more or less allowed" after the number of the quantity.

Your prompt attention to this matter will be highly appreciated.

Yours sincerely,

Cheng Qiang
Manager

Sample 3

Dear Mr. Crane,

Thank you for your L/C No. NBN 876 issued by the National Bank of Bangladesh, which arrived here yesterday.

On going through the L/C, however, we found the product specified in it is Model UX196 instead of Model UX186 as contracted.

We are able to supply UX196 in the quality you require in case you really wish to have this model. You may refer to the catalogue we previously sent you and will find that UX196 has more functions than UX186, but the price is only US$ 5.00 higher per set.

You are, therefore, requested to amend the L/C in question either by rewriting the Model Number to read UX186, or by increasing the aggregate amount to US$ 110 000 and the unit price to US$ 55.00 CIF Dhaka.

Please let us have your L/C amendment advice next week so that we may effect shipment within the contracted delivery time. Thank you.

Sincerely yours,

Zhang Fen

Sample 4

Dear Sirs,

Re:Granting Amendment to L/C No. ×××

We are in receipt of your letter dated ××× and have to apologize to you for making mistakes in the captioned L/C, which are made due to the negligence of our new employee.

We now inform that we have already instructed our Bank to amend the relevant L/C by fax with the least possible delay. We believe our Bank would certainly pay its prompt attention to this matter when they have received our instructions.

As we are in urgent need of the goods, we hope this amendment of L/C will not effect your punctual shipment of the goods.

Let's express our apology to you again. We are expecting your favorable reply.

Truly yours,

×××

4. **Requesting Extension of L/C**

Sample 1

Dear Sirs,

With reference to your L/C No. 4938 covering 3 000 cases of iron nails, we regret to inform you that it is impossible for us to fulfill the shipment before the end of September, as the earliest steamer sailing for your port is scheduled to leave Shanghai around October 2 and the next ship, as we were told, will be sailing late October or early November.

Such being the case, we have to ask you to extend the shipment date and validity of your L/C to November 15 and November 30 respectively and see to it that the amendment advice reaches us by October 1.

Your prompt attention to this matter will be highly appreciated.

Faithfully yours,

Zhang Ming
Manager

Sample 2

Dear Sirs,

We refer to your Order No. 123 for 50 tons of fish.

Owing to problems at the port and our shipping company, we will not be able to meet the stipulated delivery date of December 30.

We expect that we will be able to meet Jan. 20th, 2005 delivery deadline, **so would you please**

make an extension for the L/C?

We apologize for the inconvenience, but the delay due to circumstances is beyond our control.

Yours faithfully.

Cheng Fang

Sample 3

Dear Sirs,

Re: Requesting Extension of L/C

We thank you very much for your L/C No. ××× dated ×××, covering your order for Type ××× Children Bicycles. According to our Sales Confirmation, it is our duty to deliver the goods to you next month. But to our great regret, 3 days ago, our No. 2 Workshop was caught on fire. This fire disaster has destroyed our manufacturing equipment in the workshop and made our steel pipes deformed. As a result of this, we have to stop our production to repair our equipment and to buy new materials from the other supplier for manufacturing your bicycles. It is clear that we shall not be able to get our goods ready for shipment next month. Therefore, we request you to extend the shipment date to November 5 and the validity of your L/C to November 20.

Please amend your L/C immediately and accept our apology.

Truly yours,

×××

Sample 4

Dear Sirs,

Re: L/C No. ××× Issued by Barclays Bank, London

We wish to acknowledge receipt of the above-mentioned L/C, covering your order for ×× sets of Electronic Computers Type ××. After checking, we have found some discrepancies. Please amend the L/C as follows:

a. The amount both in figures and in words should respectively be £12 480 and Say Pounds Sterling Twelve Thousand Four Hundred and Eighty Only.
b. "Draft to be at sight" should be instead of "at 60 days after sight".
c. The port of destination should be "London" instead of "Liverpool". Your early fax amendment to the L/C will be highly appreciated.

Sincerely yours,

×××

5. Irrevocable Letter of Credit

TRANSMITTED THROUGH:
BANK OF CHINA, LONDON
BANK OF CHINA
BEIING, CHINA
Beijing, February 1, 2019

Dear Sirs,

We open an irrevocable Letter of Credit No. 846 in favor of ... Company, London for account of China National ... Corporation, Beijing to the extent of £ 30 000 (Pounds Sterling Thirty Thousand only, 5% more or less is allowed). This credit is available by beneficiary's draft(s), drawn on us, in duplicate, without recourse, at sight, for 100% of the invoice value, and accompanied by the following shipping documents marked with numbers:

a. Full set of clean "on board""freight prepaid" Ocean Bill of Lading, made out to order and blank endorsed, marked "Notify China National Foreign Trade Transportation Corporation, at the port of destination."
b. Invoice in (quintuplicate) copies, indicating Contract No. ×××.
c. Weight Memo/Packing List in duplicate, indicating gross and net weights of each package.
d. Certificate of Quality/Weight in ... copies issued by the manufacturers.

e. Beneficiary's letter attesting that 4 extra copies each of the above-mentioned documents have been distributed as follows: 1 set ship mailed along with the goods to China National Foreign Trade Transportation Corporation at the port of destination. 1 set and 2 sets airmailed to accountee and China National Foreign Trade Transportation Corporation at the port of destination respectively within 5 days after the departure of the carrying vessel.

EVIDENCING SHIPMENT OF: 20 metric tons (5% more or less is allowed) of 1 000 kilos net each of GAMMA PLCOLINE, Purity 98%-99%, £3.60 per kilo net CFR XinGang, including packing charges.

Shipment from U.K. port to XinGang. Partial Shipment is not allowed. Transshipment is allowed, through B/L required. Shipment to be made on or before March 15, 2019, per SS "Peace". This Credit is valid in London on or before March 30, 2019, for negotiation and all drafts drawn hereunder must be marked Drawn under Bank of China Head Office, Banking Department, Beijing, Credit No. 846.

We hereby engage with the drawers, endorsers and bona fide holders of draft(s) drawn under and in accordance with the terms of this credit that the same shall be honored by T.T. on presentation of the documents at this office. Amount(s) of draft(s) negotiated under this credit must be endorsed on the back hereof.

Disposal of Documents: It is a condition of this credit that the documents should be forwarded to us by two consecutive airmails, the first mail consisting of all documents except one of each item, if more than one, to be sent by second mail.

REIMBURSEMENT of this credit is available by T.T. as soon as the documents called for by the credit have been received by us and found correct. Please advise this credit to the beneficiary.

Yours faithfully,

Special Instructions:

a. This L/C is effective subject to the advising bank's sighting the relative export licenses submitted by beneficiary.

b. Certificate issued by the shipping agents is required, certifying that the carrying vessel is chartered or booked by the China National Foreign Trade Transportation Corporation, Beijing. (In case this document is called for, Charter party Bills of Lading are acceptable.)

Chapter 9 Other Methods of Payment

Learning Objectives

a. Know different methods of payment;

b. Master writing requirements of different methods of payment.

Part A Introduction

Don't lose potential business to competitors by overlooking different payment options which could be attractive to your international buyer. Explore several payment methods and find the one best suited to your needs.

Business companies must collect the receivables or the money for the products or services they sell on credit. Most buyers honor their agreement to pay. In reality, however, some buyers postpone or evade payment for various reasons. Some may forget; some may put off their payment; some may have been trapped in financial problems and cannot afford to pay; and a few never intend to pay. Under such circumstances, the sellers will have to send collection letters for the money that is due or overdue.

1. Different Methods of Payment

To succeed in today's global marketplace and win sales against foreign competitors, exporters must offer their customers attractive sales terms supported by appropriate payment methods. Because getting paid in full and on time is the ultimate goal for each export sale, an appropriate payment method must be chosen carefully to minimize the payment risk while also accommodating the needs of the buyer.

As shown in Figure 9.1, there are five primary methods of payment with different risks for international transactions. During or before contract negotiations, you should consider which method in the figure is mutually desirable for you and your customer.

International trade presents a spectrum of risk, which causes uncertainty over the timing of payments between the exporter (seller) and importer (foreign buyer). For exporters, any sale is a gift until payment is received. Therefore, exporters want to receive payment as soon as possible, preferably as soon as an order is placed or before the goods are sent to the importer. For importers, any payment is a donation until the goods are received.

Therefore, importers want to receive the goods as soon as possible but to delay payment as long as possible, preferably until after the goods are resold to generate enough income to pay the exporter.

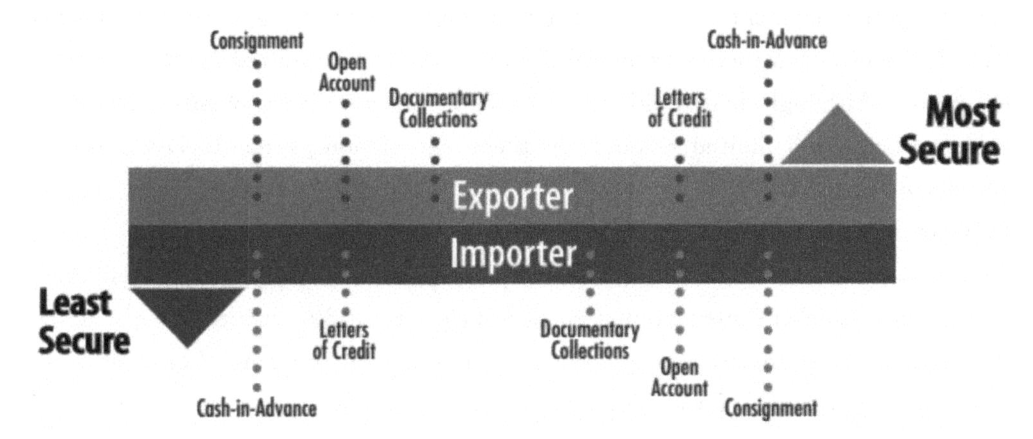

Figure 9.1 Payment Risk Diagram

(1) Cash-in-advance

With cash-in-advance payment terms, an exporter can avoid credit risk because payment is received before the ownership of the goods is transferred. For international sales, wire transfers and credit cards are the most commonly used cash-in-advance options available to exporters. With the advancement of the Internet, escrow services are becoming another cash-in-advance option for small export transactions. However, requiring payment in advance is the least attractive option for the buyer, because it creates unfavorable cash flow. Foreign buyers are also concerned that the goods may not be sent if payment is made in advance. Thus, exporters who insist on this payment method as their sole manner of doing business may lose to competitors who offer more attractive payment terms.

(2) Letters of Credit

Letters of Credit (L/Cs) are one of the most secure instruments available to international traders. An L/C is a commitment by a bank on behalf of the buyer that payment will be made to the exporter, provided that the terms and conditions stated in the L/C have been met, as verified through the presentation of all required documents. The buyer establishes credit and pays his or her bank to render this service. An L/C is useful when reliable credit information about a foreign buyer is difficult to obtain, but the exporter is satisfied with the credit worthiness of the buyer's foreign bank. An L/C also protects the buyer since no payment obligation arises until the goods have been shipped as promised.

(3) Documentary Collections

A documentary collection (D/C) is a transaction whereby the exporter entrusts the collection of the payment for a sale to its bank (remitting bank), which sends the documents that its buyer needs to the importer's bank (collecting bank), with instructions to release the documents to the buyer for payment. Funds are received from the importer and remitted to the exporter through the banks involved in the collection in exchange for those documents. D/Cs involve using a draft that requires the importer to pay the face amount either at sight (document against payment) or on a specified date (document against acceptance). The collection letter gives instructions that specify the documents required for the transfer of title to the goods. Although banks do act as facilitators for their clients, D/Cs offer no verification process and limited recourse in the event of non-payment. D/Cs are generally less expensive than L/Cs.

(4) Open account

An open account transaction is a sale where the goods are shipped and delivered before payment is due, which in international sales is typically in 30, 60 or 90 days. Obviously, this is one of the most advantageous options to the importer in terms of cash flow and cost, but it is consequently one of the highest risk options for an exporter. Because of intense competition in export markets, foreign buyers often press exporters for open account terms since the extension of credit by the seller to the buyer is more common abroad. Therefore, exporters who are reluctant to extend credit may lose a sale to their competitors. Exporters can offer competitive open account terms while substantially mitigating the risk of non-payment by using one or more of the appropriate trade finance techniques. When offering open account terms, the exporter can seek extra protection using export credit insurance.

(5) Consignment

Consignment in international trade is a variation of open account in which payment is sent to the exporter only after the goods have been sold by the foreign distributor to the end customer. An international consignment transaction is based on a contractual arrangement in which the foreign distributor receives, manages, and sells the goods for the exporter who retains title to the goods until they are sold. Clearly, exporting on consignment is very risky as the exporter is not guaranteed any payment and its goods are in a foreign country in the hands of an independent distributor or agent. Consignment helps exporters become more competitive on the basis of better availability and faster delivery of goods. Selling on consignment can also help exporters reduce the direct costs of storing and managing inventory. The key to success in exporting on consignment is to partner with a reputable and trustworthy foreign distributor or a third-party logistics provider. Appropriate insurance should be in place to cover consigned goods in transit or in possession of a foreign distributor as well as to mitigate the risk of non-payment.

The most generally used method of payment in the financing of international trade is the letter of credit, which is a reliable and safe method of payment, facilitating trade with unknown buyers and giving protection to both sellers and buyers. The process of issuing a letter of credit starts with the buyer. He instructs his bank to issue an L/C in favor of the seller for the amount of the purchase.

The buyer's bank (the opening bank) sends to its correspondent bank in the seller's country the L/C, giving instructions about the amount of the credit, the beneficiary, the currency, the documents required and other special instructions. On arrival of it, the correspondent bank advise the seller of the receipt of the credit. Sometimes a seller requires a confirmed L/C. In this case, the correspondent bank usually adds its confirmation, becoming the confirming bank and advices the seller of the same; the seller will then dispatch the goods accordingly.

2. Other Methods of Payment

Payment is the most important and complicated part in business and settlement of foreign trade, and may be made in many ways, such as payment in advance, open account terms, consignment sales, etc. But the most often adopted methods of payment in international trade are as follows: collection, remittance and letter of credit. As for the letter of credit, it has been introduced in the previous chapter, this chapter will not discuss it. Before knowing the above methods of payment, please learn something about an important instrument in payment, i. e. draft.

(1) Bill of exchange

A bill of exchange or a draft (see Figure 9. 2, Figure 9. 3 and Figure 9. 4) is an unconditional written order drawn or issued by the drawer (the exporter usually) to the drawee (the confirming bank or the issuing bank usually) or another person for certain amount of money to be paid to someone, or the ordered one, or the holder at sight, or at a fixed time in the future or at the time stated.

Payment in international trade is seldom made with cash, but mostly with the worldwide used instrument of bill of exchange, check and promissory, especially with draft in chief. It has two forms: a sight draft and a usance draft (also called a time draft or a term draft). The draft is widely used in international trade, most frequently in the payment against a letter of credit (L/C). It is also used in the open account without any L/C involved.

Exchange for US$25,000.00 No. CI-00888
March 15 20 01
AT SIGHT of this First of Exchange (Second Unpaid)
pay to the order of UVW Exports
the sum of Twenty Five Thousand U.S. Dollars
Drawn under documentary credit No. SB-87654 of The Sun Bank, Sunlight City, Import-Country, dated January 26, 2001
To The Moon Bank
5 Moonlight Blvd.,
Export-City and Postal Code, Export-Country
UVW Exports

Figure 9. 2 The draft

BILL OF EXCHANGE

Draft No. MD-01

For USD30,804.70 Date: APR 30 2008

At ***** sight of this **FIRST** of Exchange (Second the same tenor and date being unpaid)

Pay to the order of COMMERCIAL BANK, LTD.

the sum of SAY TOTAL U.S. DOLLARS THIRTY THOUSAND EIGHT HUNDRED FOUR AND CENTS SEVENTY ONLY. value received

Drawn under

Irrevocable L/C No. 073708010006 dated JANUARY 28, 2008

To AUTO CO.LTD.

Daniel

AUTHORIZED SIGNATURE

Figure 9.3 Bill of Exchange 1

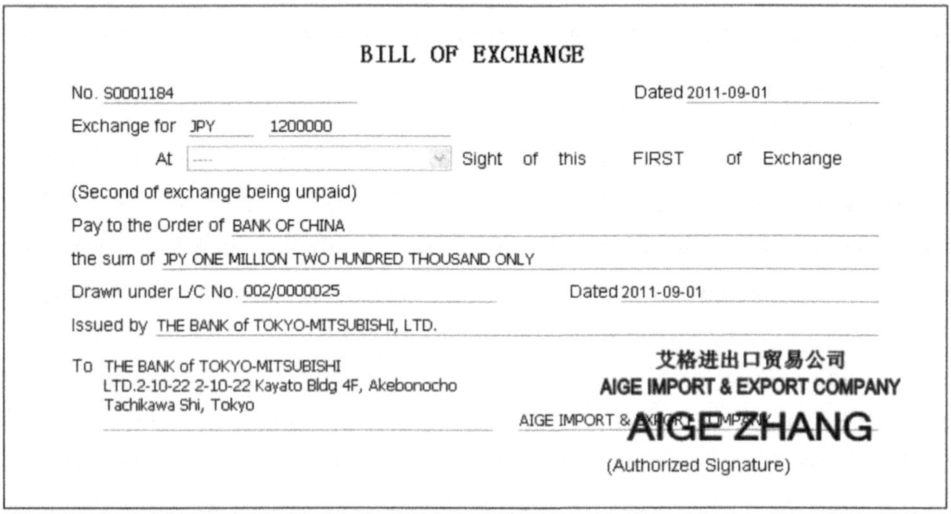

BILL OF EXCHANGE

No. S0001184 Dated 2011-09-01

Exchange for JPY 1200000

At ---- Sight of this FIRST of Exchange

(Second of exchange being unpaid)

Pay to the Order of BANK OF CHINA

the sum of JPY ONE MILLION TWO HUNDRED THOUSAND ONLY

Drawn under L/C No. 002/0000025 Dated 2011-09-01

Issued by THE BANK of TOKYO-MITSUBISHI, LTD.

To THE BANK of TOKYO-MITSUBISHI LTD.2-10-22 2-10-22 Kayato Bldg 4F, Akebonocho Tachikawa Shi, Tokyo

艾格进出口贸易公司

AIGE IMPORT & EXPORT COMPANY

AIGE IMPORT & EXPORT COMPANY

AIGE ZHANG

(Authorized Signature)

Figure 9.4 Bill of Exchange 2

(2) Collection

It means the creditor (exporter) issues the bill of exchange and entrusts the bank to collect the payment of the shipment from the debtor (importer). Documentary collection falls into two major forms: Documents against Payment (D/P) and Documents against Acceptance (D/A).

Payment is sometimes made by collection through banks under the terms of Documents against Payment (D/P) or Documents against Acceptance (D/A). In this case, the banks will only do the service of collecting and remitting and will not be liable for non-payment of the importer, while in the case of an L/C the opening bank offers its own credit to finance the transaction.

Documents against payment calls for actual payment against transfer of shipping documents. There are D/P at sight and D/P after sight. The former requires immediate payment by the importer to get hold of the documents. In the latter condition, the importer is given a certain period to make payment as 30, 45, 60, or 90 days after presentation of documents, but he is not allowed to get hold of the documents until he pays. Documents against Acceptance calls for delivery of documents against acceptance of the draft drawn by the exporter. D/A is always after sight.

As for as the seller's benefit is concerned, L/C is better than D/P. D/P at sight is better than D/P after sight, whereas D/P is better than D/A. In international trade, payment through collection is accepted only when the financial standing of the importer is sound or where a previous course of business has inspired the exporter with confidence that the importer will be good for payment.

Collection letters are sent usually one after another, with the tone and language getting more direct with each successive letter, until at least some payment is received. An effective letter of collection achieves its purpose without destroying the customers' goodwill that was painstakingly acquired over the years. Also called dunning letter. Not to be confused with collection letter.

1) Documentary Collection.

It is a process by which an exporter asks a bank to "safeguard" its interests in the foreign country by not releasing the documents. It is accompanied by a Bill of Exchange (also called a Draft). It involves a Letter of Instructions to the Presenting Bank (See Figure 9.5).

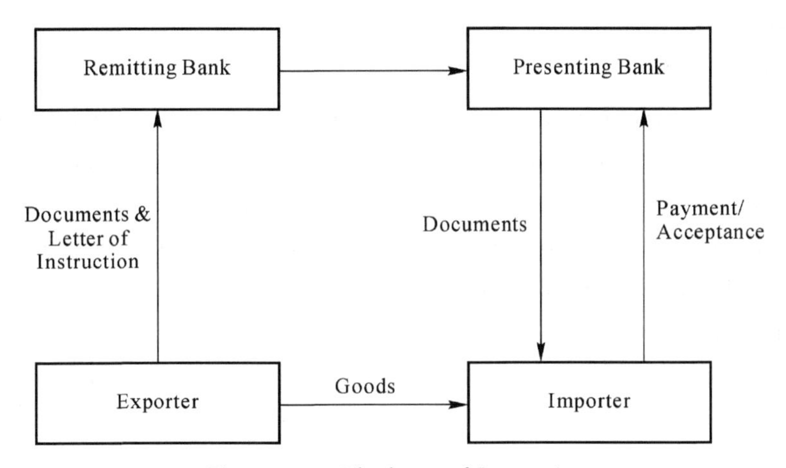

Figure 9.5 The letter of Instruction

A. Remitting Bank. Receives the documents from the exporter and then sends them to the Presenting Bank. It has no obligation to render judgment or advice on the quality of the packet of documents; it just transmits them to the Presenting Bank.

The Remitting Bank is instructed to sign the Draft on behalf of the Importer. The Remitting Bank only does so if it is convinced that the Importer will eventually pay. The Remitting Bank "avals" the Draft.

B. Presenting Bank. The bank that interacts with the importer on behalf of the exporter. Receives the documents from the exporter or from the Remitting Bank and holds them until the importer either signs a draft or pays the exporter. Follows the Letter of Instructions from the Exporter.

2)Collection Appeals.

As in other persuasive message, the primary purpose of a collection letter is to get action (payment). A secondary goal is to maintain a customer's goodwill and therefore collection letters are a special form of persuasive writing. In the following we will discuss some of the elements of persuasion that usually determine the effectiveness of a collection letter.

A. Short and written inductively. Collection letters are generally written inductively; but they are shorter than other letters. Normally, customers do not know that they owe (no need to devote space to informing them) and they expect to be asked for payment, so there is no need to get attention of the receiver, nor is there an apology. If a letter is short, its main point stands out vividly. Compared with a long letter, a short letter has a greater chance of being read in its entirety. In a long letter, the main point might be in the skipped-over portion or may have to compete for attention with minor points.

B. Avoidance of emotional appeal. People are influenced by emotions. Prior to the mild-appeal stage of the collection series, the use of emotional appeal should be minimal and subtle. The writer should adopt a businesslike, firm, yet friendly and considerate tone. Beginning with the mild-appeal stage, though, the writer can attempt to engage the reader's emotions more seriously.

C. Use of a credible, sincere image. The main principle is that we have already sent the purchaser the goods he required and, in return, as a buyer, he or she should pay for the benefits he has received. What we ask for is just something in exchange. It is a fair treatment. Therefore, the writer must appear determined to collect what is due, yet unthreatening and, at least in the early collection stages, willing to adapt to the readers' reasonable consideration.

D. Avoidance of disrupting the reader's expectations. A debtor knows for sure that the creditor will ask for payment, and therefore they are very sensitive about the respect especially at the early time, and like anyone else, they also expects to be treated like a human being. Be sure not to let your reader lose "face".

E. Careful choice of words. Wording may vary with collection series. Early stages in the collection series call for words that can create pleasant, cooperative feelings such as appreciate, cooperation and so on. In mid-stage, words like legal remedies, forced to take steps can be used to create more serious, and perhaps more motivating feelings if necessary. Only in the final stage can the writer select the words that emphasize the negative orientation to cause considerable uneasiness.

3) Collection Series.

The procedure in a collection series is one of increasing forcefulness. The stages are as follows:

A. Reminder. The first collection letter should only be a friendly reminder. Assume that the customer has forgotten to pay and courteously invite him/her to pay promptly. Most people will make a payment after a couple of reminders. If there is no response to these reminders, you should assume that the customer is not paying because of financial, medical, or other personal difficulties.

Suggestions for a typical format:

a. Send a copy of the original bill.

b. Stamp on it Reminder or Past Due and highlight the amount past due.

c. Include a short statement indicating the amount due, the due date, late charges (if any), and the account number.

d. Make sure the address where the customer should send payment is plainly indicated. Including a pre-addressed envelope for payment (with or without postage) is also helpful.

If the customer has not even made a partial payment after a couple of gentle Reminder Collection Letters, you can send a final reminder collection letter to ask why the customer is not paying. A final reminder letter should explain that there will be consequences for continued nonpayment. If no payment on the amount owed is received, then you will need to take a more aggressive approach in follow-up collection letters.

B. Inquiry. Before you employ any harsher means, try to discover if the customer has extraordinary circumstances that are preventing him/her from making any payment. You can help maintain a good relationship with the customer and go a long way toward collecting your debt if you are sensitive to any potential problems. The Inquiry Collection Letter demonstrates your willingness to help the customer solve his/her current financial difficulty by offering new terms. If you are willing to accept a partial payment now with regular payments after that, most people in financial difficulty will be grateful for this option and agree.

Remember, it is better to collect your money through a series of payments than not to collect it at all. It is also better to work with your customers than to alienate them, because their present difficulties may resolve and they may prove to be more reliable in the future.

Tip for the first inquiry letter: Make a request for prompt payment, and add your willingness to help the customer by offering new terms for repayment.

Tip for the second inquiry letter: Use positive wording, but state firmly that the customer will pay a penalty for continued non-payment, such as a late fee, a collection fee, or interest on the amount owed.

C. Appeal. If the customer fails to respond to any of the Reminder Collection Letters or to the Inquiry Collection Letters, you must take a more aggressive approach. Because the customer has not responded to date, you should assume that he/she will probably not respond to any further demands for payment. This is why many organizations at this point turn their debtors over to a collection agency. If you do choose to continue the collection process yourself, you can take two basic approaches.

Positive appeal approach: Try to appeal to the customer's sense of fairness, personal pride, or his/her desire to maintain a good credit standing and its connected privileges.

Negative appeal approach: If the positive approach is ignored, inform the customer that continued nonpayment could result in various penalties.

a. The loss of his/her good credit standing and its connected privileges.

b. The initiation of legal action to reclaim any purchased goods; any services will be discontinued.

c. He/She may incur additional debt through collection fees and/or interest on the amount owed.

D. Ultimatum. If the customer does not answer any of your collection letters, you can give him/her a final chance to pay. The Ultimatum Collection Letter needs to state the specific action you will take if the customer does not send payment by a certain date. Your statements should be fair, reasonable, and logical.

In your last letter:

a. First review the history of the account: what the customer purchased, your repeated efforts to collect, etc.

b. Give a deadline for payment or for the customer to commit to a repayment agreement—otherwise you will take legal action to reclaim the purchased goods and/or turn the account over to a collection agency.

Be careful not to use name-calling or to make accusations, which are both illegal. Always be careful with what you put in print! Simply state the facts and explain why his/her inaction is causing you to take action.

If the Ultimatum Collection Letter fails to bring results, be sure to follow through with your stated action.

Debt collection is not an enjoyable pastime, but if you follow these logical steps in preparing your collection letters, you will succeed in collecting payment on many of your delinquent accounts.

Do not suggest in any collection letter that the customer might be dissatisfied with the product or service he/she purchased from you.

4) Other tips for writing a collection letter.

A. Consider offering a discount for early payment on products or services. In this type of letter, you can remind or notify a customer that if you receive payment within a certain period, you will give him or her a discount on the purchase. Be specific about the conditions for the discount.

B. Gather all the facts about your customer's account and to encourage your customer to pay the money owed. Always be specific about how much the customer owes and about when the money was due to avoid future misunderstandings.

C. Offer assistance to a customer having difficulty paying an overdue bill. In fact, often it is the only way to collect payment. Use a sincere tone, and gently persuade the customer to contact you to talk about the problem. When discussing new terms, be sure that any new arrangement is one that the customer can handle and that you can feel comfortable about.

D. Take a firmer stand in your next letter if after writing one or more collection letters you have received no response from the customer (even after suggesting an alternative payment plan or other options). Unlike earlier letters, this one should carry a demanding rather than a requesting tone. Although this letter is less friendly than other letters, it should still make it easy for the customer to respond.

E. Let the customer know exactly what the penalty will be in the final letter unless he or she responds immediately with the payment. Don't make an empty threat, and don't send another letter asking for payment. You must be prepared to follow through with your claim.

F. If you must cancel or withdraw a customer's credit account, explain clearly your reasons for doing so. Be sure to use a courteous tone when writing this letter, as you may want to maintain this customer's business, even if you must ask for cash payments from now on.

G. If you receive a collection letter and plan to pay your overdue bill, it is a good idea to write a letter reassuring the creditor of that fact. Use simple language to clearly state your intent, and refrain from making promises that you are not sure you can keep. If necessary, you may want to consider outlining your proposed payment plan in your letter or asking about an alternative payment plan.

H. Though it is usually not necessary to send a letter acknowledging payment of an overdue balance, you may wish to do so if you feel it is important to clear the slate or ease the customer's mind, or if the customer requests it.

I. If you have sent a collection letter by mistake, you should apologize for your error and acknowledge any inconvenience you may have caused. You should also state the current condition of the customer's account.

When requesting payment of a personal loan—because the person who borrowed the money from you is most likely a friend or family member—your letter should communicate very little pressure. Don't hesitate to make the message as personal and warm as possible.

(3) Remittance

Remittance, like collection, is another mode of payment based on commercial credit. It means the buyer sends the payment through bank or other forms to the receiver initiatively. It is widely used for payment in advance, cash with order and open account business. It has three forms: mail transfer (M/T), telegraphic transfer (T/T) and demand draft (D/D).

Nowadays, there is a development of the introduction of a procedure known as "SWIFT" (Society for Worldwide Inter-bank Financial Telecommunication) system for passing and receiving international payment. The system is characterized by its uniform format, fast transfer and low costs.

Remittance is a kind of payment that the remitter pays a certain number of money to the payee by the bank transfer by using a series of settlement instruments (e. g. draft, check or promissory note), chiefly used for payment in advance, cash with order, deliver first and payment after for small quantity of goods, etc.

1)Parties involved (See Figure 9. 6).

Remitter (Payer): the importer, the buyer, or debtor;

Beneficiary (Payee): the exporter, the seller, or the creditor;

Remitting Bank: first, accept the application of the remitter; then, remit it out to the payee;

Paying Bank: pay the money directly to the payee (it is often the correspondent bank of the remitting bank).

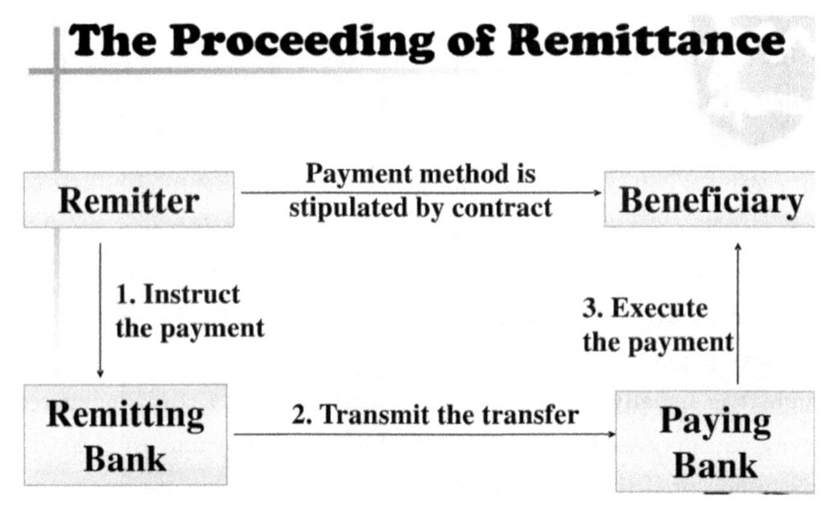

Figure 9. 6 The proceeding of remittance

2)Three forms.

A. Mail Transfer (M/T). The buyer will hand over the payment of goods to the remitting bank that will authorize its branch or corresponding bank in the country of the beneficial by mail to make the payment to him.

B. Telegraphic Transfer (T/T). The buyer will hand over the payment of goods to the remitting bank that will authorize its branch or corresponding bank in the country of the beneficial by telegraphic method to make the payment to him.

C. Demand Draft (D/D). The remitter will buy a certain kind of settlement instrument and deliver it to the payee who can then get the money from the bank designated by the remitter.

The payee will go to the bank directly to get the payment for goods without the advising of the bank. The settlement instrument under D/D is endorsable so that it can be transferred while the M/T and T/T cannot.

3) Advantages and disadvantages.

a. Feature: There have no procedure for documents examination by bank.

b. Advantages: convenient, fast.

c. Disadvantages: It is a kind of commercial credit rather than bank credit so there always exists some potential danger.

Remittance uses commercial credit and hence in adopting this method the parties involved need have trust in each other. If it is used for payment in advance or cash with order, it will put the seller in an advantageous position. The buyer may suffer losses if the seller does not make delivery after he receives the payment for goods.

If it is used for payment remittance against documents, it means only when the seller offers the shipping documents to the buyer, will the buyer make the remittance. It is safer for buyer than that under payment in advance or cash with order, but as the buyer can cancel the remittance so the seller should get the money from bank as soon as he makes the delivery.

A remittance is a transfer of money by a foreign worker to his or her home country or simply sending amount from one country to another. Money sent home by migrants constitutes the second largest financial inflow to many developing countries, exceeding international aid. Remittances contribute to economic growth and to the livelihoods of people worldwide [citation needed]. Moreover, remittance transfers can also promote access to financial services for the sender and recipient, thereby increasing financial and social inclusion.

4) Letter of remittance.

Letter of remittance is basically a document that accompanies checks or drafts that are submitted for collection. It lists the number of checks (items) being sent along with the total dollar amount mentioned in the checks. The checks presented to other banks for payment accompanies a cash letter. A remittance letter is primarily used when the bank does not possess an account at the receiving bank. The three basic pieces of information are contained in any kind of remittance letter. It has the identification of sender with name and mailing address of the debtor. In addition to sender's contact information, it also mentions the reference of the name and address of the creditor. It also has the details of the amount of the enclosed payment in the body of the letter.

In addition to the above mentioned details, there are other types of information that may be included in the body of the remittance letter. The account number of the debtor can be included along with a reference to any invoice number to which the payment needs to be applied. It also contains the goods or services that were bought by the customer. The due date of invoice can also be mentioned.

The entire format for a remittance letter is kept short and brief. The remittance letter starts with the date of the correspondence and it is followed by the recipient name and mailing address. It should have a simple salutation where the sender can mention the details including reason for the payment, and any other data in one or two paragraphs. The information contained in the letter should assist the receiver in applying for the payment effortlessly. In the end of the letter, the standard closing along with the signature of the sender should be followed.

5) Potential security concerns.

The recent internationally coordinated effort to stifle possible sources of money laundering and/or terrorist financing has increased the cost of sending remittances directly increasing costs to the companies facilitating the sending and indirectly to the person remitting. As in some corridors a sizable amount of remittances is sent through informal channels (family connections, traveling friends, local money lenders, etc.). According to the World Bank, some countries do not report remittances data. Moreover, when data is available, the methodologies used by countries for remittance data compilation are not publicly available.

Remittances can be difficult to track and potentially sensitive to money laundering and terror financing concerns, especially when using the emerging "cryptocurrencies" such as bitcoin. Since 9/11 many governments and the Financial Action Task Force (FATF) have taken steps to address informal value transfer systems. This is done through nations' Financial Intelligence Units (FIUs). The principle legislative initiatives in this area are the *USA PATRIOT Act*, Title III in the United States and, in the EU, through a series of EU Money Laundering Directives. Though no serious terror risk should be associated with migrants sending money to their families, misuse of the financial system remains a serious government concern.

3. Writing Tips

It is often the case for customers to ask for other methods of payment in their transactions: payment extension, payment in installments, D/P at sight or D/A, cash in advance, etc. It is a hard job, because you need to try to make the receiver of your letter understand and accept your request, while you are keeping sensitive to maintain relations with your trade partners.

In presenting your request, you will have to provide your reasons or other convincing evidence to prove the merit of your request, including facts, figures, expert opinions, examples, and details. If it is possible, you can suggest direct and indirect benefits for the receiver. But at the same time announcement of your request should be clear but understated, trying to avoid anything blunt to damage the climate for your possibly successful request. If your request is very likely to be refused, you should identify what

factors will be obstacles to the receiver and offer your arguments. But your tone should not sound emotional. Where it seems natural, you can include compliment or anything else to make the receiver feel better.

Part B Sample Letters of Other Methods of Payment

1. Asking for D/P

Dear Sirs,

We thank you for your order No. 1368 and are pleased to inform you that the goods required have been dispatched by S. S. "Garden", due at Singapore on the 19th, August.

We are sure that you can understand our position that on this occasion it is necessary to make this a "Document against Payment" transaction, since we have not had time to secure credit references on your firm. We have drawn a sight draft on you for the amount of US$8 500 through the Merchant Bank Ltd. of Singapore, who will approach you in a few days for the payment of the draft. They will then hand to you the full documents to enable you to take delivery.

We hope that in due course we will be able to establish regular trading with you. In such circumstances we would be prepared to give you a three-month credit once your references are secured. We hope that this will be only the first of many orders you will place with us.

Faithfully yours,

2. Buyer Proposes Payment by D/A

Dear Sirs,

We wish to place with you a trial order for 150 cases of Canned Luncheon Meat at your price of US$300 per case CFR Kuwait for shipment during October/November.

As this particular order involves a relatively small amount and we have only moderate means at hand, **we would suggest payment by D/A at 60 days' sight.** If the trial sale proves successful, you may count on us for further orders.

We hope you can give our proposal your most favorable consideration and await your early reply.

Truly yours,

×××

3. Asking for Earlier Payment Terms

Dear Sir,

In the past, our purchases of steel pipes from you have normally been paid by confirmed, irrevocable letter of credit.

This arrangement has cost us a great deal of money. From the moment we open the credit until our buyers pay us normally, funds have been tied up for about four months. This is currently a particularly serious problem for us in view of the difficult economic climate and the prevailing high interest rates.

If you could offer us easier payment terms, it would probably lead to an increase in business between our companies. We propose either cash against documents on arrival of goods, or drawing on us at three month's sight.

We hope our request will meet your agreement and look forward to your early reply.

Yours faithfully,

×××

4. Suggesting Payment by D/P Instead of D/A

Dear Sirs,

We thank you for your letter of 24 this month, from which we have learnt that you suggest our accepting payment by D/A as you think it does not pay to open a L/C for a small order.

After taking your suggestion into due consideration, we think the best we can do at present is to agree to payment by D/P at 30 days'sight. And with the development of our business, we will consider more flexible ways to cooperate with you in the near future. The goods under your order have been ready for shipment and we will deliver them within the contracted time after receipt of your confirmation of payment terms.

We hope that you will find the shipment satisfactory to you and are looking forward to your regular orders.

Yours faithfully,

×××

5. Refusing Payment by D/ A

Dear Sirs,

Thank you for your order of August 15 and we are pleased to learn that you intend to give our Canned Luncheon Meat a trial sale in your market.

While we appreciate your good intention, we regret being unable to accept your request for payment by D/A at 60 days' sight. As we generally require payment by irrevocable letter of credit available by draft at sight, we cannot make any arrangement contrary to our usual practice, especially for a new customer. May we suggest that we do business on the basis of payment by L/C first and leave the matter to be discussed at a later date?

We hope the above payment terms are acceptable to you and look forward to your confirmation.

Yours faithfully,

×××

6. Payment by T/T

Dear Sirs,

We have received your statement for the quarter that ended September 30 and found that it agrees with our books. As requested, we have instructed our bankers to send the sum of US $ 5 000 **by T/T for the credit of your account of the Bank of China**, Beijing Branch.

This payment that clears your account up to August 31 the unpaid balance of US$ 2 000 for the goods supplied during September will be telegraphed by our bankers on or before November 15.

Yours faithfully,

×××

7. Asking for T/T Payment

Dear Sirs,

We have studied the specifications and price list of your new paints and varnishes and now wish to place the enclosed order with you. As we are in urgent need of several of the items, we should be glad if you would make up and ship the order as soon as you possibly can.

In the past we dealt with you on sight credit basis. Now, we would like to propose a different way of payment, i. e. when the goods purchased by us are ready for shipment and freight space booked, we will remit you the full amount by T/T. The reasons are that we can thus more confidently assure our buyers of the time of delivery and save a lot of expenses on opening the letter of credit. As we feel this would not make much difference to you but would facilitate our sales, we hope you will grant our request.

We look forward to your confirmation of our order and your affirmative reply to our new arrangements of payment.

Yours faithfully,

×××

8. **Asking for Accepting the Draft**

Sample 1

Dear Sirs,

As to this business, we will draw our draft at 30 days on you against the 200 units of the construction machines for a sum amounting to US$150 000 under the L/C.

We ask you to accept it on presentation and honor it on maturity.

Faithfully yours,

×××

Sample 2

Dear Sirs,

We thank you for your order of 25th July for 10 000 meters of poplin shirting at the quoted price of US$1.24 per meter.

The shirting is now ready for dispatch and will be shipped by the S. S. Tripoli sailing from Liverpool on 18th August.

We are pleased to enclose the shipping documents. Also enclosed is our sight draft drawn at 30 days as agreed.

Please accept and return it immediately.

Yours faithfully,

×××

9. **Asking to Change the Method of Payment**

Dear Mr. Smith,

Thank you for being so prompt in sending the sales confirmation against our last order No. KK78901. We have established the covering L/C, and the bank should be sending you an advice in no time.

We have been dealing with you on the L/C basis for over a year and would like to change to payment by 30-day bill of exchange, documents against payment.

When we first contacted you in March last year, you told us that you would be prepared to reconsider terms of payment once we had established a trading association. We think that sufficient time has elapsed for us to be allowed the terms we have asked for. If you need references, we will be glad to supply them.

As we will be sending another order within the month, could you please confirm that you agree to these terms of payment?

Attached is the Sales Confirmation No. 980654 we have countersigned and returned for your file.

Yours sincerely,

×××

10. **Paying by cheque**

Amsterdam, 16th September 2020

To: Mykia Furniture
(address)

Dear Sir,

We thank you for your consignment of garden furniture on the 15th September 2020, the goods have been received in good condition.

We enclose a cheque for EUR € 1 000 (EUR One Thousand Only), in full settlement of account towards supply of goods as per your invoice number 82615.

Please acknowledge the receipt of the above mentioned cheque and credit us with the amount. Thank you in advance.

Sincerely yours,

×××

11. The Reminder of Overdue Payment

Sample 1

Dear Sirs,

We have not received your payment for Order No. 625, which was due on Oct. 16, 2019. It would be appreciated if you could have it remitted to us by Oct. 30, 2019.

Yours faithfully,

×××

Sample 2

Dear Sirs,

Have you overlooked the unpaid balance from your recent purchase? If your payment is already on the way to us, please accept our thanks. Otherwise, won't you check and mail the remittance right now?

Thank you for cooperation.

Your truly,

×××

12. The Inquiry for Overdue Payment

Sample 1

Dear Sirs,

RE: Account No. 8675

According to our closing accounts for the first quarter of the year, our account for the paint and wallpaper supplied to you on 16 March has not yet been settled.

We enclose a detailed statement, which shows the amount owing to be US $ 68 000, and hope you will be able to make an early settlement.

Yours faithfully,

×××

Sample 2

Dear Sir or Madam,

We have not heard from you for the past two months.

Your Order No. 687 for the printers is still unpaid, which is past due. We believe something special has prevented you from continuing your prompt paying practice.

Will you please either remit the unpaid balance of US$6 000 to cover the overdue payment or give us your plan for meeting your obligation?

We are looking forward to your reply.

Faithfully yours,

×××

13. Urgent Appeal for Overdue Payment

Sample 1

Dear Sir or Madam,

I have recently sent you a letter regarding the outstanding balance of your account with this shop.

According to our records, you have failed to make any repayments whatsoever and the sum of HK$5 000 is now overdue.

We understand that it is sometimes difficult to meet our debts. We are therefore prepared to overlook the fact that you have missed the first three repayments if you undertake to meet the repayments schedule from now on.

Also, if you would like to extend the period of credit so that repayments are made easier, we should be happy to discuss the matter with you.

We certainly would not like to reduce your credit limit for future purchases. I urge you in the strongest terms, therefore, to contact me within the next seven days so that this unfortunate situation can be sorted out.

I look forward to hearing from you within the next week.

Yours truly,

×××

Sample 2

Dear Mr. Smith,

How much is it worth to you? It is your credit record I am referring to, and it's a most important question to you, now that it hangs in the balance.

The good reference we were given on you when you opened your account told us that you have successfully handled your promises to pay promptly for a long time. We know that you must want to maintain this good rating, for it means so much to you. Aside from the obvious advantages of credit buying, it is important to your CI (company image). The business would judge you by how you fulfill your promises.

Because your credit record means so much to you, it is hard to understand how you have permitted your account of US$ 8 000 to run six months past due.

Send us your payment today.

Yours sincerely,

×××

14. Ultimatum

Sample 1

Dear Mr. Alexander,

When we agreed three months ago to ship medical supplies and equipment, you agreed that you would pay US $ 6 000 within 30 days. Yet the 30 days have gone by, then 60. Now more than 90 days have elapsed.

Because our overdue notices and letters have gone unanswered, our patience is exhausted; however, our interest in you and in your welfare is not. Your name will be submitted as non-pay unless we receive now check for US$ 6 000 by July 29. The effect of a bad report could restrict your ability to purchase medical supplies and equipment on credit. In addition, our legal department would be forced to bring suit for collection.

We have every right to enforce legal collection. You have until July 29 to retain your good record and to avoid legal embarrassment.

Sincerely yours,

×××

Sample 2

Dear Mr. Wilson,

Is there any reason you have not paid your bill of US$ 3 680?

In the credit agreement you signed, you agreed to pay off your bill in three payments. Your total bill is now overdue. Please send US$ 3 680 within 10 days. If you have any questions or concerns regarding this bill, please contact me at 800-666-9765 by October 21, 2019.

Failure to send the full amount by October 21 may mean that your bill is turned over to a collection agency. Your prompt attention is urgent to protect your credit.

Sincerely yours,

Mary West
Credit Manager

Sample 3

Dear Mr. Johnson,

Subject: Overdue Loan Repayments (Account No. 067809)

I refer to my letter of 17th August regarding your failure to meet your loan repayments. According to my records, repayments totaling US $20 000 are currently overdue. This represents repayments for the last three months.

I spoke to your assistant on the telephone today and he informed me that you had no intention of repaying the money owed to us. I should remind you that the US $300 000 you borrowed from the Third Bank of Chicago was used to expand your premises, and that it has led to increased profits on your part. We do not, therefore, feel it unfair to expect you to honor our agreement.

I have written to you several times asking you to contact me to discuss the matter so that we might come to an arrangement. However, on all occasions, you have ignored my letters.

It is regretful that I must inform you that unless we receive full payment within the next three days, I shall be compelled to instruct our legal department to begin proceedings against you.

Yours sincerely,

Peter Lusardi
Overdue Accounts Division

Chapter 10 Packing

Learning Objectives

a. Master the general concept and characteristics of packing;

b. Master writing requirements of packing.

Part A Introduction

Packing is of particular importance in foreign trade because goods have to travel long distance before reaching their destinations—often across oceans or across continents. Accidents, rough weather, unloading and reloading on the way, everything has to be taken into consideration.

As the buyer has the right to expect that his goods will reach him in perfect condition, the seller has to get them into a nice, compact shape that will stay that way even during the roughest journey.

Packing must be strictly marked. Conveniently, outer packing marks mainly include transport marks, directive marks and warning marks. The transport marks consist of:

a. consignor's or consignee's code name;

b. number of the contract or the L/C;

c. the port of destination;

d. numbers of the packed goods.

And sometimes weight and dimensions, all of which can greatly facilitate identification and transportation. For example, directive marks are eye-catching figures and concise instructions concerning manner of proper handling, storing, loading and unloading of the packed goods like "USE NO HOOKS." "THIS SIDE UP. "KEEP DRY.", etc. Warning marks are obvious symbols or words to warn people against the hidden danger of inflammation, explosives and poisonous products.

Packing usually varies with the nature of the contents. The most commonly used packing containers are cartons, cases, crates, drums, barrels, bales, tins, and carboys.

Details such as manner of packing, kinds of packing materials and the burden of packing cost should be unmistakably stipulated in the contract concerned and strictly observed by both the selling side and the buying side.

Letters about packing issues should be concise and clear. In such letters, the seller can describe in detail to the buyer his customary packing of the goods concerned and also indicate clearly that he may accept any required packing at the expense of the buyer. The buyer can inform the seller of any formerly unexpected requirements or fears about the packing. Any changes regarding packing stipulated in the contract should be mutually discussed and determined before shipment.

1. What is a Packing Slip?

Primarily, a packing slip contains a list of items or products in details included in the shipment and usually comes with an order that is inside the shipping pouch or the package itself. This is intended not only for the customers but also for transport agencies, government authorities, and other related parties in the transaction for them to handle the package or shipment accordingly.

The details included in general in the packing slip are the quantity, description, and weight of the items contained in the shipment excluded the pricing for each content. More of the details to be included in a packing slip are discussed in the next section.

A packing slip is created either by the seller or by the shipping company and sent to the recipient, to where the goods are located, in order for the person handling the shipment to have an accurate tally of the goods being shipped as it is sent along with the items to their destination. They are only required if there are products being shipped and received for sale.

This is also referred to as packing list, shipping list, waybill, bill of parcel, or unpacking note.

2. What to Include in a Packing Slip?

(1) Product description

Generally, a product description must be included in a packing slip. It is important to include the color of the product so it will not be interchanged with another product of similar type.

(2) Reference number

A reference to the relevant commercial invoice number or item number must also be included in the packing slip as this is important to compare if the two numbers matched when it arrives in the destination.

(3) Type

The type of package must also be specified, for example, box, carton, and vials. This gives the authorized person the knowledge on how to handle appropriately the product that is being shipped.

(4) Weight

The net and gross weights of each package must also be present in the packing slip, and these must be stated in pounds or tons and converted into a metric equivalent, except where the buyer or government regulations require otherwise. The weight should be made known to the handler of the goods so they can use appropriate measures in handling the product or the shipment. There are also times when the cost of the shipment depends on the weight of the items to be shipped. Hence, it is important that the weight must be disclosed.

(5) Legal measurements

The legal measurements should also be included in the details. This must be expressed in inches and cubic feet and converted into a metric equivalent, except where the buyer or government regulations require otherwise. Similar to weight, the dimension of the item or product to be shipped may also be a factor for the cost of shipping.

(6) Package markings

Specific identifiable markers, if any, should also be written down in the package slip to have a specific identification of the shipment.

(7) Buyer and seller references

There are times when there are specifications and preferences requested by the buyer or seller. This must also be included in the packing slip.

3. Reasons Why Packing Slips are very Useful

These commercial documents can be a very important medium for creating a strong and a fruitful relationship between the seller and his or her customers.

If a seller meets all the expectations of the customers there is surely that they come back to the business premises in order to increase their purchases. On the other hand, the seller will enjoy more profits, and increase his or her sales.

This kind of business documents is cost effective, thus assisting in saving money.

They assist in increasing trust and loyalty between the seller and the buyer.

They provide a suitable means of liquidating commodities that are hard and heavy to transport from the seller to the buyer. This helps in maintaining mutually beneficial relationships between the buyer and the seller.

A buyer is not supposed to pay for this document because the cost is already cared for.

4. Importance of Packing Slips

Packing slips are the most important business documents, this due to the fact that they possess vital information to parties involved in any business transaction. The data in this document is not limited to involve delivery address, quantity and measurements, order details, delivery dates, package and PO numbers, and any other unique information or directions.

The following are some of the important uses of packing slips.

It involves the calculation of the goods that are supposed to or are being discharged and delivered to the premises of the customer(s).

They help in sustaining derivation of the offshore price of the shipment.

They provide the necessary information needed to formulate certificate of origin of the goods or services.

They have the necessary data that is used by law enforcement agencies to document any business transaction carried out in a different part of the country. An example of these agencies is Automated Export System (AES).

This types of documents ensure that all the goods will be delivered safely and minimize any form of risk that may arise in the process of transporting goods.

If one is purchasing his or her products on international markets and the products need to be delivered in different countries. The document assists in formulating bookings for international deliveries and the application for the derivation of the offshore price of the shipment.

The documents are used to allow the passage of imported goods into the country.

The documents are used in demanding any compensation for goods spoiled or damaged goods or any stolen goods.

It enables the buyer to accurately verify the goods received, and compensation of the goods is made easier because they will not be any form of misunderstanding. Due to this conflict of interest is also minimized.

This document may be utilized in assisting compensation under the message of a loan.

The most important thing which you should always keep in mind is always ensuring that you have created an awesome experience for your clients. By going further beyond your own expectations, you will always leave your customers smiling and this will give them reasons to shop again from your business premises or your company.

5. How is it Different from an Invoice?

Both packing slips and invoice are documents sent to customers by owners of business premises but they differ a lot.

They differ in terms of purpose. It is a document sent to customers to show details of the products that are supposed to be transported from the seller to the buyer.

The packing slips are most preferably used in the transportation of physical goods, on the other hand, an invoice is a document sent to customers to show details of goods purchased or services offered by your company. Business enterprises that offer services do not offer packing slips because they do not offer physical or tangible goods.

Recipients also vary. This is the major difference between the two. An invoice is sent to an individual accountable for paying the bills of the goods bought or services offered.

While a packing slip is part of the goods that are supposed to be transported to the customer. In some cases, individuals may buy goods but sent them to others to receive them such as purchasing a gift to your spouse. The person buying the gift will pay for the gift but he or she will not receive it.

Their contents of both documents vary. The details of an invoice comprise of the number of goods purchased, the amount to be paid and the deadline on which all payments should be completed.

Also, the invoice contains a specific date, an explanation about the goods bought or services offered and the basic addresses of the customer. The details of a packing slip differ according to one's business and goods. Every delivery done must be accompanied with a packing slip showing all the details which include, the date on when the order was made or requested, quantities of goods involved and the goods involved in an orderly sequence. The weight of the goods may be included as part of the contents of this commercial document.

It is mainly used by a lot of customers when unpacking their goods this enables them to verify that their purchase has been delivered in full, if something is absent, the customer will confirm on the packing slip and then communicate to the seller in order to notify him or her.

Their merits also differ. Packing slips have some sort of limited merits. Once the products are finally delivered, packing slips do not possess any other objective because the main objective has already been achieved. On the other hand, all the original copies of each and every invoice ought to be securely kept by the seller and the purchaser of the goods or purposes of record keeping.

Details of their prices vary. The packing slip will not include the amount of each product or tax incurred after purchasing the products, but invoices comprise of a detailed summary of all the products purchased accompanied by the amount of taxes deducted after the purchase was completed.

Services offered differ a lot. A business enterprise that is service oriented does not require the need to use the packing slip because it does not offer tangible products. Although, the company will surely require the services of an invoice to show the cost of each service offered, maybe charged on hourly rating and the cost charged on each hour.

The actions needed both documents vary a lot. One requires the usage of a packing slip mostly when offloading the goods, for purposes of confirming the amount and the state of the goods delivered. Although, the invoice ought to be paid while the original copies should remain in the hands of both the buyer and the seller in order to prevent any form of misunderstanding. The original copies are kept by both parties for purposes of record keeping, tax, and legal basis.

It is recommended for one to have a clear knowledge on the type of document he or she is dealing with. This is due to the reason that the same document can be referred by different names, such as the packing slip has a variety of names that are used to name it. These words are a shipping list, manifest, or a waybill. On the other hand, an invoice can be called in the following names, a tab, a bill or a purchase invoice.

The most important thing is regular communication between the seller and the buyer, this will easily enable them to solve and prevent any misunderstanding that may arise.

6. Types of Packing Slips

Order fulfillment is the most important thing for both parties. This kind of fulfillment comprises of meeting the agreed terms of every purchasing order. There are different types of packing slips which include, packing slips with return form, packing slips with order and ship quantity, and packing slips with buyer and vendor codes.

(1) Packing slips with return form

This type of packing slips lists the amount of the goods either in kilograms or in tones that are supposed to be delivered or shipped to a certain client. It is usually accompanied with a return form. The purpose of this form is to make it easier for customers in filing complaints on issues relating to the goods delivered.

The issues may include the presence of damaged or spoiled goods or the goods delivered are not enough. Return forms are useful for the replacement of any missing or damaged merchandise. By having this type of packing slip enables sellers to gain the trust of their customers and help them sustain a mutual relationship with them.

(2) Packing slips with order and ship quantity

This kind of packing slips has the details of the order and the amount in terms or kilograms or tons. It has all the details of the customers. But the most important part of this kind of packing document is the details and quantity of the order. It also includes the means of transport used to transport the goods.

(3) Packing slips with buyer and vendor codes

Vendor codes are special economical codes which all vendors are allocated at the point they are offered a contract, business traction has taken place or payment is to be completed.

These codes represent each business owner or customer without the necessity of knowing the name of the customer or the business enterprise. This type of document makes it easier for record keeping especially if the seller uses computerized record keeping systems.

7. Document Packing Slips Data Right into the Marketplace

There are electronic packing slips which formulate a record of the goods received contrary to Purchase Order (PO). It is precisely related to the Purchase Order; it can also be kept and asked contrary to the shopping place.

Utilizing these kinds of documents is very simple thus time-saving. You only have to add the date on which the delivery was completed. Enter the packing slip code or serial number and other important details which include the name of the means used to transport the goods, tracking codes and any other interested parties.

Using this kind of commercial document for packing slip template which is electronically generated has lots of benefits. These kinds of benefits include;

a. This kind of commercial document can be documented and kept alongside the shopping PO.

b. They replace the requirement of restoring hard copies.

c. They are easy to access provided you are logged in the database or in the shopping area.

d. It is a simple and efficient way of documenting.

e. They assist in running delivery reports in the business premises.

f. The most important issue about this kind of business documentation is that you do not require the utility of hard copies which are easily exposed to hazardous conditions compared to the soft copies.

8. Utilizing the Packing Slip Template

These are the most important things that you should always take caution when using this kind of a commercial document.

You should add rows. This is the section where you are supposed to list all your items. Although at the bottom of it, you should include a reference space for listing the total number of the items.

You must include the date at the upper right and use the present tense. One can easily fill the date manually but he or she will not be able to alter the date.

You must leave a section for comments, on which clients or customers can leave their comments. Outside the printing position, one is required to list feedbacks which he or she uses on a regular basis in order for him or her to copy and write the suitable feedbacks in the section reserved for comments.

A sample of packing slip template (See Figure 10. 1) will assist people in transferring their goods from one point to another. One can easily visit various websites where he/she can easily download it either for free or for a given a price.

The importance of printing your own packing slip template:

- It enables one in gaining control.
- This enables you in formulating it in your own style.
- It allows one to complete plasticity.
- It also enables one to include a personal design which makes it unique.
- One can formulate quotes to be part of the document.
- This act helps individuals in saving time.
- You can easily print it and mail it on the same day.
- You do not have to keep on waiting or wait for approvals from anyone.
- You can easily update changes any time you wish.
- It also assists in saving money.
- Unmarked goods can be utilized for more than one e-mail all over the year.
- It is much easier to minimize wastes.
- It does not require any hidden prices.
- It also does not require any limitation on quantity or higher prices on smaller amounts.

• It is cost favorable by printing it in-house instead of using outsourcing.

Company Name			PACKING SLIP
Street Address		Date	
City, State, Zip Code		Invoice #	
Phone: (123) 456-7890		Customer ID	
Fax: (123) 456-7890			
Website: www.myaccountingcourse.com			

Bill To:	Ship To:
Customer Name	Customer Name
Street Address	Street Address
City, State, Zip Code	City, State, Zip Code
Phone	Phone

Order Date:	Order Number:	Invoice Number:	Contact:
12/31/16	2098	2.83943E+11	Steve

Item #	Description	QTY Ordered	QTY Shipped
12	Product #1	50	23
	Total:	50	23

Other Information:
Shipping and Return Information Here

Please let us know if you have any questions. We are here to help!
(Company Name and contact info here)
Thank you for your business!

Figure 10.1 Packing slip template

Part B Sample Letters

1. Packing Requirements

Sample 1

Dear Sir or Madam,

We enclose the countersigned copy of contract No. 350 of the 4th May 2019 for 350 bales of printed cottons. The letter of credit is on its way to you.

Please mark the bales with our initials, with the destination and contract number as follows:

KT
LONDON
250

This will apply to all shipments unless otherwise instructed.

Please advise us by fax as soon as shipment is effected.

Yours faithfully,

×××

Sample 2

Dear Sirs,

Thank you for your quotation of March 23 and the sample sweaters sent to us recently. We find both the price and quality satisfactory and herewith enclose our order form for 300 dozen each of men's and women's woolen sweaters at the prices stated in your quotation.

As this is our first order, we would like to state our detailed packing requirements. We want the sweaters to be packed each in a polybag, 6 dozen to a carton lined with waterproof paper. If the cartons are not strong enough, most of them will be liable to go broken on arrival. So we would require that the carton be bound with double iron straps outside.

We hope these packing requirements can be met and await your early shipment.

Yours faithfully,

×××

Sample 3

Dear Sirs,

Please pack the captioned machines in a strong wooden case and wrap and pad generously all polished parts of the machine to avoid scratches and knocks against the container.

Also please put the machine in a case of about 12 cubic meters covered with waterproof cloth and strapped vertically and horizontally with metal bands and cut ventholes in the case to minimize condensation.

Thank you for your sincere cooperation.

Yours faithfully,

×××

Sample 4

Dear Sirs,

We regret to inform you that the 145 cartons of iron nails you shipped to Dubai on May 12, 2019 were badly damaged, which is of course not your fault.

We are now writing to you about the packing of these nails, which we think necessary to clarify for our future dealings.

The packing for Dubai is to be in wooden cases of 112 lbs net, each containing 7 lbs 16 packets. For Malta, we would like to have the goods packed in double gunny bags of 50 to 60 kilos each. As for the British market, our buyers prefer 25 kilo cartons.

Would you please tell us whether these requirements could be met?

Your faithfully,

×××

2. Negotiation over Packing Marks

Dear Sirs,

Sales Confirmation NO. 89A/56

We thank you for your letter of October 12, 2020, enclosing the above Sales Contract in duplicate but wish to state that the packing clause in the contract is not clear enough. The relative clause should read:

Packing: Seaworthy export packing, suitable for long distance ocean transportation.

The shirts under the captioned contract should be packed in plastic bags, 5 dozen to one carton, 20 cartons on a pallet, and 10 pallets in FCL container. On the outer packing please mark our initials: JHCL in a triangle, under which the port of destination and our order number should be stenciled. In addition, directive marks like fat WATERPROOF, etc., should also be indicated.

We have made a footnote on the contract to that effect and are returning herein one copy of the contract, duly countersigned by us. We hope you will find it in order and pay special attention to the packing.

We look forward to receiving your shipping advice soon and thank you in advance.

Faithfully yours.

×××

3. Packing Seller Advising Packing and Shipping Marks

Dear Sirs,

We thank you for your letter dated June 5 inquiring about the packing and the shipping marks of the goods under Contract No. B321, and are pleased to state as follows:

All milk powders are wrapped in plastic bags and packed in tins, the lids of which are sealed with adhesive tape. Ten tins are packed in a wooden case, which is nailed, and secured by overall metal strapping.

As regards shipping marks outside the wooden case, in addition to gross, net and tare weights, the wording "Made in Australia" is also stenciled. Should you have any special preference in this respect, please let us know and we shall meet your requirements to the best of our ability.

We assure you of our close co-operation and await your further comments.

Yours faithfully,

×××

4. Negotiation on Carton Packing

Dear Sirs,

We are pleased to inform you that for your future orders we shall pack our garment in cartons instead of in wooden cases, as packing in cartons has the following advantages:

(1) It will prevent skillful pilferage, for the traces of pilferage will more in evidence.
(2) It is fairly fit for ocean transportation.
(3) Our cartons are well protected against moisture by plastic lining.
(4) Cartons are comparatively light and compact, so they are more convenient to handle.

Our comments about come from a comparative study of the characteristics of the two modes of packing, i. e. carton packing and wooden case packing, as well as the results of shipments already made.

We hope you will accept our carton packing and assure you of our sincere cooperation.

With best regards.

Yours faithfully,

×××

Reply to the above

Dear Sirs,

We have received your letter of August 13 with pleasure and immediately approached our clients about the packing. After our repeated explanation, they say they will have no objections to your packing of the garments in cartons if you guarantee that you will pay compensation in all cases wherein they cannot get indemnification from the insurance company for the reason that the cartons used are not seaworthy.

We deem it our duty to inform you of this and consider it a tacit understanding that you would hold yourselves responsible for the losses our clients might sustain on account of your using such cartons if the insurance company refuses compensations.

We think you will understand that our candid statements are made for our mutual benefits as packing is a sensitive subject, which often leads to trade disputes.

We appreciate your cooperation.

Yours faithfully,

×××

5. Packing and Shipping Marks Suggestion

Dear Sirs,

We thank you for your packing instruction, but regret our inability to comply with your request for special packing.

In order to finalize this initial trade activity between us, we would like to make the following suggestions for your consideration.

(1) The bed spreads will be packed 6 dozen to a packet, 4 packets to a carton and 8 cartons to a crate.
(2) Your initials will be printed in a diamond instead of the full name.
(3) The name of the country of origin of the goods will be marked on the carton and crate, not on every packet.
(4) Special directions and warnings will be stenciled on the crate, not on every carton.

Please inform us your comments by return fax.

Yours truly,

×××

6. Suggestion for Improvement of Packing

Dear Sir or Madam,

We regret to inform you that of the 160 cartons of machine parts delivered to us last week, 2 were found broken and some of the contents were badly damaged clearly through improper packing.

In view of our long-standing business relations, we would not lodge a claim against you for the loss this time. But we feel it necessary to stress the importance of seaworthy packing for our future dealings.

Usually valves and all delicate machine parts should be wrapped in soft material packed in cardboard boxes. These in turn are to be packed in wooden cases in such a manner that movement inside the cases is impossible. Besides, rope and metal handle should be fixed to the cases to facilitate consignment.

We look forward to your comments on the above.

Yours faithfully,

×××

Chapter 11 Shipping

Learning Objectives

a. Know different means and the procedure of shipping;

b. Master writing requirements of shipping.

Part A Introduction

In international trade, the exporter has various means of shipment, for instance, by ship, by truck, by train, or by airline, to ship consignment. The choice will be made according to the nature of product, the distance to be shipped, available means of transportation, time limit as well as freight cost.

One popular method of shipment is to use containers chartered from carriers. These containers vary in size, material and construction, and accommodate most cargoes, but they are best suited for standard package sizes and shapes. Also refrigerated and liquid bulk containers are usually readily available.

Usually there are three parties involved in most transportation of goods, the consignor, the carrier and the consignee. Shipment covers rather a wide range of work, such as:

a. Buyers sending shipment instructions;

b. Sellers sending shipping advice;

c. Booking shipping space;

d. Chartering ships;

e. Appointing shipping agent;

f. Arranging shipment;

g. Nomination of vessels, etc.

In case of an export business covering a large amount of goods, it is necessary to make shipment in several lots by several carriers sailing on different dates. When there are no or few ships sailing direct to the port of destination at the time or the amount of cargo for a certain port of destination is so small that no ships would like to call at the port, transshipment is necessary. Of course, partial shipment and transshipment should be allowed by the buyer in advance.

After the shipment is made, the seller should promptly advise the buyer of its effectiveness, no matter whether the transaction is concluded on FOB, CFR, or CIF basis. For FOB and CFR transactions, the buyer will have to effect insurance to shipment upon receipt of shipping advice from the seller. It has been a customary practice that in the case of FOB transactions, the seller, before shipping, should ask the buyer to name the vessel on which the goods are to be shipped unless otherwise specified in the contract of L/C.

Letters regarding shipment are usually written for the following purposes: to urge an early shipment, to amend shipping terms, to give shipping advice, to dispatch shipping documents and so on. Taking advantage of this occasion to advise the buyer of the shipment, the seller may also review the course of the transaction and express the desire for further development of business.

Part B Simple Letters

1. Urging Shipment

Sample 1

Dear Sirs,

We wish to call your attention that we have extended the L/C No. 6789 for some time, but up to now we have got no definite information from you about delivery time. It may have some reason for the delay.

It's impossible for us to extend the L/C No. 6789 again, which expires on July 5th and our customers are in urgent need of these goods.

As the long delay in delivery has caused us considerable inconvenience and loss. We ask you to deliver the goods in time, otherwise we shall cancel the orders in accordance with the stipulations of the contract.

Please make your best efforts to get the goods dispatched with the least possible delay for our long-established relationship.

Yours faithfully,

×××

Sample 2

Dear Mr. Smith,

Our Order No. TB－286

We are now very anxious to know about the shipment of our above order for 3 000 "Changhong" brand DVD players, which should be delivered before March 26 as contracted.

Now the shipment is approaching rapidly, but so far we have not received any information from you concerning this lot. When we placed the order we explicitly pointed out that punctual shipment was of special importance because our customers were in urgent need of the goods and we had given them a definite assurance of early delivery.

We hope you will make every effort to effect shipment within the stipulated time as any delay would cause us inconvenience.

Sincerely yours,

×××

Sample 3

Dear Sirs,

Our order No. 8236 covering 200 Electric Fans

As it is more than two weeks since we opened a letter of credit in your favor, we wish to draw your attention to its expiration date—27 February.

For the reason is approaching, our buyers are badly in need of the goods. We would like you to effect shipment as soon as possible, thus enabling them to catch the brisk season in business.

We would like to emphasize that any delay in shipment will undoubtedly involves us in trouble.

Please look into the matter and give us your definite reply without further delay.

Yours faithfully,

×××

2. A request to Advance Date of Shipment

Dear Sirs,

We refer to our order No. 358 for six tons of processed polyethylene due to be shipped at the end of next month. When this order was placed, our stocks were considered to be sufficiently high to last until December.

However, there has been such a demand for this type of polyethylene recently that we must now ask you to arrange for immediate shipment.

As soon as we receive the above consignment we shall be in a position to judge our requirements with greater accuracy and order accordingly.

Yours faithfully,

×××

3. Proposing Partial Shipment

Dear Mr. Smith,

We are pleased to receive your letter dated October 8th. As to the issuance of L/C, we assure you that you will receive the irrevocable L/C opened by Bank of China, Jiangsu Branch by the end of this month.

Regarding the delivery, as we urgently need the products to recommend to our clients, may we propose to advance the initial shipment for 50% of the total quantity from May/June to March/April and the remaining 50% to be shipped during May/June? We can accept the transshipment terms if it is necessary and bear the extra expenses incurred.

We thank you for your cooperation in advance and are looking forward to your favorable reply.

Yours sincerely,

Cheng Gang
Manager

4. Shipping Instruction

Dear Mr. Johnson,

We thank you for your Order No. 536 for the 3 machine tools, and we are glad to inform you that a letter of credit in your favor has been opened last week. We have booked shipping space on S. S. "Good Luck" which is due to sail from London to Dalian, Liaoning Province at the end of next month. Please get the goods ready for shipment at an early date and try your utmost to ship them by that vessel without delay.

We would like to let you know that the machines must be packed in special crates with reinforced bottom. Meanwhile, please see to it that the shipping marks indicated in our order and the gross and net weight are to be stenciled on each crate.

We believe that the above instructions are clear to you and the shipment will give our users good satisfaction.

Yours sincerely,

×××

5. Shipping Notification

Sample 1

Dear Sirs,

We are pleased to have received your L/C No. 9785, covering 2 000 dozen electric drills under our Sales Confirmation No. FC9891 and inform you that shipment was loaded on M. V. "Shunfeng" on August 6 for transshipment at Singapore.

Enclosed is a set of the duplicate shipping documents, which consists of:

(1) A non-negotiable copy of Bill of Lading;
(2) A signed Invoice No. 889;
(3) Packing List;
(4) Certificate of Origin No. 1001;
(5) Insurance Policy.

I would like to take this opportunity to assure you of our close cooperation.

Yours faithfully,

×××

Sample 2

Dear Sirs,

We are writing to inform you that mowing machines have been loaded on board M. V. "Dongfeng", which is scheduled to leave Montreal on May 24, and is due by the end of this month.

We enclose our invoice and shall present shipping documents and our draft for acceptance once through the Royal Bank, Shanghai Office, as agreed.

All items were individually examined before being packed and we trust they will reach you safely. We should be pleased if you would unpack and examine them as soon as possible after delivery, and in the event of any breakage, notify us at once.

Yours faithfully,

×××

Sample 3

Dear Mr. Goodman,

Order No. 975

We are pleased to advise you that the above order has been dispatched.

The electric drills are in fifty separate crates marked UMT IND MANILA and numbered 1 to 60.

The consignment is the M. V. "Mermaid", which left Shanghai on June 21 and is due in Manila on July 12.

We have presented to the Overseas Chinese Banking Corporation our draft for the amount of your L/C together with a full set of shipping documents consisting of Clean, Shipped on board Bills of Lading in triplicate, Certificate of Insurance, Certificate of Origin and our invoice in triplicate.

We hope that the drills will prove suitable for your customers' needs and look forward to receiving your next order.

Sincerely yours,

×××

Sample 4

Dear Sirs,

We are pleased to inform you that the following goods under our Contract No. BE1508 have now been shipped by S. S. "Feng Fan" sailing tomorrow from Guangzhou to Sydney.

Order No. C120 10 Bales Grey Cotton Cloth
Order No. C135 10 Bales White Cotton Cloth

Copies of the relative shipping documents are enclosed, thus you may find no trouble in taking delivery of the goods when they arrive.

We hope this shipment will reach you in time and turn out to your entire satisfaction.

Yours faithfully,

×××

6. **The Reply on Transshipment**

Sample 1

Dear Sirs,

Thank you for your letter of May 21, and we are pleased to provide you the following information for your reference.

(1) There are about 2 to 3 sailings weekly from Shanghai to Hong Kong.
(2) Arrangements have been made with the ABCA Line, which has one sailing approximately on the 11th every month from Hong Kong to West African ports, such as Lagos, Accra, etc. Shipping space is to be booked through their Shanghai Agents, who communicate with the line by fax. After receipt of the Line's reply accepting the booking, their Shanghai Agents will issue a through bill of lading. Therefore, with the exception of unusual condition, which may happen accidentally, the goods will be transshipped from Hong Kong without delay.
(3) In general the freight for transshipment from Hong Kong is higher than that from the UK or continental port, but ABCA Line agrees to the same freight, the detailed rates of which are shown on the 2 appendices to this letter.

If you want to have the goods transshipped at Hong Kong, your L/C must reach us well before the shipment month so as to enable us to book space with the Line's agents.

We assure you of our best attention at all times.

Yours faithfully,

×××

Sample 2

Dear Sirs,

We thank you for your L/C No. BC243 amounting to US $ 600 000. 00 issued in our favour through Citi Bank.

With regard to shipment, we regret very much to inform you that, despite strenuous efforts having been made by us, we are still unable to book space of a vessel sailing to Jakarta direct. The shipping companies ports told us that, for the time being, there is no regular boat sailing between ports in China and Jakarta. Therefore, it is very difficult, if not impossible, for us to ship these 6 000 metric tons of sugar to Jakarta direct.

In view of the difficult situation faced by us, you are requested to amend the L/C to allow transshipment of the goods in Hong Kong where arrangements can easily be made for transshipment. Please be assured that we will ship the goods to Hong Kong right upon receipt of the L/C amendment. Since this is something beyond our control, your agreement to our request and your understanding of our position will be highly appreciated.

We are anxiously awaiting the amendment to the L/C.

Yours faithfully,

×××

7. Delay Delivery Caused by Supplier

Dear Mr. Gates,

Your order No. 651

Because of unavoidable difficulties with our own suppliers, and with a defective machine, which has now been repaired but cause a disorder in production, we regret that we cannot keep the scheduled delivery date of 5 July.

We are writing to advise you with maximum advance notice that the delivery date is now revised to 7 July. We have taken strenuous measures after considerable difficulties, to maintain delivery to you after minimal delay.

Yours faithfully,

×××

Chapter 12 Insurance

Learning Objectives

a. Know the importance and benefits of insurance;

b. Master writing requirements of insurance.

Part A Introduction

Insurance is very closely related to foreign trade. In international trade, the transportation of goods from the seller to the buyer is generally over a long distance by air, by land or by sea and has to go through the procedures of loading, unloading and storing. During this process it is quite possible that the goods will encounter various kinds of perils and sometimes suffer losses. In order to protect the goods against possible losses in case of such perils, the buyer or the seller before the transportation of the goods usually applies to an insurance company for insurance covering the goods in transit.

The purpose of insurance is to provide compensation for those who suffer from loss or damage; in other words, it is a contract of indemnity, a contract to restore to someone, either the full amount of the loss that may be incurred, or a specified percentage of the amount of the loss.

A contract of insurance, which is generally made in the form of an insurance policy, is one between a party who agrees to accept the risk (the insurer) and a party seeking protection from the risk (the insured). In return for payment of a premium, the insurer agrees to pay the insured a stated sum (or a proportion of it) should the event insured against occur. The premium, being the name given to the sum of money paid by the insured, is quoted at percentage of the sum insured.

There are mainly two types of insurance coverage, basic coverage and additional coverage. Basic coverage mainly includes FPA (Free from Particular Average), WPA (With Particular Average) and All Risks. Additional coverage includes general additional coverage and special additional coverage. General additional coverage includes coverage of such risks as Theft, Pilferage & Non-Delivery Risks (TPND), Fresh and/or Rain Water Damage Risks, Shortage Risk, Contamination Risks, Leakage Risk, Clash & Breakage Risks, Taint of Odor Risk, Sweating & Heating Risks, Hook Damage Risk, Rust Risk, Breakage of Packing Risk. Special additional coverage covers the risks of War Risk, Strikes Risk, Failure to Delivery Risk, Import Duty Risk, On Deck Risk, Rejection Risk. etc., among which War Risk and Strike Risk are more common.

An insurance claim, if any, should be submitted to the insurance company or its agent as promptly as possible. In order to substantiate an ordinary average claim on cargo, the following documents must be presented: insurance policy or certificate, B/L, original invoice, survey report, master's protest and statement of claim. When you write a letter of covering insurance, see to it that you should write down clearly the following information: subject matter, duration of coverage, insurance amount and premium, scope of cover, etc. Import and export cargo are subject to damage or loss incurred by a variety of risk in the course of transit, loading and unloading, storage, etc. They must be insured against these risks according to the mode transport used, the nature of the goods and the contract stipulations, so that they can be compensated in time after the damage or loss.

Sales and purchase contracts generally have the stipulation as to who (the buyer or the seller) should cover insurance and bear the expenses. If the goods are sold on FOB/CFR terms, insurance shall be arranged by the buyer and the premium for his account. Provided the goods are sold on CIF terms, the seller is under obligation to take out insurance and bear the expenses.

For CIF transactions, we usually effect insurance for 110% of the invoice value against ... (risks) as per Ocean Marine Cargo Clauses of the PICC. That is to say, 100% is for CIF invoice value and 10% is to cover a reasonable profit and some expenses. Sometimes, buyers may request insurance to cover more than 110%. In such cases, the extra premium will be for buyer's account.

Insurance was originally applied to losses at sea, where risks were always great. Now it has become a vast subject, entering into almost every activity of human beings.

Part B Reasons Why Insurance Policies are Important in the Workplace

Insurance has proven to be useful as a shield in all the uncertainties that could happen in business. Insurance policies will help you effectively and keep you secure in whatever form of loss you and your business will face and will mitigate, reduce, or eliminate the risk of having your business go down to zero. Here are some reasons why insurance policies are helpful in business.

1. Protection and Security, and Reduction of Business Losses

Insurance is a shield that protects and secures business from any possible risks. For example, one of the branches of a popular fast food chain has turned into ashes due to a big fire. Even though millions have been lost, the business owners would be unable to feel the great impact of the loss of one of their branches because they have an insurance that will compensate from the actual loss the fire caused. Imagine if the business owners did not have an insurance, a lot of companies will be affected, particularly the best asset every business has—their employees.

Without an insurance, you would not be able to have a new construction or even put up a new branch of your business. If your business does not offer insurance to the employees, no one would like to apply for a job since one of the things that people look into when looking for a job is the insurance they will receive upon employment or regularization.

Business owners must always try to expect all the possible things that could happen for the business as well as what could happen with the people in the business and one of the things they could do is not only to have an insurance but as well as insurance policies to manage it.

2. Business Becomes Productive and Effective

If you and your business are secured with an insurance, you will become productive since you would not anymore exert useless effort in worrying about what could happen for you and your business since you already have an insurance that will back you and your business up. with the appropriate insurance, you and your employees tend to work well without worries, hence, you become productive and effective and that also includes your business and all your undertakings.

3. Business Continuation

With an insurance, plus an insurance policy to go with that, you will have funds that assist you when your partner leaves. With the help of an insurance, you and the business you two put up together is protected and will be able to continue whatever disastrous events that might bring you business to waste or more loss.

4. Employee's Security and Welfare

You have to keep in mind that that best asset you have in your company is your employees and that is why you must, at all costs, protect and keep their security and welfare. That is not only your responsibility; that is what you are really ought to do. Do not repay their service to you and your business with a lousy insurance. Always have an insurance policy to back your employees' insurance in order for them to feel secure and safe working for you.

There are some employees' who have known how uncertain life could be due to all the extreme hardships they have faced. That is why with the presence of an insurance as well as an insurance policy to go with it, the employees will become productive as well. This would also create harmony between the employers and the employees.

Part C Benefits of Insurance Policies

Here are some of the benefits that insurance policies bring to you and your employees.

A. When your business would face losses, particularly on the finances, if you have an insurance, you will be able to compensate for your losses. Your employees will benefit from it, too.

B. Having insurance policies is in compliance with the law. You will not be able to put up your business or meet statutory and contractual requirements without an insurance.

C. Insurance policies mitigate risk and put risks at bay. Anything could happen that is why, with the help of your insurance policies, you would still be able to lessen the impact. Insurance policies can help in implementing an effective loss control program that will aid you and your employees in case something bad will actually happen in the business.

D. Insurance secures your resources, and the common resource we know is financial. With an effective insurance policy, you will not only be able to secure your finances but you can also use it efficiently.

E. Insurance and insurance policies are actually a form of investment. An investment is defined as an asset or item that is purchased that is expected to be of use in the future.

F. Insurances decrease any kinds of the financial burden. Anything could happen to us, and that includes accidents. If you have a secured insurance, even if it does not help in paying your entire bills in full, it would at least reduce your burden.

G. Insurances are seen, particularly by employees, as benefits. This would increase your employment opportunities since prospect employees would choose your company over a company that has no insurance policies since its absence would make them question the stability of your business.

Part D Sample Letters of Insurance

1. Inquiring about Insurance Rate

Dear Sirs,

We will be sending a consignment of 1 000 refrigerators to Fortune Trading Company, Ltd., Pusan, the Republic of Korea. The consignment is to be loaded on to the S. S. "Prince" which sails from Xiamen on December 18 and is due in Pusan on December 23.

Details with regard to packing and values are attached, and we would be grateful if you could quote a rate covering all risks from port to port.

As the matter is urgent, we would appreciate a prompt reply. Thank you.

Yours truly,

Zhang Bing
Export Manager

Attachment:

Reply to the above

Dear Mr. Zhang,

Thank you for your fax of 8 December, in which you inquired about cover for a shipment of refrigerators from Xiamen to Pushan.

I have noted from the details attached to your letter that the net amount of the invoice is US$ 9 000 and payment is by letter of credit. I would therefore suggest a valued policy against all risks for which we can quote 0.005 8.

We will issue a cover note as soon as you complete and return the enclosed declaration form.

Yours sincerely,

×××

2. Importer Asks Exporter to Cover Insurance

Dear Sir or Madam,

Re: Our order No. 245. Your S/C No. 867

We wish to refer you to our Order No. 245 for 1 500 cases of electric drills, from which you will see that this order was placed on CFR basis.

As we now desire to have the consignment insured at your end, we shall appreciate it if you will arrange to insure the same on behalf of us against All Risks at invoice value plus 10%, i. e. US$ 8 700.

We shall of course refund the premium to you upon receipt of your debit note or, if you like, you may draw on us at sight for the amount required.

We sincerely hope that our request will meet with your approval.

Yours faithfully,

×××

Reply to the above

Dear Sirs,

Re: Your order No. 245. Your S/C No. 867

Thank you for your letter requesting us to effect insurance on the captioned shipment for your account.

We would like to inform you that we have covered the above shipment against All Risks for US$ 8 700 with the People's Insurance Company of China, which is a state-run enterprise enjoying high prestige in settling claims promptly and equitably. The policy is being processed and we will forward to you by the end of the week together with our debit note for the premium.

We are now making arrangements to ship your ordered consignment from Shanghai to New York, by S. S. "Dasun", sailing on or about the 15th of July.

Yours faithfully,

×××

3. Asking for Improvement of Insurance

Dear Sir or Madam,

Thank you for making your rates available to us immediately. We have obtained quotations from various insurance companies and found your quotation most competitive. After consideration, we think that the premium rate you quoted to us does not meet our expectations. Therefore, we are able to sign a general policy with your company this time. Please insure us against All Risks at the rate of 0.005% for the sum of US$15 000 value of 1 200 sets of Changhong Color TV shipped at Qindao, on board S. S. "Princess", sailing for New York on July 15. Please send us the policy, together with a note for the charges.

We would be thankful if you could handle this business quickly.

Yours faithfully,

×××

4. Asking for Additional Insurance

Dear Sirs,

We have inadvertently written in our Order Confirmation No. OR231 "WPA & War Risk Insurance to be effected by seller", whereas we should have asked for broader coverage.

Please hereafter take out cover on all our purchases of leathers against TPND, Contamination, Fresh and/or Ram Water Damage in addition to WPA.

We enclose an Amendment to Order Confirmation, which is to supersede the one previously sent.

Yours faithfully,

×××

5. Asking for the Information about Special Rate of Insurance

Dear Sirs,

We write this letter to you in the hope of getting some information about special rate of insurance. Regularly we arrange consignment of chinaware to London by both passenger and cargo liners of the International Shipping line. Would you please tell us whether you can cover All Risks for the consignments and, if so, on what terms?

Particularly, we wish to know whether you can issue a special rate for the promise of regular monthly shipments.

We are awaiting your early reply.

Yours faithfully,

×××

6. Requiring the Change of Insurance Clause

Dear Sir or Madam,

We thank you for your L/C No. 168 covering glazed wall tiles. Please note that we do not cover breakage. Therefore, we hope you will delete the word "breakage" from the insurance clause in the credit. Furthermore, we have to inform you that for such articles as window glass, porcelains, etc., even if additional Risk of Breakage has been insured, the insurance is subject to a franchise of 5%. In other words, if the breakage is surveyed to be less than 5%, no claims for damage will be entertained.

We believe we have now made our position clear. Please fax the amendment immediately.

Yours faithfully,

×××

Chapter 13 Complaints and Claims

Learning Objectives

a. Know writing principles and basic information of complaints and claims;

b. Master writing requirements of complaints and claims.

Part A Introduction

In business activities, no matter how perfect an organization may be, complaints from the customers are certain to arise. Generally speaking, complaints may be of several kinds, and may arise from the delivery of wrong goods, damaged goods, or too many or too few goods or quality may have been found unsatisfactory, and etc.

If a complaint or claim has to be made by the buyer, the matter should be investigated in detail and these details should be laid before the party charged.

People must handle complaints or claims in accordance with the principle of "on the first grounds, to their advantage and with restraint" and settle them amicably to the satisfaction of all parties concerned. Usually a complaint or claim letter should follow the following principles.

a. Begin by regretting the need to complain.

b. Mention the date of the order, the date of delivery and the goods complained about.

c. State the reasons for being dissatisfied and ask for an explanation.

d. Refer to the inconvenience caused.

e. Suggest how the matter should be put right.

f. Be careful in choosing the wording in the correspondence so as to avoid any misunderstandings.

Sometimes, a reference to the previously satisfactory deliveries and services may help to win more sympathetic consideration of the present complaint or claim.

Having been given a complaint or claim letter by the buyer, the seller should deal with the matter according to the following rules without delay.

a. The first thing that has to be decided is whether the complaint is justified.

b. If so, then the seller has to admit it readily, express his/her regret and promise to make the matter right.

c. If the complaint is not justified, point out politely and in an agreeable manner. It would be a wrong policy to refuse the claim offhand.

d. If the seller cannot deal with a complaint promptly, acknowledge it at once. Explain that he/she is looking into it and that he/she will send a full reply later.

e. All complaints should be treated as serious matters and thoroughly investigated.

Letters concerning disputes should be written tactfully and reasonably. They must be confined to a statement of facts and insist on the absolute truth.

Part B How to Write a Complaint Letter

Writing a complaint letter or a claim letter may seem like a simple task, but it is not.

In many cases, the tone, the words, the forms people use when writing the letter, will condition its result.

Here are some tips on how to write a complaint letter.

A. Never write the complaint or claim being angry and irritated, because you will only succeed in negatively altering the recipient. Insulting is not a smart way to achieve something. Take your time, think carefully about what you will say when you write your complaint letter, study what are the points you have in your claim, and then try to also think about what things could play against you when making your complaint.

B. Be clear on what you want to communicate in your complaint or claim letter. If you are not very good at writing, ask someone else to read your letter to see if they understand what you want to convey.

C. Watch your spelling and grammar. If you submit a letter of complaint or claim with faults, nobody will take you seriously.

D. Convey confidence in your letter. Don't say you think you're right. Prove it! It requires that you be compensated for the damage to the service or product you purchased.

E. Find out which consumer protection associations protect your claim. Know well before writing the letter of complaint or claim, because—and always remember—the information is power.

Effective complaint letters explain the problem and how you'd like the company to resolve it. Try to be clear and include only the details you need to describe the problem and the resolution you want.

1. Information To Include in Your Letter

Avoid writing an angry, sarcastic, or threatening letter. The person reading it probably didn't cause the problem, but may be very helpful in resolving it.

1) Give the basics.

a. Include your name, address, and phone number.

b. Include your account number, if you have an account with the company.

c. Give the product name and its serial or model number.

d. State the date and place of purchase.

2) Tell your story.

a. Explain the problem.

b. Give a brief history of your efforts to resolve the problem, if the information helps explain why you're writing to the company.

3) Tell the company how you want to resolve the problem.

a. State the solution you want, like a refund, repair, exchange, or store credit. Or, consider asking the company to suggest a resolution.

b. List the documents you're enclosing, if any. Remember—only send copies, not originals.

c. Let them know how to reach you.

4) Be reasonable.

a. Say how long you'll wait for a response. Allow time for the company to take action.

b. Tell them what you plan to do next: for example, report it to the Better Business Bureau or your state attorney general or consumer protection office.

5) File your complaint.

a. Send your letter by certified mail, return receipt requested. Keep a copy for yourself.

b. If you file your complaint online, print the screen or take a screenshot before you hit "submit".

2. Examples

Study the examples to write a complaint about a product or service.

Example 1

Your Address

Your City, State, Zip Code

[Your email address, if sending by email]

Date

Name of Contact Person [if available] Title [if available] Company Name

Consumer Complaint Division [if you have no specific contact] Street Address
City, State, ZIP Code

Dear [Contact Person or Consumer Complaint Division],

Re: [Your account number, if you have one]

On [date], I [bought, leased, rented, or had repaired/serviced] a [name of the product, with serial or model number or service performed] at [location and other important details of the transaction].

Unfortunately, [your product has not performed well (or) the service was inadequate] because [state the problem, like the product doesn't work properly, the service wasn't performed correctly, I was billed the wrong amount, or something was not disclosed clearly or was misrepresented, etc.].

To resolve the problem, I would appreciate a [state the action you want, like a refund, store credit, repair, exchange, etc.]. Enclosed are copies [do not send originals] of my records [include receipts, guarantees, warranties, canceled checks, contracts, model and serial numbers, and any other documents] concerning this purchase [or repair].

I look forward to your reply and a resolution to my problem. I will wait until [set a reasonable time limit] before seeking help from a consumer protection agency or other assistance. Please contact me at the above address or by phone at [phone number with area code].

Sincerely yours,

Your name

Enclosure(s)

Example 2

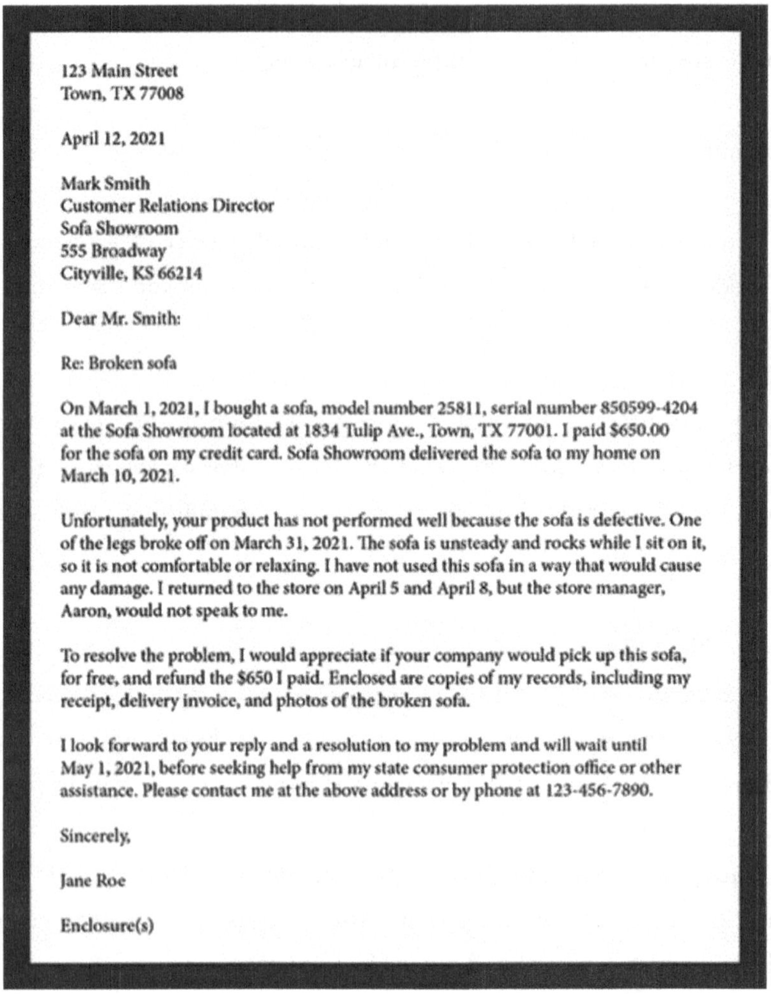

123 Main Street
Town, TX 77008

April 12, 2021

Mark Smith
Customer Relations Director
Sofa Showroom
555 Broadway
Cityville, KS 66214

Dear Mr. Smith:

Re: Broken sofa

On March 1, 2021, I bought a sofa, model number 25811, serial number 850599-4204 at the Sofa Showroom located at 1834 Tulip Ave., Town, TX 77001. I paid $650.00 for the sofa on my credit card. Sofa Showroom delivered the sofa to my home on March 10, 2021.

Unfortunately, your product has not performed well because the sofa is defective. One of the legs broke off on March 31, 2021. The sofa is unsteady and rocks while I sit on it, so it is not comfortable or relaxing. I have not used this sofa in a way that would cause any damage. I returned to the store on April 5 and April 8, but the store manager, Aaron, would not speak to me.

To resolve the problem, I would appreciate if your company would pick up this sofa, for free, and refund the $650 I paid. Enclosed are copies of my records, including my receipt, delivery invoice, and photos of the broken sofa.

I look forward to your reply and a resolution to my problem and will wait until May 1, 2021, before seeking help from my state consumer protection office or other assistance. Please contact me at the above address or by phone at 123-456-7890.

Sincerely,

Jane Roe

Enclosure(s)

Figure 13.1 A complaining letter

3. Report Fraud or Deception

If you think a company or seller has been dishonest, contact your state attorney general or consumer protection office. Tell the Federal Trade Commission (FTC) too, at ReportFraud.ftc.gov. The FTC doesn't resolve individual complaints, but your report helps law enforcement detect patterns of wrongdoing and may lead to an investigation.

Part C Sample Letters of Complaints and Claims

1. Complaint about Low Quality

Dear Sirs,

The green beans under S/C No. ED034 dispatched on May 4th, 2019 arrived at our port last week. The Commodity Inspection Bureau has carefully examined the quality of the beans, and we regret to say that they found it is far below the standard stipulated in the S/C and the covering Inspection Certificate is going to be airmailed to you as soon as it comes to hand.

We think you will look into the matter at once and take immediate measures to correct the mistakes and ensure that nothing like this will happen in the future.

The inferior quality of these beans causes us considerable difficulty and it is hard for us to dispose it, even at a rather low price. We think we can reserve the right to lodge a claim against you for the loss we have suffered.

Yours faithfully,

×××

Reply to the above

Dear Sirs,

We are sorry to learn from your letter of May 28th , 2019 that the green beans dispatched on May 4th 2019 were below the standard stipulated in the contract and that you are reserving the right to lodge a claim against us.

Naturally we hope that the transaction will be concluded to your satisfaction. Now that you have found the quality of the beans do not comply with that stipulated in the contract, we want to have the problem clarified without any delay. So we have sent our representative to investigate the matter in detail. We would not give any comments before our representative inspects the goods. We will soon let you know the date of his visit and hope you will give him your best cooperation.

You may be assured that the matter will be settled in a reasonable manner to our mutual benefits.

Yours faithfully,

×××

Further Reply by the Exporter

Dear Sir or Madam,

We have got the news from our representative that through his careful study he has found deterioration of a very small part of the green beans delivered on May 4th, 2019, under the S/C No. ED034. First please accept our sincere apologies for the inconvenience caused to you.

Nevertheless, as you may be aware such deterioration can hardly be avoided during the long period of transportation and storage, we hope that you will not take this case as a breach of the contract and refrain from making any claims against us as the loss can be negligible, and you know well, in fact, we have delivered more quantities than that stipulated.

Please be assured that in our future business, we will take great measures to ensure nothing like this to happen again.

Yours faithfully,

×××

2. Complaining about Delay in Shipment

Dear Sirs,

We enclose herewith the figures of sales in your product during the past six months, from which you will see that our sales of the special line are quite disappointing.

Because the end-users here are in urgent need of the goods, we requested your prompt shipment of them, which you had accepted. However, five weeks went by before the goods arrived instead of three weeks, and we lost a wonderful opportunity of sales.

On inquiry we found that the goods were not shipped until four weeks after the date of dispatch. We have been put to considerable inconvenience through long delay and have to ask you to make us allowance corresponding to our loss.

Yours faithfully,

×××

3. Apologizing for the Delay in Shipment

Dear Sirs,

We have received your letter complaining our delay of shipment, and we are very sorry that we have not been able to deliver your order on time. The delay was caused by the late arrival of some of the raw materials.

It is due to the events that are entirely beyond our control. We are pleased, however, that your order will be ready for shipment next week, and we hope that they will arrive in time for the season. Please accept our apologies to you for the delay and the inconvenience it has caused you.

Yours faithfully,

×××

4. Complaining about Poor Packing

Dear Sirs,

We regret to inform you that the cotton goods covered by our Order No. 8632 and shipped per S. S. "Peace" arrived in such an unsatisfactory condition that we cannot but lodge a complaint against you. It was found, upon examination, that nearly 20% of the packages had been broken, obviously attributed to improper packing. Our only recourse, in consequence, was to have them repacked before delivering to our customers, which inevitably resulted in extra expenses amounting to U. S. $ 860.

We expect compensation from you for this, and should like to take this opportunity to suggest that special care be taken in your future deliveries as prospective customers are apt to misjudge the quality of your goods by the faulty packing.

Yours faithfully,

×××

5. Claim for Damages

Dear Sirs,

The captioned goods you shipped per S. S. "Changhong" on May 14 arrived here yesterday. On examination, we have found that many of the electric heaters are severely damaged, though the cases themselves show no trace of damage.

Considering this damage was due to the rough handling by the shipping company, we claim on them for recovery of loss; but an investigation made by the surveyor has revealed the fact that the damage is attributable to improper packing. For further particulars, we refer you to the surveyor's report enclosed.

We are therefore, compelled to claim on you to compensate us for the loss, US $ 20 000, which we have sustained by the damage to the goods.

We trust that you will be kind enough to accept this claim and deduct the sum claimed from the amount of your next invoice to us.

Yours faithfully,

×××

Reply to the above

Dear Sirs,

We have received your letter of 5th July, informing us that the electric heaters we shipped to you arrived damaged on account of improper packing on our part.

On receiving your letter, we have given this matter our immediate attention. We have studied your surveyor's report very carefully.

We are convinced that the present damage was due to extraordinary circumstances under which they were transported to you. We are therefore not responsible for the damage; but as we do not think that it would be fair to have you bear the loss alone, we suggest that the loss be divided between both of us, to which we hope you will agree.

Faithfully yours,

×××

6. A Reply to the Claim

Dear Mr. Cooke,

Policy No. EIL 3258

I have now received our assessor's report with reference to your claim CR8653 in which you asked for compensation for damage to two marble polishers, which were shipped ex-Qingdao on the S. S. "Taishan" on May 5, for delivery to your customer, Hitek Industries, Bangkok.

The report states that the B/L, No. 5326, was claused by the captain of the vessel, with a comment on cracks in the cashing of the machinery.

Our assessor believes that these cracks were responsible for the casing weakening during the voyage and splitting, which eventually caused damage to the polishers themselves.

I am sorry that we cannot help you further, but the company cannot accept liability for goods unless they are shipped clean. See clause 13C of the Policy.

Yours sincerely,

×××

7. Complaints and Reply

Sample 1

Dear sirs,

We regret to complain about the late delivery of canned mushroom ordered on July 8. Although you guarantee a delivery in the middle of September, we haven't received the goods until this week. We placed the order on the basis of your assurance.

Unfortunately, late delivery has occurred several times recently, and we have no choice but to make it clear that business will be canceled in this case.

We feel it necessary to clarify that if the supplier can not deliver the goods on time, we are unable to explain to our customers.

We hope you can understand our situation and assure us of prompt shipment from now on.

Yours faithfully,

×××

Sample 2

Dear sirs,

We are sorry to learn from your letter of the 10th May that 100 pairs of leather shoes supplied under the above order are damaged when they reached you. We would certainly replaced them and have in fact already done so. Replacement have been sent by parcel this morning.

Despite the care we took in packing shoes sent by post, there have been recently several reports of damage. To avoid further inconvenience to customers and expenses to ourselves, we are now seeking advice of a packaging consultant and hope we will be able to make improvements.

We regret the need for you to write to us and hope the steps we are taking will ensure the safe arrival of all your orders in the future.

Faithfully yours,

×××

Sample 3

Dear Sirs,

RE:CLAIM FOR SHORT WEIGHT

1 500 cartons of canned mushroom under the contract No. FA1770854 have been shipped to Antwerp by "YONGFENG" steamer on 10th September. When taking the delivery, 145 cartons have been found missing. We were told by the shipping company that only 1 355 cartons had been shipped on the steamer.

Because the weight is short in large quantities, please make up a deficiency of 145 cartons of the missing goods when you deliver the last three items. You are kindly requested to check whether these 1 500 cartons of mushroom were loaded on ship in whole at the port of shipment.

Please reply by cable.

Yours truly,

×××

Sample 4

Dear Sirs,

CONTRACT NO. 23HBSF/1008CN

Thanks for your fax dated April 26, 2004. We are terribly sorry our last shipment arrived badly damaged.

The T-shirts under the above contract are packed as per your requirements. Under normal condition this should have been enough protected. As you mentioned on your fax undoubtedly the damage of the goods results from rough handing.

We are grateful to you for pointing this out. We will take precautions to avoid such a thing from occurring again.

We realize the need to reduce your selling price for the damaged T-shirts and readily agree to the special allowance of 10% which you suggested.

Yours faithfully,

×××

Sample 5

American Zhong Nong Trading Co. Ltd.
PO Box 58090 Santa Clara, California, USA 95052 - 8090

July 6, 2020

China Zhenyuan Trade Co, Ltd
No. 13 Zhen'an Road, Guangzhou,
Guangdong, China.

Dear Mr. ××,

We have duly received the shipment of our 1 200 tins of Longjing Green Tea ordered at CNY 38/tin FOB New York but regret to find them in unsatisfactory condition. We cannot but lodge a claim against you.

After carefully examining, it was found that nearly 50 tins are completely wet, obviously attributed to improper packing. We stressed in our last letter the importance of packaging strictly according to your Export Standard. But we found some of them are not packed in water-proof materials before put in the tin with a result that the materials become inferior in quality.

We expect compensation from you for this and should like to take this opportunity to suggest that special care be taken in your future deliveries.

Yours faithfully,

American Zhong Nong Trading Co. Ltd.
Touis Tomas
Manager

Sample 6

Dear Sirs,

We have received your fax dated May 11 filling a claim against us for the damage of the captioned goods.

We regret for the loss you have suffered. The S. S. "SUNSHINE" encountered heavy weather incessantly with torrential rains on the voyage from Shanghai to Surabaya. The log showed that the hold ventilators had to be closed for some time to guard against ingress of fresh water into the hold. It is precisely because of this protective measure that sweat formed in the hold resulted in the garlic's sprouting.

This is an event beyond our control and on the strength of the provision of the B. L we cannot hold ourselves responsible for the loss. We propose you approach the shipping company or the insurance company for compensation.

We hope this unpleasant case will not cast a shadow on our future business.

Your faithfully,

×××

Sample 7

Dear Sirs,

Thank you for your letter of 20 May.

We agree with you that our shoes should last longer than one month. If they do not, we like to know the reason why.

We have carefully examined the pair you returned to us. Our production manager reports that the shoes have been thoroughly soaked and then dried by heat. Even the best quality shoes will not withstand this treatment.

For this reason, we regret that we cannot agree to your request for a replacement pair.

Yours faithfully,

×××

Chapter 14 Agreements and Contracts

Learning Objectives

a. Know different forms of agreements and contracts;

b. Master writing requirements of agreements and contracts.

Part A Introduction

A contract is an agreement having a lawful object entered into voluntarily by two or more parties, each of whom intends to create one or more legal obligations between them. The elements of a contract are "offer" and "acceptance" by "competent persons" having legal capacity who exchanges "consideration" to create "mutuality of obligation".

Proof of some or all of these elements may be done in writing, though contracts may be made entirely orally or by conduct. The remedy for breach of contract can be "damages" in the form of compensation of money or specific performance enforced through an injunction. Both of these remedies award the party at loss the "benefit of the bargain" or expectation, which are greater than mere reliance damages, as in promissory estoppel. The parties may be natural persons or juristic persons. A contract is a legally enforceable promise or undertaking that something will or will not occur. The word promise can be used as a legal synonym for contract, although care is required as a promise may not have the full standing of a contract, as when it is an agreement without consideration.

Contract law varies greatly from one jurisdiction to another, including differences in common law compared to civil law, the impact of received law, particularly from England in common law countries, and of law codified in regional legislation.

A contract is founded on agreement, and agreement arises from offer and acceptance. One person makes an offer, another person accepts that offer. When that has happened, there is a contract.

1. The Form of a Contract or an Agreement

Contracts or agreements don't have unified or fixed forms. In practice, complete and valid contracts or agreements usually consist of three parts: head, body and end.

(1) Head

The head covers the following contents:

a. The title of the contract or agreement, e. g. Purchase Contract, Agency Agreement, Exclusive Sales Agreement, Contract for Export of Labor Service, etc. The title indicates the character of the contract or agreement.

b. The number of the contract or agreement.

c. The date and the place of signing the contract or agreement (some contracts or agreements put the date and the place in the End)

In the preface of the contract or agreement, there are the parties' names, state clearly the Sellers and the Buyers or Party A and Party B, explain the principles and the purposes of signing the contract or agreement, e. g. ×× Company, ×× Country (hereinafter called Party A) and ×× Company, PRC (hereinafter called Party B) through friendly negotiation reached the following agreement on the basis of equality and mutual benefit.

(2) Body

The body is the most important part in the contract or agreement. You may use the style of stipulations or the style of forms or you may combine the two styles together to state clearly the contents negotiated by the parties concerned.

For instance, the stipulations in an Import or Export Contract are the name and the specification of the commodity, quantity, unit price and total value, package, the time of shipment, the port of shipment, the port of destination, payment, insurance, inspection, claim and arbitration, etc.

The contents of other contracts or agreements (e. g. Agency Agreement, Joint Venture Contract, Investment Agreement, the Contract for Export of Labor Service, the Agreement for Technology Transfer) are complicated. The terms and conditions are different. But they have certain forms and formulas. When you write them you can consult example versions.

(3) End

The contents in this part are usually the following: the copies and the conserves of the contract or agreement, the language(s) used, the full names of the parties, and the seals affixed by the parties, etc. If the contract or agreement is companied by some enclosure(s), you should state clearly the name(s) of the enclosure(s) as well as the number of the copies as the integral parts of the contract.

2. The requirement of writing a contract or an agreement

1) The contents of contracts or agreements should conform to the principle of equality and mutual benefit and through common negotiations.

The versions of the contract or agreement are legal documents. The parties concerned are equal in legal status. Neither party has privilege to force the other party to accept its own will(s), so both parties should respect the other side's interests. The stipulations should be discussed by the parties concerned and reach an agreement.

2) The stipulations of contracts or agreements should be complete, concrete, definite and without careless omissions, in order to avoid unnecessary economic losses.

For example, in an Import and Export Contract, the stipulation of shipping marks seems to be an unimportant term, but if it is indefinitely and unclearly stated, that would cause trouble when deliver the goods.

Another example, the arbitration clause is the most important term in all the contracts. Though it is not used in the execution of every contract, but if you neglect it, it will be a great problem when a dispute occurs and no agreement can be reached. Such things happened to some companies in the past. When disputes occurred the foreign party directly sued to a court of their own country that thrown the other party into passivity—if the other party responded to the action, the foreign laws might not be beneficial to the other party; if the other party did not response, the foreign court would make a judgment by default.

3) Using words and expressions accurately, arrange the contents properly, logically and without mistakes.

The words and expressions used in the contract should not be ambiguous and no different meanings. For example, for the term of package you should state clearly and definitely the packing materials and methods, i. e. pack in cartons, wooden cases, casks, gunny bags, etc. and mark clearly the volume, weight (net weight and gross weight) and quantity, avoid using "seaworthy packing" or "packing as usual", for these expressions are too ambiguous. The expression of "Ship the goods in two lots. " is not complete and unclear, you'd better add "50% for each lot", or "60% for the first lot and the rest for the second" to the clause. These expressions are rigorous.

A contract or an agreement set forth bonding obligations of the parties concerned. Once entered into, a contract or an agreement is enforceable by law. Neither of the parties has the right to amend or cancel it as their pleases. If some terms should be amended or supplemented, or if a contract (an agreement) should be ended for some special reason, the parties need to consult and agree upon the matter first. Then they should sign an agreement for the amendment or cancellation. Any party who fails to fulfill its contract obligations (except caused by force majeure) should bear the economic losses of the other party (or parties).

Part B Samples of Agreements and Contracts

Sample 1

Sole Agency Agreement

This Sole Agency Agreement is entered into through friendly negotiations between China National ××× Import and Export Corporation, Xi'an, China (hereinafter called Party A), and ××× Company, New York, U. S. A(hereinafter called Party B) on the basis of equality and mutual benefit to develop business on the terms and conditions set forth below:

(1) Party A agrees to appoint Party B to act as its Sole Agents in the territory of North America for the sale of Type MD－4×××Brand Medical Device.

(2) Price: Party B is under obligation to push sales energetically at the price quoted by Party A. Each transaction is subject to Party A's final confirmation.

(3) Quantity: During the under-mentioned period, Party B shall place orders with Party A for not less than 6 000 sets of Type MD－4×× Brand Medical Device. Party B shall order at least 3 000 sets in the first six months from the date of signing this agreement. Should Party B fail to fulfill the above mentioned quantity (namely 3 000 sets) in this duration, Party A shall have the right to sell the goods under this agreement to other customers in North America.

In case Party B places orders for less than 1 000 sets in three months from the date on which the agreement is signed, Party A shall have the right to terminate this agreement by giving notice in writing to Party B.

(4) Payment: Payment is to be made by confirmed, irrevocable letter of credit, without recourse, available by sight draft upon presentation of shipping documents. The letter of credit for each order shall reach Party A 30 days before (prior to) the date of shipment. Should Party B fail to establish the letter of credit in time, any loss or losses including bank interest, storage, etc. , which Party A may sustain shall be borne by Party B.

(5) Commission: Party A agrees to pay Party B a commission of 5%(five percent) on FOB value of orders. The commission is to be paid only after full payment for each order is received by Party A. As slated in Article(3) of this agreement, no commission shall be paid on orders secured and executed by Party A itself.

(6) Reports on market conditions: Party B shall have the obligation to forward once every three months to Party A detailed reports on current market conditions and on consumers' comments For Party A's reference. Party B shall, from time to time, forward to Party A samples of similar commodity offered by other suppliers, together with their prices, sales position and advertising material.

(7) Advertising & publicity expenses: Party B shall bear all expenses for advertising and publicity within the above-mentioned territory in the duration of this Agreement and submit to Party A all drafts and/or drawings intended for such purposes for prior approval.

(8) Validity of agreement: This Agreement, when duly signed, by the parties concerned, shall remain in force for one year to be effective as from January 1, 2008 to December 31, 2008. If a renewal of this Agreement is desired, notice in writing should be given by either party within one month prior to its expiry. Should one of the parties fail to comply with the terms and conditions of this Agreement, the other party is entitled to terminate this Agreement.

(9) Arbitration: All disputes arising from the execution of this Agreement shall be settled through negotiation between both parties. In the event that no settlement can be reached, the case in dispute shall then be submitted for arbitration to the Foreign Trade Arbitration Commission of the China Council for the Promotion of International Trade, Beijing, in accordance with the Provisional Rules of Procedure of the Foreign Trade Arbitration Commission of the China Council for the Promotion of International Trade. The decision made by this Commission shall be regarded as final and is binding on both parties.

(10) Other Terms & Conditions:

a. Party A shall not supply the contracted commodity to other buyers in the above-mentioned territory. Direct inquiries, if any, will be referred to Party B. However, should any other buyers insist on dealing direct with Party A, Party A shall have the right to do so. In the latter case, Party A shall send to Party B a copy of relevant S/C and reserve ... per cent (... %) commission for Party B on the net invoice value of the transactions concluded.

b. Should Party B fail to send their orders to Party A for a minimum of ... for a period of ... months, Party A shall not be bound to this Agreement.

c. For any business transacted between governments of both parties, Party A shall have full right to handle such direct dealings as authorized by Party A's government without binding themselves to this Agreement. Party B shall not interfere with such direct dealings, nor shall Party B bring forward any demand for compensations or commission there of.

d. Should Party B fail to send their orders to Party A for a minimum of ... for a period of ... months, Party A shall not be bound to this Agreement.

e. For any business transacted between governments of both parties, Party A shall have full right to handle such direct dealings as authorized by Party A's government without binding themselves to this Agreement. Party B shall not interfere with such direct dealings, nor shall Party B bring forward any demand for compensations or commission there of.

f. Other terms and conditions shall be subject to those specified in the formal S/C signed by both parties.

This agreement is made out in quadruplicate, each party holding two copies.

Party A (Supplier) Party B (Agent)

Sample 2

Exclusive Sales Agreement

Through friendly negotiations, this Agreement is entered into between China National

×××Import and Export Corporation, Jiangxi, China (hereinafter called Party A), and ×××Company, Russia (hereinafter called Party B) on the following terms and conditions:

(1) Party A entrust Party B with the exclusive sales in the territory of Russia for "YAYA" Brand Down Coat. This Agreement is valid from 1st September, 2008 to 31st August, 2010.

(2) Quantity: During the above-mentioned period, Party B shall endeavor to push sales of not less than ... of "YAYA" Brand Down Coat, the quantity of which should be spread over quarterly periods in approximately equal proportions.

(3) During the validity of this Agreement, Party A refrain from offering the above-mentioned goods to other merchants with any place of Russia as place of destination, while Party B undertake to refrain from purchasing, pushing sales of or acting as agents for the commodity of other suppliers same as or similar to that stated in Article 1 and guarantee not to transship in any way the said goods supplied by Party A to any area, where exclusivity or sales agency has been granted by Party A. If any violation of the above is found, Party A have the right to cancel this Agreement.

(4) Should other buyers in the territory under exclusivity approach party A for the purchase of the above-mentioned goods, Party A should refer them to Party B. If such buyers insist on concluding business direct with Party A, Party A may do so. Party A may likewise conclude business with Russian buyers who come to visit China or attend the Chinese Export Commodity Fair at prices not lower than those quoted to Party B. In the above event, Party A agree to reserve for Party B a commission of 1% on basis of FOB value of the business thus concluded and send a copy of the relative contract to Party B.

(5) During the period of this agreement, both parties should strictly abide by the terms and condition of this Agreement. In the event of any breach of them by one party, the other party are entitled, when necessary, to claim the termination of this Agreement.

(6) Party B should be responsible for the sending of reports every month to Party A for their reference, setting forth local market conditions of the said goods (including details of price level and demand for variety in articles).

(7) This Agreement is not binding on inter-government (authorized state enterprises and cooperatives in the nature of a state-owned enterprise) tenders and barter transactions of any nature.

(8) At its expiration, the termination or renewal of this Agreement will be decided by both parties through negotiation.

(9) This Agreement is made out in Chinese and Russian languages, both texts being equally binding. One copy each is kept by either party.

Party A　　　　　　　　　　　　　　　　　　　　　　　　Party B

Sample 3

Consignment Agreement

China National Light Industrial Products Imp. & Exp. Corp., Beijing Branch (hereinafter called Party A) held talks with U. S. Max Factor & Co., (hereinafter called Party B) about the consignment of Max Factor Cosmetics. Through friendly negotiation both parties confirm the principal points as stipulated hereunder:

(1) Item for Consignment

It mainly covers four product categories, i. e. Treatment, Fragrance, Cosmetics, and Toiletries. The detailed specification, unit price and quantity of the above goods shall be provided in a list to Party A by Party B. After confirmation by Party A, a concrete contract signed by both parties will then be effective.

(2) Terms of Consignment

1) Period of Time. Both parties agree that sales of Max Factor Cosmetics will commence on or about January 15, 1999 and continue through December 31, 1999.

Party A agrees to sell exclusively Max Factor Cosmetics during this one year time in Beijing and agrees that no other cosmetics lines including perfumes, beauty cosmetics, cosmetics for protecting skin, hair lotions and nail enamels will be sold in Beijing Hotel, Beijing Friendship Store or any other location in Beijing.

In order to facilitate Party A's work of starting the consignment sales on time, Party B should ship the first lot of consignment goods to Party A before Dec. 31, 1998. On or about March 15, 1999, Party A and Party B shall meet to mutually determine on acceptable sales level for the remainder of the consignment period.

2) Port of Destination. Xingang, Tianjin (by sea) and Beijing (by air). Party B agrees to sell CIF named Chinese Port.

In assurance certificate will be ALL RISKS with a warehouse to warehouse clause. While the goods are in the warehouse and during the course of selling Party A shall take the responsibility of insurance on behalf of Party B.

3) Party B will submit to Party A the actual retail prices of aforesaid articles in Hong Kong and Japanese Markets for Party A's reference. Party B has no right to interfere with Part A's selling price, spot and method, but it has the right to make positive proposals. Party A is responsible to submit Party B regular reports to selling situation (covering retail prim), problem arising in the course of selling and making proposals to improve sales. Party B should provide Party A with various arrangement are conductive to sales (including samples free of charge, articles for trial sales, data for promoting cosmetic goods, technical exchange and conditions for storage, etc.)

4) All expenses for advertisement of these items should be paid by Party B. The contents of advertisement are subject to the approval of Party A.

5) In the case of problems occurring due to quality, damage or any other matter of Party

B's responsibility, Party B should compensate such a loss to Party A by the replacement of goods or the deduction of the sum in question from Party A's remittance to Party B against Party A's certificate. One percent of the sum from Party A's remittance to Party B should be dedicated by Party B as a damage allowance during the course of selling.

6) During the consignment period if Party A wishes to increase the quantity of salable items, Party B should cooperate on this matter through best efforts. For those articles which can not be sold Party B should make readjustment, replacement or withdrawal of the goods in question.

(3) Terms of Payment

1) Within one month after expiration of the consignment period, Party A shall remit Party B the total sum in U. S. Dollars based on the contracted unit price for those items which have been sold.

If at any time the total value of goods sold exceeds the amount of U. S. Dollars 150 000, Party A shall remit the total sum in U. S. Dollars to Party B within one month's period of time.

2) For those items which cannot be sold, Party A should send a list of these items to Party B in order to make an appropriate settlement by sending these items back or any other method.

(4) All disputes arising in the course of the consignment period shall be settled amicably through friendly negotiation. In the case that no settlement can be reached through negotiation, both parties agree the case should be submitted for arbitration to a third country which can be accepted by both parties.

(5) At the beginning of December, 1999, both parties shall meet and discuss the future business possibility in Beijing in 2000.

Sample 4

Purchasing Equipment Contract

Contract No.

Dated:

The Buyers: ××× Company Ltd.

People's Republic of China

Fax No. (0755)6694008

The End-Users: ××× Corporation

Chengdu, Sichuan

People's Republic of China

Fax No. (028)3324333

The Sellers: ×× Inc.

12345 Market Street, Livonia, Michigan, U. S. A
Fax No. (313)591-1111

1. Scope

This contract (including Appendices I through V) defines total scope of work to be performed by the three parties. Seller recognizes that over the course of contract execution, End-Users may wish to amend the scope of work. Should such amendments be necessary, Seller shall promptly submit additional proposals for End-Users' review. Seller will not, make any amendments unless they have been agreed to in writing by the contracting parties. However,Seller reserves the fight to change the details of construction to Seller fabricated equipment, as specified in the Seller's proposal if, in its judgment, such changes of substitutions shall be to the best interest of both End-Users and Sellers.

2. Contract Effective Date

This contract will go into effect on the latest date at which all approvals required by the contracting parties have been obtained. Such approvals will be obtained within sixty(60) days of the signing of the contract. Seller reserves the right to revise the contract price if Buyer fails to obtain approvals within the sixty(60) days period. Buyer and Seller shall notify each other by fax immediately upon receipt of approvals. With respect to the Seller, the contract must be ratified by an officer of Seller's Parent Company.

3. Contract Equipment

This contract is made by and between the Buyers, the End-Users, and the Sellers, whereby the Buyers and End-Users agree to buy and the Sellers agree to sell the under-mentioned commodity (here-in-after referred as the Contract Equipment) according to the terms and conditions stipulated herein:

Base Prices (Omitted)
Accessories (Omitted)
Spare Parts (Omitted)
Subtotal
Less Discount
Final Sales Price

4. Payment

4.1 Terms of Payment

① 15% down payment within thirty (30) days of the contract date.
② 20% upon receipt of Floor Plan.
③ 65% immediately upon shipment.

4.2 Conditions of Payment

① Payment No. 1

By Telegraphic Transfer to Seller's account number 551-17-001 at First National Bank of Boston when Buyer receives the following documents:

—Three (3) copies of Seller's Invoice
—Two (2) copies of Sight Draft

—Seller's standby Letter of Credit (sample attached as Exhibit I)

② Payment No. 2

By Telegraphic Transfer to Seller's account number 551-17-001 at First National Bank of Boston when Buyer receives the following documents:

—Three (3) copies of Seller's Invoice

—Two (2) copies of Sight Draft

—Floor Plan drawing

③ Payment No. 3

Against a Confirmed Irrevocable Letter of Credit (sample attached as Exhibit 2) at sight when following documents are submitted:

—Three (3) copies of Seller's Invoice

—Clean on Board Ocean Bill of Lading

—Packing List

—Certificate of Quality and Quantity

—Seller's standby Letter of Credit (sample attached as Exhibit 3)

Copy of fax to Buyer notifying shipment Buyer shall establish this Letter of Credit in favor of the Seller at the ×× Bank, ×× Branch within thirty (30) days after contract effective date.

4.3 Late Payments

All late payments will carry an interest at a rate of Prime rate plus 3% per annum prorated to the actual delay with a grace period of fifteen (15) days.

5. Export License

Requirements regarding United States Export License change periodically. Sellers will make a determination whether a license is required. Buyer will cooperate with Sellers in signing the certificates which may be necessary to complete the application for the license. Seller assures the Buyer that this requirement has never in the past impeded execution of such types of contracts.

6. Shipment

Date of shipment is to be in October, 1998. Port of shipment will be an East Coast Port, U.S.A. Port of Destination will be Guangzhou, P.R. China. All equipment is to be shipped C.I.F.

7. Terms of Shipment

7.1 The Sellers shall, 40 days before the date of shipment stipulated in the contract, advise the End-Users by telex of the Contract No. ××, commodity, quantity, value, number of packages, gross weight, and measurements.

7.2 The Sellers shall, no later than 10 days before the estimated date of arrival of the vessel from the port of shipment, notify the End-Users of the name of vessel and estimated date of loading. If the schedule of the vessel is changed, Seller's shipping agents shall promptly notify the End-User.

7.3 The Sellers shall bear all expenses and risks of the commodity until it arrives at the port of destination. Once the goods arrive at the port, any and all charges shall be borne by the End-User.

7.4 If goods need to be stored at the docks, the responsibility for safekeeping of same shall rest with the End-User.

7.5 Bills of Lading shall constitute Proof of Delivery.

8. Storage at End-User's Plant

All material must be stored by the End-User indoors in a warm and dry place. Damage to material due to improper storage (regardless of how packaged) will not be Seller's responsibility. If End-User unpacks the goods in the absence of Seller's representative, Seller will not be responsible for missing parts and shortages.

9. Delays and Escalation

In the event the End-User delays shipment of material and equipment, directly or indirectly, the seller shall have a right to impose escalation and/or storage charges for the term of the delay.

10. Cancellation & Default

End-User may cancel only upon written notice to Seller and upon payment to Seller of reasonable and proper cancellation charges, including direct and indirect costs with proportionate profit.

11. Documentation

Seller shall provide documentation as outlined in Appendix Ⅱ.

12. Training

Seller shall provide training to End-User's personnel as outlined in Appendix Ⅲ. End-User must recognize that the Seller can accommodate only a limited number of trainees at any given time. End-User shall be responsible for the conduct of its personnel while in the U. S. all expenses relating to trainees will be borne by the End-User; however, Seller will arrange for the daily transportation on working days from the hotel to Seller's plant and provide a working lunch. The training shall, under no circumstances, include information which Seller deems proprietary.

13. Field Supervision and Start-Up

Seller shall provide supervision and start-up services as out lined in Appendix IV.

14. Force Majeure

Seller shall not be responsible for any loss, damage, delay in shipment or non-delivery of the goods due to Force Majeure (causes such as fires, theft, acts of war, insurrection or riot, strikes and lockouts or any other cause beyond Seller's control) which might occur during the process of manufacturing or in the course of loading or transit. The Sellers shall advise the End-Users immediately of the occurrence mentioned above. As soon as possible thereafter, the Sellers shall send by airmail to the End-Users for their acceptance a certificate of the accident.

Under such circumstances, the Seller however, is still under the obligation to take all necessary measures to hasten the delivery of the goods. In no event shall the Seller be liable for any special, indirect or consequential damages or loss of profits for causes attributed to Force Majeure.

15. Taxes and Duties

End-User will be liable for all taxes and import or export duties outside the Seller's country. In addition, End-User shall be responsible for all port charges, demurrage, etc., at the port of destination. End-User further agrees to indemnify Seller against all liabilities for such taxes or duties and legal fees or costs incurred by Seller in connection herewith.

16. Arbitration

All disputes in connection with the execution shall be settled through friendly negotiations. Where no settlement can be reached, the disputes shall be submitted for arbitration. Arbitration shall take place in Stockholm. Each party shall appoint an arbitrator within thirty (30) days after receipt of notification from the opposite party and the two Arbitrators thus appointed shall jointly nominate a third person as umpire to form an Arbitration Committee.

The said umpire shall be confined to the citizens of Swedish nationality. The decision of the Arbitration Committee shall be accepted as final and binding upon both parties; neither party shall seek recourse to a law court or other authorities to appeal for revision of the decision. Arbitration expenses shall be borne by the losing party.

Improper or negligent use and operation of the equipment.

Equipment not manufactured by the Seller will be guaranteed on the same terms as Seller's vendor's guarantee. In such case, Seller will provide full assistance to End-User's manufacturing process or the quality of End-User's product. Losses or damage resulting from equipment failure or from the time consumed in delivering, installing, or testing the equipment are not covered by the guarantee.

In no event shall the Seller be liable for any special indirect or consequential damages or loss of profits for causes covered under this guarantee. Seller will make no guarantee for repairs of alterations to the product made by the End-User, unless made with the advance written consent of Seller. Seller will not assume liability for costs of disassembly, reassembly, or re-machining of defective product. Seller makes no guarantee, express or implied, other than the above.

Buyer　　　　　　　　Seller　　　　　　　　End User

Sample 5

SALES CONTRACT

Contract No. :CE102　　　　Date:Jun. 2, 20××　　　　Signed at:Qingdao

Sellers: ××Shandong Import & Export Group Corporation
20, ×× Road, Qingdao, China

Buyers: Pacific Trading Co. , Ltd.
1118 Green Road, New York, U. S. A.

This Sales Contract is made by and between the Sellers and the Buyers whereby the Sellers agree to sell and the Buyers agree to buy the under-mentioned goods according to the terms and conditions stipulated below:

Name of Commodity Specifications & Packing	Quantity	Unit Price	Total Amount
Lithopone ZnS content 28% min. Paper-lined glass-fibre bags	100 M/Ts	USD 36 000 per M/T CIFC 3% New York	USD 36 000.00

1. Shipping Marks:

PTC
New York
No. 1 - 1000

Insurance: To be covered by the Sellers for 110% of the invoice value against All Risks and War Risk as per the relevant Ocean Marine Cargo Clauses of the People's Insurance Company of China. If other coverage or an additional insurance amount is required, the Buyers must have the consent of the Sellers before shipment, and the additional premium is to be borne by the buyers.

2. Port of Shipment: Qingdao, China.
3. Port of Destination: New York, U. S. A.
4. Time of Shipment: During August, 20××, allowing partial shipments and transshipment.
5. Terms of Payment: The Buyers shall open with a bank acceptable to the Sellers an Irrevocable Letter of Credit at sight to reach the Sellers 30 days before the time of shipment specified, valid for negotiation in China until the 15th day after the aforesaid time of shipment.
6. Commodity Inspection: It is mutually agreed that the Certificate of Quality and Weight issued by the State General Administration for Quality Supervision and Inspection and Quarantine of P. R. China at the port of shipment shall be taken as the basis of delivery.
7. Discrepancy and Claim: Any claim by the Buyers on the goods shipped shall be filed within 30 days after the arrival of the goods at the port of destination and supported by a survey report issued by a surveyor approved by the Sellers. Claims in respect to matters within the

responsibility of the insurance company or of the shipping company will not be considered or entertained by the Sellers.

8. Force Majeure: If shipment of the contracted goods is prevented or delayed in whole or in part due to Force Majeure, the Sellers shall not be liable for non-shipment or late shipment of the goods under this Contract. However, the Sellers shall notify the Buyers by fax or E-mail and furnish the latter within 15 days by registered airmail with a certificate issued by the China Council for the Promotion of International Trade attesting such event or events.

9. Arbitration: All disputes arising out of the performance of or relating to this Contract shall be settled amicably through negotiation. In case no settlement can be reached through negotiation, the case shall then be submitted to the Foreign Economic and Trade Arbitration Commission of the China Council for the Promotion of International Trade, Beijing, China, for arbitration in accordance with its Provisional Rules of Procedure. The award of the arbitration is final and binding upon both parties.

10. Other Terms: ...

THE SELLERS (Signature)　　　　THE BUYERS (Signature)